Derek M

ROUGH HILLS

An East End Story

Rough Hills, Wolverhampton,
Its History, People and Places

Derek Mills

ROUGH HILLS

An East End Story

Rough Hills, Wolverhampton,
Its History, People and Places

MEREO
Cirencester

Mereo Books

1A The Wool Market Dyer Street Cirencester Gloucestershire GL7 2PR
An imprint of Memoirs Publishing www.mereobooks.com

ROUGH HILLS - AN EAST END STORY: 978-1-86151-875-0

First published in Great Britain in 2017
by Mereo Books, an imprint of Memoirs Publishing

Copyright ©2018

The address for Memoirs Publishing Group Limited can be found at
www.memoirspublishing.com

The Memoirs Publishing Group Ltd Reg. No. 7834348

Typeset in 11/16pt Helvetica
by Wiltshire Associates Publisher Services Ltd.
Printed and bound in Great Britain by Biddles Books

DEDICATION

To members of the Mills and Bateman families
Past and Present
Young and Old

CONTENTS

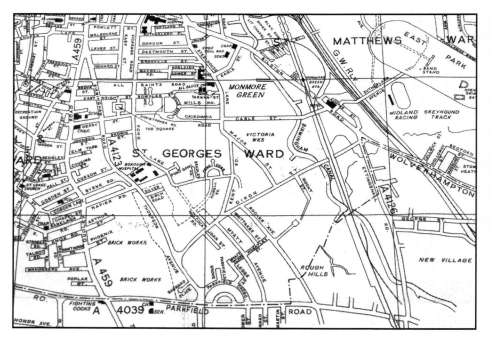

A Town Map from 1946

(Photograph reproduced with the permission of Wolverhampton
Archives and Local Studies).

INTRODUCTION

> *'Rough-hills, a locality so called from the "bowels" of the earth having been piled up upon its surface.'* Birmingham Daily Gazette, Tuesday 24 September 1867.

In 1953, a shy 4-year-old moved with his parents from the warmth and security of life with his grandparents in Bushbury to start a new life in a new house on a new estate. We were the latest residents of Rough Hills Estate: a construction site, work in progress. We had shops, a pub and the promise of a new neighbourhood school and community centre. The lack of tarmac, street lighting and a bus service were dismissed as temporary inconveniences.

This was to be my home for the next 18 years: the focal point of my childhood and my transition into a young adult. Life's experiences were played out in the houses, streets and neighbourhoods of Rough Hills against a background of national and global events like JFK's assassination,

Figure 1: 250, Bushbury Lane – my birthplace.

Beatlemania and England's World Cup victory.

In 2015, it was time to reappraise that estate, its history and the years I spent there. As the project developed, my initial area of interest expanded to include the neighbourhoods: All Saints, its school and surrounding streets; Monmore Green with its railways and speedway stadium and Parkfields, the original 'Rough Hills' estate. The 1946 map shown earlier illustrates how these locations fit together in the south east area of the town. By including these neighbourhoods, I hoped a more comprehensive account of my experiences from 1954 to 1968 would

Figure 2: Cheviot Road on the Rough Hills estate.

become evident. The motives for my research were simple: a chance to revisit my memories of people and places, an opportunity to explore the history and identity of an area that played an important part in Wolverhampton's industrial heritage. Ultimately, it was nostalgia: the desire to put on those rose-tinted glasses and to wallow in the past.

My initial research, based on books of Wolverhampton, revealed very little. The History of Wolverhampton by Gerald Mander is a wonderful book of its time but fails to mention the Rough Hills area by name. Chris Upton's book on the town makes a fleeting reference as does George Barnsby's comprehensive 'History of Housing in Wolverhampton'. Both refer to the time in the 1850s when Wolverhampton Waterworks Company supplemented its supplies from Rough Hills. Concerns about its quality appear to have been confirmed by an alderman at a council meeting. When he added the water to his glass of brandy, he described how it immediately 'turned as black as ink'.

Fortunately, research in the 21st century is immeasurably easier thanks to the internet and deep inside the bowels of the World Wide Web I found valuable pieces of information which have helped to reveal a more rounded picture of Rough Hills and its surroundings. While confirming its importance in the first half of the 1800s as a centre for coalmining and ironmaking, the Web has started to reveal details of these enterprises: the succession of owners who operated these businesses, the mining communities which grew up in the area and the tragedies that inevitably transpired. It chronicles the rise and fall of the neighbourhood's factories, such as John Thompson, which provided work and a social life for its employees for most of the 20th century. A sporting history going back to the 1880s has been uncovered which remarkably includes a successful world record attempt at the local running ground. The book looks at the area's close involvement in the development of the country's canal and railway networks and follows the landscape's slow transition from pits and furnaces to housing estates and playing fields. It also explores the impact of religion, education and leisure on the lives of the people who settled in the area.

To complement these articles, I have included, where appropriate, my family's involvement in events as well as my own memories of life in the 1950s and 60s: my formative years as described above. I have also been lucky enough to find a number of people who were kind enough to share their own memories, in some cases going back to the 1930s, and I formally pass on my gratitude to them in the 'acknowledgements' chapter at the very end of the book. To emphasise these two sets of recollections, I have put the relevant text in italics, with a grey panel for the contributions made by the general public and for milestones in the town's history.

In an ideal world, I would have gleaned more information on the pre-1800 history of Rough Hills, acquired the legal skills to interpret the deeds that document land transactions in the 19th century and showed greater perseverance with the microfilm machines which taxed my eyesight and fortitude. It is appropriate at this point to thank all the staff at Wolverhampton Local History Archives (Wolverhampton City Archives) who displayed great patience with this project. The Archives comprise a vast and varied collection of maps, books, newspapers and other materials relating to the history of the city and it provided the majority of the resources used in this book.

I take full responsibility for the inconsistencies, mistakes and significant gaps in the book and encourage everyone who has an interest in the subject matter to draw my attention to them. It is hoped that future researchers of Rough Hills can now look beyond the notoriety of the water in the brandy. It ignores the significant contribution that Rough Hills has made to the transport, industrial and sporting history of the town. This book will attempt to redress these omissions and convince sceptics that Rough Hills deserves a more substantial place in the annals of Wolverhampton.

1

WOLVERHAMPTON'S EARLY HISTORY

No man is an island and the same is true of a Council estate. The story of Rough Hills estate will inevitably run in parallel with that of the city of Wolverhampton and the nation itself. Incidentally, as city status was not granted to Wolverhampton until 2000, the book will refer to the 'town' of Wolverhampton.

Much of Wolverhampton's early history is shrouded in speculation. It may have been the site of an Iron-Age hill-fort but robust archaeological evidence has not yet been found. Following the Anglo-Saxon invasions in the fifth century AD, it probably became one of many settlements in Mercia, one of the seven Kingdoms that formed Anglo Saxon England, and inhabited by one of the many tribes that made up this kingdom. We have to wait until 985 before we find the settlement named as Heantune, the 'High Town'. In an Anglo-Saxon charter of that year Aethelred, King of Mercia, grants ten pieces of land at 'Heantune' to Lady Wulfruna, a Mercian noblewoman. In 994, another charter records an endowment by Lady Wulfruna of land and possessions to a minster Church at Heantune. In recognition of her gift the name of the settlement was prefixed by Wulfrun. Despite the familiarity of this version of events amongst 'Wulfrunians', doubts exist among academics about the authenticity of these two charters, particularly the second one. More convincing evidence about the city's early history comes from a royal charter dated around 1080 which refers to a church, dedicated at that time to St Mary, as 'the church of Wolvrenehamptonia'. By the 15th century the church was dedicated to St Peter and, over time, the place-name evolved into its present form.

Although there are question marks about the validity of these two charters, there is no doubt about its Anglo-Saxon heritage. Wolverhampton provides a good example of a place-name conferred by Anglo-Saxon invaders. While hills and streams and other natural phenomena were allowed to retain their old British names (e.g. Barr, "a summit," and Tame, "a flood water"), towns, villages, and other political divisions were very generally renamed by the Saxon conquerors. In many instances, the places were called after the personal names of their owners:

Bilston signifies "the town of Bil's folk".

Ettingshall was "the hall of the Etri family".

In contrast, Monmore, as in Monmore Green, is a Celtic place-name which signified 'the boggy mere' in the tongue of the ancient Britons.

The original settlement of Wolverhampton was probably centred around the Church with a market held on a Sunday in the churchyard. Many markets developed out of the informal trading which would took place after church services. In 1258 a Royal Charter from Henry III for a weekly market was obtained by the Dean of Wolverhampton and it moved to an area nearby known at the time as High Green but better known today as Queen Square. The market was held on a Wednesday and its presence boosted the growth of the town so that by the 15th century Wolverhampton had become an important centre for the woollen industry. Raw wool was brought in from Wales and the borders, spun into yarn and woven into cloth in the town. The Borough coat of arms granted in 1898 includes a woolpack as a symbol of the wool staple or market formerly held in the town. Street names like Blossoms Fold and Farmers Fold in the town centre reflect this heritage: a 'fold' being the place where sheep were penned before or after going through the market.

Lock making, for which the town later became famous, had started by the 17th century and by the mid-18th century the prosperity of Wolverhampton was based on metal trades and mining rather than wool. The town was visited in 1754 by R. R. Angerstein, a Swedish industrial expert, who travelled around Europe reporting on the industries of each country. Wolverhampton received a good deal of his attention because it was described as 'one of the three towns in England famous for the fabrication of iron and steel-ware'. He noted that it is 'particularly renowned for all kinds of polished articles, such as buckles, watch chains, candle-snuffers, etc'. Wolverhampton's position in the west of the midlands of England gave the town a dominant position in trade arrangements with Shrewsbury and central Wales, and it was as a trading as well as an industrial town that Wolverhampton developed faster than other neighbouring towns.

*By **1744** the construction of Molineux House had begun. This later became home to Wolverhampton Wanderers F.C.*

We can follow the development of Wolverhampton from 1750 thanks to a detailed map of the town engraved by Isaac Taylor. At this time metal trades dominated the town's economy. Water power was non-existent and the main tool was said to be the file. According to Isaac Taylor, there were 7,454 inhabitants occupying 1440 houses. While the map shows a familiar layout of streets, most of the names were different. The centre of the town was High Green (the present Queen Square and part of Dudley Street) with 214 houses and workshops in and around the area. A dotted line on the map shows the old division of Wolverhampton into two manors, the Deanery to the west and Stowheath to the east. Running north from 'The Roundabout' at the western end of High Green were Goat Street and Tup Street (the present North Street) while continuing south were Cock Street and Boblake (the present Victoria Street). Beyond Boblake was Worcester Street. Running east of High Green was Lichfield Street which finished near the site of the present Princess Square. Nearby were Stafford Street and Rottons Row (Broad Street). These were already heavily populated and in time were to become the most notorious slum areas of Wolverhampton.

In 1777, Parliament passed an Improvement Act for Wolverhampton, under which 125 Commissioners were appointed to govern the town.

The Godson map and rate plan of Wolverhampton of 1788 shows that the town was expanding rapidly: the number of inhabitants had increased to 11,368 and the number of houses to 2270. Godson also identifies the main landowner in the town as William Pulteney of the Leveson-Gower family. The Levesons had prospered from the wool trade and now owned about 300 acres including much coal bearing land in the eastern manor of Stowheath which included the site of Rough Hills. In the 19th century, the family by marriage became Dukes of Sutherland, the largest landowners in the United Kingdom and responsible for the notorious Highland clearances in Scotland.

The Godson map reveals a few landmarks in the south east of the town that we would recognise. One is the Red Lion pub shown on an unnamed track we now know as Parkfield Road. Bilston Road is clearly shown and branching off it is a road named as Hell Lane. This road is known today as Ettingshall Road but the Hell Lane name persisted well into the 1800s, as we will see later.

2

ROUGH HILLS' EARLY HISTORY

The Taylor map showed roads radiating outwards from the town centre. Worcester Street, Dudley Street and Bilston Street were clearly shown, directing travellers to the respective towns. The two roads leading to Dudley and Bilston formed roughly the west-east perimeters of the area we now identify as Parkfields and Rough Hills.

The origin of the Rough Hills name is far from clear with one popular assumption that it arose from the mounds of cinder heaps in the locality. The area does not appear to be mentioned in documents until the early 1700s, by virtue of a deed dated 9 July 1725. This covers the 'mortgage by demise of a parcel of land by the name of Rough Hills in the manor of Stowheath' involving five named individuals:

John Wishaw of Lad Lane, London, mercer.
John Preist of Cheapside, London, mercer.

Henry Price of Wolverhampton, ironmonger.

Thomas Turnpenny of Wolverhampton, tobacconist.

Paul Stubbs of Wolverhampton, founder.

Figure 3: The No. 30 bus stop – close to the site of Rough
Hills Furnaces in the early 1800s.

A 'mortgage by demise' referred to a temporary transfer of property in order to secure a loan of money.

Despite this apparent existence, it does not make an appearance in the Isaac Taylor map of 1750 referred to earlier. Nor is it named as such in Godson's 1788 map. The south east corner of the town is shown as an expanse of empty parcels of land. Many tracks and some roads are visible but few are identified. There are isolated signs of industry with furnaces marked on the site of the Dixon Street playing fields, an area where the Wolverhampton Ironworks is labelled on maps of the 1800s. A furnace is also shown a little further to the south east, around the present Cheviot Road/ Rough Hills Road area, seen in the photograph. A short length of canal is marked coming off the Birmingham Canal towards these particular

Figure 4: Cockshutts Lane - a road to nowhere.

furnaces. Slightly north are indications of a settlement but it is not deemed worthy of a name. In contrast, a small isolated settlement named as Cockshutts is shown on the map, well to the west of the furnaces, with no obvious industrial activity around it. Its legacy remains today as Cockshutts Lane. Originally forming a continuation of Green Lane (the present Birmingham Road) onto Parkfield Road, it now sits anonymously behind Thompson Avenue. No one is sure about the origin of the Cockshutts place-name. According to John Freeman's Black Country Stories and Sketches, the name derives from the huts, the Cocks Hutts, in which fighting cocks were kept. This seems a likely explanation as the area is not far from the cross roads known as Fighting Cocks after the pub which once stood there. Alternatively, and just as likely, the name arose from the cock shut, a name for a strip of land at the head of a field.

3

BLACK COUNTRY OR NOT?

It was said in the early 1800s that in this part of the West Midlands 'there was a colliery in almost every field'. Even as late as 1873, a Mine Inspector reports that 'they (collieries) may be said to spring up very much like mushrooms; they are here today and gone tomorrow'. By then, this area had become known as the 'Black Country'. The introduction of the term is often attributed to Elihu Burritt by way of his 1868 book "The Black Country and its Green Borderland", but bearing in mind that two years earlier, the 30 July 1866 edition of the Birmingham Daily Gazette was already referring to the 'ironworks of the Black Country', this credit may not be justified.

There are two related explanations for this 'Black Country' term. One says that the name arose from the abundance of coal in the 'ten-yard seam', the legendary bed of coal made up of ten or more distinct but closely packed layers. Others say it was because of the smoke from the many thousands of ironworking foundries and forges. The Royal Commission report for South Staffordshire in 1842 on the Employment of Children in Mines contains the following description of the area, 'No one who has ever passed between Birmingham and Wolverhampton during the night ever can forget that scene. The blazing fires on every side, from the coal burning upon the ground in the process of conversion into coke, the blazing fields of bituminous shale and indurated clay, the flames proceeding from the chimneys of the great towers of the iron furnaces, present an impressive and even awful prospect, to which nothing usually seen by mortal eyes can be compared.'

Although the term 'Black Country' is entrenched in the culture of this part of the West Midlands, Burritt's 'definition' of its location would now be discredited. In his opinion, it lay within a 20-mile radius of Birmingham Town Hall to include, bizarrely, the towns of Kenilworth and Warwick. Nevertheless, he would only ascribe Wolverhampton as 'the border town of the district'. In contrast, Samuel Griffiths, in his 1872 Guide to the Iron Trade of Great Britain, considered Wolverhampton as the capital of the Black Country. While the capital is now widely recognised as Dudley, the exact boundaries of the Black Country have always been open to interpretation and indignant argument. In his 1980 book, British Coalminers in the Nineteenth Century: A Social History, John Benson lists six mining towns of South Staffordshire but does not even include Wolverhampton. To traditionalists the Black Country is the area where the coal seam comes to the surface, so West Bromwich, Oldbury, Blackheath, Cradley Heath, Old Hill, Bilston, Dudley, Tipton, Wednesfield and parts of Halesowen, Wednesbury and Walsall are included. Wolverhampton is excluded despite the fact that 'The Memoirs of the Geological Survey of Great Britain' of 1858 records 26 collieries in Wolverhampton. While not as high as the 59 in Bilston, it exceeds the number in neighbouring areas like Tipton. Indeed, we will see in a later chapter that in areas of Wolverhampton like Parkfields, Cockshutts and Rough Hills, the mining of coal and ironstone and the production of pig iron became well established enterprises supporting mining communities in the surrounding areas. While there is a clear case for the westernmost and agricultural parts of Wolverhampton to be ignored, the historical occurrence of both iron production and coalmining in this south eastern part of the town justifies putting it firmly within the Black Country.

4

THE CUT

The Godson map of 1788 also shows the Birmingham Canal, the Cut, running to the east of these furnaces. Until the 18th century this part of the town would have been predominantly agricultural. The plan to build the canal was first discussed at a public meeting in Birmingham on 24 January 1767 held by a number of prominent Birmingham businessmen, including Matthew Boulton and others from the famous Lunar Society based in that city. The canal would extend from Birmingham to the Staffordshire and Worcestershire Canal near Wolverhampton, taking in the coalfields and furnaces already established in the area. The eminent canal engineer James Brindley was commissioned to set out a route and came up with one, largely level, passing through Smethwick, Oldbury, Tipton, Bilston and Wolverhampton, finishing at Aldersley. An Act of Parliament to allow the building of the canal was passed on 24 February 1768

Figure 5: 'Miller's Bridge' on Dixon Street.

and construction of the Birmingham Canal began in the same year. The canal opened in stages from the Birmingham end and in 1771 the Wolverhampton section opened. The canal was then joined to the Staffordshire and Worcestershire canal at Aldersley via a flight of twenty-one locks. Termed 'the extension', it opened in September 1772, a few days before the death of Brindley.

The canal measured 22 miles and 5 furlongs and followed the contours of the land as far as possible, with deviations by way of wharves and basins to factories, workshops and collieries. The photograph shows the canal making its way underneath the bridge, known locally as Millers Bridge, on Dixon Street. Not only did it create a change in the landscape it also provided a strategic transport system for raw materials and goods. A clause in the 1768 Act entitled 'owners … of Coal-mines, Ironstone, Limestone or other Mines, lying within the Distance of One Thousand yards from the Canal (to) … make Railways, cuts or … or roads to convey their minerals to the said Canal'. Once established, it became a major factor in the industrial growth of the Monmore Green and Rough Hills areas spawning numerous factories, workshops and foundries along its banks. South of Bilston Road bridge, one short basin served the Mitre Works east of Eagle Street. In the last section, south of Cable Street, two short basins served the Victoria Iron Works and Chemical Works respectively.

The Birmingham Canal was one of many that made up a dense network across the country. A canal boat pulled by one horse could carry thirty tons and the system proved a great economic success with private industrialists using the network to move raw materials and products around the country. For a time, canal companies were seen as a worthwhile investment. As late as 1836, local coalmasters and ironmasters such as John Turton Fereday from Monmore Green colliery were looking at ways of reducing journey distances and freight charges by putting their name to a proposal to create a new 'line of canal conveyance' between Birmingham and London. Unfortunately for these investors, railway mania was soon to sweep the country and by the middle of the century the railway network was transporting goods faster and in far larger quantities. The majority of the canal companies struggled to compete with some bought out by the railway companies. This was not the case with the Birmingham Canal Company which bucked the trend by sharing with the London to Birmingham Railway Company (later known as the L.N.W.R.) the cost of building the Birmingham, Wolverhampton and Stour Valley Railway (later known as the Stour Valley Line). As part of this arrangement, it created rail interchange wharves for the deliveries and collections of goods and raw materials.

Despite their positive impact on local industry, canals regrettably became linked with drowning accidents. The stretch of the Birmingham Canal around Rough Hills was no exception with local papers such as the Staffordshire Advertiser reporting a number of incidents. In 1834 Mary Ann Murray, aged 8 or 9, was sent to collect water from the canal but fell in and drowned. Two youngsters Catherine and William Higgins drowned in the canal by Rough Hills colliery in 1836 while playing among some boats. Edward Allen, a sixteen-year-old youth, died near Rough Hills bridge in 1868 while bathing with a friend. Some deaths may have been linked with excessive drinking, as in the case of William Trevitt in 1862, while others remained unsolved. The canal was reported in newspapers as being 5 or 6 feet deep, much deeper than we were led to believe, and on one occasion provided the scene for a distressing suicide cum murder. On the 16 June 1885, the Birmingham Daily Post reported the disturbing deaths of Edith Jones, aged 4, and her mother Ann. Witnesses saw Ann, with Edith in her arms, standing by the side of the canal at Rough Hills before jumping into the water. When the bodies were retrieved from the water, Edith was already dead but Ann was alive and taken to hospital. Before she died the following Sunday, the newspaper reported that she said to her husband, "I don't blame you for this. It is my son that has caused this. They have left us in our old age to work for ourselves. I wish I had begged from door to door with my child before I had put her in the water." The jury at the Bridge Inn, Ettingshall returned a verdict of 'Wilful Murder' against the mother.

In contrast, generations of local youngsters adopted the canal or 'cut' as their adventure playground. George Cartwright who was born in Dixon Street in 1938 remembers the area where the canal ran under the Rough Hills railway bridge, near what is now D'Urberville Road.

'There was a lovely meadow for horses. That's where we all learnt to swim in the cut. We had some great times over by the narrow. It was like Blackpool when on holiday for weeks.' For George and his friends, the first warm day of the year provided the annual race to be the first one to swim in the canal. As the event was often announced at very short notice, swimwear was optional but as it was a boys-only contest, this caused no embarrassment. Swimming in the canal seems to have been restricted to boys and George cannot recall local girls getting involved.

George was one of many from the area who learned to swim there. Brian Hall from Parkfield Grove also made the trek to the same spot in the summer.

'... by the railway bridge, that's where I learned to swim - in winter we would go down Sankey's as the water came into the canal out of the furnaces giving a nice, warm bath.'

George Paddock from Thompson Avenue used the same area for swimming and remembers altercations with the bargemen.

We often made our way down to the 'cut' to swim. Our 'gang' was boys only and trunks were optional. If we got too close to a barge, the bargeman would use his pole to move us away. Some were quite aggressive and an exchange of words was not uncommon.

The 'narrow', referred to by George Cartwright, was not the remains of a lock, despite its appearance. Instead it was a gauging point used to slow down the commercial narrowboats so that a toll based on the weight and type of cargo could be

16

Figure 6: The 'Cut' narrow.

collected. A cottage by the 'narrow' functioned as a tollhouse. The photo alongside shows a modern day narrowboat making its way along the 'gauging narrow'. The old cottage has been modernised and is out of sight on the right hand side.

This was the first genuine adventure playground for our 'gang' from Cheviot Road. It introduced us to 'dares', rites of passage invented by ourselves or passed on by older groups. One of the 'dares' was to jump the 'narrow' but I cannot remember anyone of us even attempting the challenge – the consequences of failure were too awful to contemplate and we were more than happy to watch others have a go. It is sad to find that this particular rite of passage would not even be a possibility now: the land on the estate side is completely overgrown, curtailing any run-up.

Our attitude towards the canal was in marked contrast to that of George Cartwright and his friends. We treated the canal with respect if not fear. None of us had yet learned to swim. We had no older brothers who were confident in the water and could look after us. Although there were rumours that the canal was actually very shallow, we dared not put them to the test. Even on the warmest day the water would not tempt us in. Our other concern was leeches. Our phobia probably originated from watching films such as 'The African Queen'. To relieve the boredom of waiting for the next train to arrive, we made our first

Figure 7: The scene of our 'dare'.

attempts at angling and occasionally caught tiddlers of an unknown variety. When we first found a leech on a fish, it freaked us out. No more angling for us.

Another of the 'dares' was to walk under the railway bridge along a narrow ledge, a shortcut from one side of the train line to the other. We were more confident, even complacent, about succeeding at this one, despite the potential fall into the canal. Unfortunately, during one of our afternoons of trainspotting, one of our 'gang', Ronnie Bagnall, fell in. Most of us panicked and ran back to the safety of Cheviot Road. A few minutes later, someone came back and told us that Ronnie was alive and had climbed out of the water. Greatly relieved we tried to carry on as normal. Mrs Bagnall must have suspected something was amiss and came out of her house to ask where her son was. We said we were not sure, which was true if not a little misleading. Later we were to learn he had stayed down by the canal waiting for his clothes to dry out but the British summer was not doing Ronnie any favours so he eventually gave up and walked home to face the music. We had already disappeared. After standing in the street in silence and embarrassment for a short time, we made our way home and waited for the uproar that was to follow.

5

WOLVERHAMPTON AND ROUGH HILLS, 1800 TO 1850

Industrialisation

In an attempt to monitor the population of the country, to discover whether it was increasing or decreasing and also incidentally to establish the number of men able to fight in the Napoleonic Wars, decennial censuses were introduced in 1801 in England and Wales. From the returns the population size was estimated to be 9.4 million. Wolverhampton was by now the largest town in the area with a population of 12,565 with 2,344 houses and 3,087 families. This was made up of 6,207 males, and 6,358 females. The wool trade was still taking place on open fields but these were now few in number and much employment was now based around the diverse trades associated with the metal industry. Only 125 worked the land compared to 3,356 employed in trades, and 9,084 involved in other work.

As well as using census returns, the growth of towns such as Wolverhampton during the 1800s can be monitored by other means. Trade directories were published by a number of people such as William White from Sheffield. His 1834 History, Gazetteer and Directory for Staffordshire gives a comprehensive review of Wolverhampton and also includes a complimentary portrayal of the town: 'Though not remarkable for the beauty of its streets and buildings, and though seated in the heart of the great midland mining district, the town is salubrious and very picturesque'.

It has even been suggested that by the late 1830s Wolverhampton had become a fashionable place and visitors to the racecourse on the site of West Park may even have included Prince Albert, Queen Victoria's husband. Confirmatory evidence has not been found. Indeed, the following description by a young Princess Victoria on a visit to the town in 1832 reads, 'We have just changed horses at Wolverhampton a large and dirty town but we were received with great friendliness and pleasure', making this suggestion all the more unlikely.

An 1835 map by Lt Robert Dawson showed that while housing was concentrated in the town centre, surrounding the centre were situated a small number of settlements. Some names such as Compton, Oxley and Aldersley are familiar while others like Tunstall have presumably evolved into Dunstall. Rough Hills makes an appearance on the map and is prominently marked in the south east of the town although one is unable to make out its boundaries.

More informative data about settlements like Rough Hills became available following the release of the 1841 census records. This was the first census to ask individuals specific questions about their occupation and whether they were born in the county. Evidence could also be gleaned from government reports published during this period. In his 1840 evidence to the Poor Law Commissioners, Doctor J. Dehane from Wolverhampton makes the point that: 'The larger portion of the population is employed in the coal and ironstone mines in the neighbourhood, in the iron works, and in getting up, principally in their own residences, a variety of articles in the iron, brass and tin trades.' In his Report to the Commissioners on the Employment of Children and Young Persons in the Iron trades and other Manufactures of South Staffordshire written in 1841, R. H. Horne describes Wolverhampton as 'extremely rich. It is not only rich considering its size, but even when compared with much larger and populous towns and cities, such as Birmingham'. Its population of 36,382 in 1841 put it tenth in the ranking of British towns by population.

The town's wealth was based on the manufacture of all kinds of metalwork and Horne drew attention to the proximity of coal and iron ore. Tin toys, hinges, locks and screws, made from iron, tin, steel and brass, were some of the diverse products made in the town for export. One particular trade for which Wolverhampton and its neighbouring town, Bilston, became world famous was japanning. Items made of tin plate and papier mache such as coal scuttles and trays were decorated with lacquer and varnished.

Despite the scale and quality of its products, initially there were surprisingly few large manufacturers. Horne remarked on the numerous workshops hidden away in passages and courtyards around the town centre with few craftsmen advertising their trade. He also noted with dismay that the majority of children over the age of 8 were already employed in these workshops, working long days of up to 13 hours, lacking education and in many cases suffering malnutrition and ill treatment. The productivity of these workshops created great wealth for the ironmasters and factory owners with some on average worth over £100,000. Their lifestyle, however, was in marked contrast to those of the working-class members of the town.

The Great Divide – the Workhouse

Nothing illustrated more miserably the gap between wealth and poverty at this time than the Union Workhouse. Built across the country in the late 1830s in response to the Poor Law Amendment Act of 1834, their aim was to reduce the cost for ratepayers of looking after the poor people (paupers) in a parish. At the Workhouses, paupers would be given accommodation, clothing and food in return for working. Described by some campaigners as 'Prisons for the Poor', the conditions in a workhouse were grim with basic facilities and manual labour intended to act as a deterrent to the able-bodied pauper. If an able-bodied man entered the workhouse, his whole family was expected to enter with him.

Wolverhampton's Union Workhouse, built in response to this Act, was opened around 1837 on the south side of Bilston Road near to its junction with Steelhouse Lane. By the 1850s, the majority of those forced into the workhouse were not the work-shy, but the old, the infirm, unmarried mothers, orphaned children and the physically or mentally ill. Entering its strict regime and spartan conditions was still considered the ultimate degradation but 'residents' could, in principle, leave whenever they wished. Some people, known as the 'ins and outs', entered and left quite frequently if temporary work became available, treating the workhouse almost like a guest-house. Some, however, would stay for the rest of their lives.

This unfortunately was the case for my 3rd great grandfather William Bateman. By 1841 he was living aged 65 in the Union Workhouse on Bilston Road. There are no records to confirm when he was admitted and the census returns for 1841 show no close relatives had been admitted with him. In 1845 he died. I assume that he died at the Workhouse, but there is no corroborative evidence.

Wolverhampton's was probably designed by George Wilkinson and adopted the relatively uncommon 'St Andrew's Cross' plan which Wilkinson had also used in Oxfordshire. The entrance was at the north of the site and connected to a central hub used for administration. It cost around £9,000 to build and provided four accommodation wings radiating outwards for the various classes of inmate (male/female, old/young). The enclosed areas between the wings were used as exercise yards. Various additions were made to the buildings including an infirmary and new infectious wards in 1867, and new accommodation wards in 1881. In 1867, Wolverhampton was the subject of one of a series of articles in the medical journal, The Lancet, investigating conditions in the country's workhouse infirmaries. Although the report was generally positive, it included a number of unfavourable comments describing many of the wards as overcrowded, the kitchens and system of food distribution as inadequate and the reception and tramp ward as 'very bad'.

Despite the austerity of the workhouse, every effort was made to make Christmas Day a memorable day for the inmates.

The 31 December 1879 edition of the Wolverhampton Chronicle describes the celebrations that had taken place a week earlier. Over 1000 persons were present to enjoy the roast beef (over 88lbs) and 'good sized and luscious looking' plum puddings (127 of them). Each adult pauper received with his roast beef an extra quantity of ale and after dinner there was a plentiful supply of dessert for the children and tobacco and snuff for the adult inmates. The article describes how 'the dining hall and the sick and imbecile wards had been very tastefully decorated with holly, ivy etc ...'. As well as the inmates of the workhouse, invitations had been sent out to those young people who had been apprenticed or sent to service out of the workhouse. Local businesses also played their part. Mrs Hadley, for example, from the Blue Bell Inn in Bilston Street sent a parcel of sweets for the children and tobacco for the elder people.

The capacity of the workhouse eventually reached 1,000. However, any further expansion was impossible as it was now hemmed in by houses and factories. Air pollution from the neighbouring factories added to the problems. Faced with ever increasing demands on space, the town's Board of Guardians sent 50 inmates in 1885 to the Westbury-On-Severn Union in Gloucestershire which had spare capacity. By the end of the century it was clear that a new workhouse was required and a site was chosen at New Cross in Wednesfield. This was opened in September 1903, after which the Bilston Road workhouse was closed and demolished.

The Bateman family continued their unhappy association with the Union workhouse and three of William's grandsons, William, John and Thomas were 'residents' at the New Cross workhouse when the 1911 census was taken.

Health and Welfare

The Report of Doctor J. Dehane from Wolverhampton to the Poor Law Commissioners on 24 January, 1840 painted a less salubrious image of the town than the one presented by William White six years earlier. The report was one of many made on the Sanitary Condition of the Labouring Population of England. In his report Dehane conceded that it was not an unhealthy town, but stressed that the least pleasant areas were those most subject to disease. He went on the say in his report that 'few, if any, of the larger provincial towns in the United Kingdom have been suffered to continue in so neglected a condition'.

His report read: 'The principal thoroughfares are narrow, and what is worse, it is in their immediate neighbourhood that close courts and alleys abound ... A dense population is consequently congregated in these places, almost excluded from the public view, and a stranger would pass through the town with little or no idea of the immense numbers by which these precincts are inhabited ... A great disregard to decency also exists in connexion with these dwellings many of them have only one privy allotted for the use of several families ... Dirt and disarrangement mark their (houses') interior, and it is only to the free consumption of coal, to which their comparative healthiness can be attributed. Damp is expelled, and with it a train of disease.'

Horne's graphic descriptions in his 1841 report add to the image of poverty and squalor: 'In front of some of the small houses in these and other places, there are stagnant pools, the colour of dead porter, with a glistening metallic film over them ... .' In another part of his report, he notes that: 'There is often a common dunghill at one end, or in one corner, where everything is cast ... .'

As in most towns across the country, general conditions in Wolverhampton at the start of Victoria's reign in 1837 were appalling. The town centre had grown rapidly with a build-up of courts and alleys in the Stafford Road and Littles Lane area and the development of Caribee Island. The most notorious part was undoubtedly Caribee Island, regarded as the Irish and prostitute quarter of the town and described around the time as 'a collection of the most squalid looking houses on the north side of Stafford Street inhabited by the lowest class of Irish'. By 1851, the Irish community made up 12% of the population of Wolverhampton.

Following his marriage in 1846, my 2nd great grandfather William Bateman moved to Littles Lane in the Caribee Island area of Wolverhampton and raised a family of seven children. Born in Wolverhampton in 1815, I am not aware of any Irish ancestry. For most of his working life, William was a porter at local shops such as the grocer, moving on a regular basis around the immediate area from Littles Lane to Carberry (Caribee) Street and Montrose Street before settling in Junction Street in nearby Springfield around 1870.

An examination of the hospital registers of the day revealed that the particularly unhealthy areas were Caribee Isle (49 cases of typhoid), Rawlinson's Entry, Back Lane, and the two Castle-places, Smithfield, Lichfield Street. Berry Street, Market Street, Wheelers Fold and Canal Street; many of these street names are familiar today.

Following the 1848 Public Health Act, a Government inspector, Robert Rawlinson, visited Wolverhampton and his report to the General Board of Health made alarming reading. It stated that one in six children in the town died in their first year, life expectancy at birth was only just over 19 years and two thirds of houses had no sewerage or drains.

> *In 1849, Wolverhampton was incorporated as a municipal borough under the Municipal Corporations Act 1835.*

Despite these stark reports, William White continued to paint an agreeable picture of the town. In his last Directory of Staffordshire, published in 1851, Wolverhampton is still described as the largest town in the county, retaining its salubrious and picturesque location, despite being 'seated in the heart of the midland mining district, surrounded by extensive coal and iron works, and having within its own limits, …, a great variety of sooty manufactories, … Its reputation for craftsmanship is still celebrated for the manufacture of almost every article in the ironmongery line, and other goods of which iron, steel, brass and tin are the component materials'.

6

IRON AND COAL PRODUCTION IN WOLVERHAMPTON

While Wolverhampton was building up a glowing reputation for producing quality goods from iron, brass and steel, the miners, otherwise referred to as colliers, around Rough Hills, Parkfield, Cockshutts and Monmore Green were extracting the raw materials for making many of these goods. Iron production by the start of the 19th century required iron ore (ironstone), coke (from coal) and limestone and all three materials were available in the vicinity. In fact, one specific type of iron ore, known as Rough Hills white ironstone, was unique to the area between Wolverhampton and Bilston, having first been worked at that location.

Mining for coal is believed to have started in the Wolverhampton area in the 14th century. The town lay on the edge of the famous South Staffordshire coalfield made up of 14 closely compacted seams and widely known as the 'ten-yard seam', the thickest seam in Great Britain, high in quality as well as in quantity. Coal is known to have been dug at Bradley by 1315, near Wednesfield in 1325 and at Bilston by 1401. A coalmine was being worked in Ettingshall in 1490. Dr. Robert Plot, the professor of Chemistry at Oxford University visited Wolverhampton in the 1670s and remarks, in his book 'Natural History of Staffordshire', that he found the town's high position made it healthy despite the 'fumes' from the coalmines.

Until the late 1500s, the coal would have been used exclusively by the local blacksmiths but it then became increasingly used for domestic heating. In the 17th and 18th centuries the area was experiencing the growth of the iron industry. Since coal was needed for its production from iron ore, the mining industry rapidly expanded. By 1790 the metal industries of the area alone consumed 845,000 tons of coal with the ironmaster John "Iron Mad" Wilkinson of Bilston using 800 tons of coal each week. Thousands of people across the country were drawn off the land and into the coalmines. The coal in parts of South Staffordshire could be extracted so cheaply that investing in the mining industry proved attractive to local landowners and businessmen and it was not uncommon for one owner to run several mines.

Dudley Road extended southwards from the town centre and created an east-west divide in the landscape. The land to the west of the road was generally made up of field systems, while to the east the land was either dominated by active industrial use or was derelict as a result of such uses. In this area, the ground was rich in mineral resources containing coal, ironstone, limestone and brick clay. The coal seams were erratic with the 'ten-yard seam' and the 'thin coal' found side by side. The Lord Dudley map of 1812 shows several collieries in the area named by location or owner: Monmore Green; Mount Pleasant; Cockshutt; Timmins and Co.; Rough Hills while the Fereday and Co. Furnaces were shown at Rough Hills to the west of the Birmingham canal.

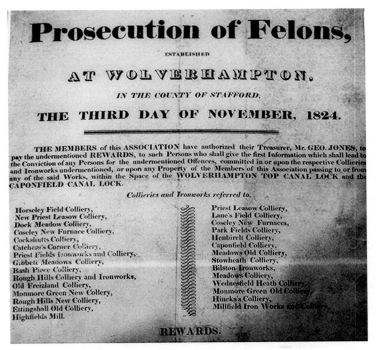

Figure 8: Reward Poster from Association of Coal and Ironmasters. (Photograph reproduced with the permission of Wolverhampton Archives and Local Studies).

Despite the economic and social disruptions which ensued when the Napoleonic Wars ended in 1815, mining had clearly become established in the area and by 1824 an Association of Coal and Ironmasters had been set up in Wolverhampton for the Prosecution of Felons. In November of that year, they printed a poster offering rewards of up to £10 to members of the general public who provided information about crimes such as 'Capital Felony', 'unlawfully, riotously, and tumultuously assembling together in disturbance of the Public Peace', or 'unlawfully, and with force, demolishing, pulling down, destroying or damaging any Engine, Bridge, Wagon Way, or Erection'. The reward poster listed 29 collieries in the areas of Wolverhampton and Bilston including the new and old Monmore Green collieries, the new Rough Hills Colliery, the Rough Hills Colliery and Ironworks and Cockshutts Colliery. The 1833 Ordnance Survey map of the SE of Wolverhampton shows the distribution of collieries and furnaces in the area. The scale of 1:50,000 precludes details of their precise position and boundaries but the collieries of Rough Hills, Cockshutts, Parkfield and Lanesfield as well as the furnaces of Wolverhampton and Parkfield are shown lying north and south of the road we now know as Parkfield Road.

In the next two chapters we will look in more detail at the development, during the 19th century, of mining and ironmaking in the Rough Hills area and the communities that grew up in the locality.

7

THE HISTORY OF THE COLLIERIES AND IRONWORKS IN AND AROUND ROUGH HILLS

Lord Dudley's 1812 map of mines provides a useful starting point in terms of the names and locations of mines and furnaces in the area. A colliery and furnace are both marked at Rough Hills under the ownership of Fereday. There is no sign of the Wolverhampton Ironworks shown on the Godson map but to the west is marked the colliery of Timmins and Co. Further west towards the Fighting Cocks junction is found the Cockshutts Colliery under the ownership of Gibbons and Bickley. The Monmore Green colliery is shown near the junction of the Birmingham canal and Bilston Road. Another colliery called the Mount Pleasant Colliery is shown to its south but subsequent research has not produced any further information about it.

In 1824, the Wolverhampton Association of Coal and Ironmasters for the Prosecution of Felons released a poster listing 29 collieries in their locality. Two were confirmed at Rough Hills: the Rough Hills Colliery and Ironworks and the Rough Hills New Colliery. Another two were listed for Monmore Green. Cockshutts Colliery was included but no mention was made of the Wolverhampton Colliery. Regrettably, the poster gave no further information about the precise location or ownership of the individual mines and during my research these two issues have led to much frustration.

By the 1840s, detailed evidence is obtained from the 1842 Tithe map of Wolverhampton which shows a large swathe of coalmines, furnaces and ironworks with Cockshutts and Rough Hills marked as distinct areas. The map confirms the important role that Rough Hills played in mining and ironmaking and provides important evidence about the ownership of each parcel of land.

Figure 9: The corner of Rooker Avenue and Rough Hills Road - the site of the Rough Hills colliery in the 1800s.

In an article published on 26 July 1843 in the Wolverhampton Chronicle, Staffordshire and South Wales are described as 'the two great seats of the (iron) trade'. Even as late as 1861, the number of furnaces in the Wolverhampton and Bilston area (130) was well in excess of any other district in England, including Yorkshire (36) and Stockton and Darlington (86).

By the time we get to the start of 1860, one of the Rough Hills collieries, the Cockshutts Colliery as well as the Wolverhampton Ironworks and Colliery were all owned by Isaiah Aston and his domination continued well into the 1860s. If there is a perception that the collieries around the Rough Hills area were insignificant enterprises, run by men looking to make a quick, trouble-free profit from mineral resources readily available below ground, I hope my research will quash that supposition. Isaiah Aston who died, aged 59, in 1878 was one of the most prominent coalmasters. A practising nonconformist: he laid foundation stones at Methodist chapels in Wolverhampton, held a Christmas service for his employees in one of his colliery pits and provided Christmas meals for over a hundred of his miners and ironworkers. In the Birmingham Daily Gazette of 30 July 1866, Aston was described as possessing 'an amount of experience of mining operations equal to any mining engineer in South Staffordshire and is esteemed and respected by all'. The article also pointed out his estate was 'on the borders of the Red Sandstone Fault and on this account the mines are found in continual displacement and are, consequently, difficult and expensive to win'. The coal and ironmasters like Isaiah Aston who ran the companies around Rough Hills deserve more recognition for their achievements.

Despite this substantial history, locating books and articles on the ironworks and coalmines around the Rough Hills area has proved elusive. Indeed, much of the information I have gathered has been obtained indirectly from newspaper reports on the internet of events such as auctions, accidents and even civil disturbances, and matching the owner and location to each colliery has not always been achieved in the most convincing manner. Nevertheless, some sense of the chronological order of events in the area is beginning to emerge.

Rough Hills Colliery and Ironworks

Although it is not clear when Rough Hills Colliery opened, the accounts books detailing its sales of ironstone verify it was already operating by 1803. The 1812 map of Lord Dudley's mines clearly shows the colliery, located south west of the Birmingham canal, near what is now Rough Hills Road. Adjacent to the colliery, close to what is now Cheviot Road, was the site of an ironworks. It is marked on the Godson map of 1788 as a furnace and accounts for the sale of refined iron at Rough Hills Ironworks also go back to at least 1803.

It was an age of integrated enterprises and some ironmasters not only owned the furnaces and foundries but the collieries as well. Evidence from the accounts books for the sale of refined iron suggests the Rough Hills collieries and ironworks were owned by Fereday and Co. This was a partnership of Samuel Fereday, John Read, Richard Smith and George and Thomas Stokes which owned a number of furnaces in the area. After the death of John Wilkinson in 1808, Samuel Fereday was probably the most important industrialist in the area until the slump in the iron trade which started in 1815 after the end of the Napoleonic Wars. The next seven years were some of the most difficult and troubled in British economic and social history. Reduced demand for iron in peacetime meant many ironworks and collieries closed down or cut their workforce. Fereday started to sell off his shareholdings but, despite this, he was declared bankrupt in April 1817. The estate was sold off to two Firmstone brothers: John Parsons and William. At the time, the estate comprised two blast furnaces capable of making between 120 and 140 tons of pig iron per week for local forges such as the one at Tipton. Plans for Furnace No.2 reveal that it was 27 feet high and the 'recipe' for making the pig iron was two tons of coal, one ton of ironstone and two barrow loads of coke. A third furnace was under construction. The estate was well organised with a basin link to the Birmingham Canal as well as tramways connecting the mines with the furnaces. By 1822, the Firmstone brothers had also been declared bankrupt with John Parsons carrying the bulk of the debts. The lease of the Rough Hills estate was advertised for sale in The Birmingham Gazette on 23 February 1824 and acquired in the same year by William Aston, another iron industry entrepreneur, for the sum of £22,000 The sale details made for impressive reading. It was described as 'a complete and connected Colliery and Ironwork' raising 400 to 500 tons of ironstone per week and enough coal to supply the three blast furnaces capable of making 130 to 150 tons of iron per week. There are 39 acres of 'New Mines' under lease for the remainder of 50 years, in addition to 22 acres of land and existing mines. The sale included engines capable of draining the mines, pit frames, gins, waggons and railway tracks connecting both the colliery and ironworks to the adjacent Birmingham Canal.

It was one of the ten businesses covering ironworks, collieries, furnaces and rolling mills in the Black Country that Aston bought between 1824 and 1826. Despite the unstable financial climate that existed at the time, Aston's order books

37

for 1825 and 1826 show the sale of plates, bars and other items to a number of companies, based mainly in the north west of England: Rogers and Parker in Oldham, Bridge Foundry in Warrington and Phillip Norris, an anchor smith, from Liverpool. Very quickly it became clear that Aston had overstretched his financial resources and in June 1826, he too fell victim to bankruptcy. The furnaces ceased to be used and were eventually demolished.

Despite this setback, coal production at Rough Hills Colliery continued and by 1826 it was owned by W and G. Firmstone, Bishton and Underhill. Whether this is the 'Old' or 'New' colliery is unclear. Accounts for a four-week period ending 14 May 1831 reveal the following figures:

Mineral		Raised (Tons)	Sold (Tons)
Coal	Coal	355	11 by Land, 344 by Canal
	Lumps	175	175
	Slack	70	70
	Coke	452	424
White Ironstone	Robins		
	Balls	278	270
	Blue Flats		
	Gubbins		

While all the ironstone seems to have been sold to Gospel Oak Furnaces, the coal was purchased by a number of companies including Wolverhampton Gas Company, Gospel Oak Furnaces, Jenks and Company from Horseley Fields and Timmins and Company who owned Wolverhampton Ironworks, a short distance away. The table also illustrates how important the canal network was to the coal trade at that time.

Another notable owner at Rough Hills was Thomas William

Giffard from Chillington Hall near Brewood. Along with the Duke of Sutherland, Giffard was the joint lord of the manor of Stowheath and thereby owned the land on which the collieries and ironworks were located. There is evidence that by 1830 Giffard had sold off other mines in the Stowheath area but retained one colliery at Rough Hills. Accounts published for the two quarters ending in October 1830 reveal the colliery made a profit of £758 while the next accounts, published in July 1831, show another profit of £629. In 1832, records show that Rough Hills coal was being distributed to The Sutton Company, Wolverhampton Gas Company and the Eagle Furnace Company, while most of the ironstone went to the Birmingham Coal and Iron Company. The 1834 History, Gazetteer and Directory of Staffordshire lists John Turton Fereday, a nephew of Samuel, as the coalmaster of Rough Hills Colliery.

The 1841 census records appear to show that when the Tithe map was being drawn up, the mining community of Rough Hills was relatively small with only 29 dwellings and 164 residents of whom 47 were miners, nearly one third of the population. The collieries around Rough Hills had spread to cover a large area of about 78 acres, extending from Parkfield Road beyond the Birmingham canal towards Ettingshall Road. The principal landowners and occupiers (tenants) in the Rough Hills area at the time of the map were:

Landowner	Occupier	Acreage
Duke of Sutherland	John Turton Fereday	12 (two separate sites)
Benjamin Bickley	John Turton Fereday	7
J. and W. Firmstone Trustees	Themselves	35
Bate and Robins	Phineas Bullocks Devisees	3
John Dixon and Others	Themselves	21

Most of these landowners had local connections. Bate and Robins were bankers from Stourbridge, John Dixon lived at Merridale, Wolverhampton, while the Firmstones from Kingswinford, before their death, were coal and ironmasters. Even the Duke of Sutherland had a local connection, going back to the 1500s, when his Wolverhampton ancestor, James Leveson, bought Trentham Priory and its lands. In contrast, Benjamin Bickley was a merchant from Bristol. The role of the occupier (tenant) is described in the next chapter.

The largest colliery site, by far, was owned by the trustees of J and W. Firmstone. Situated just south of the modern Rough Hills estate, it was surrounded by small plots of land, described as 'House or Garden', occupied by the workers and their families. In most cases, these homes will have been constructed by the workers themselves, using assorted materials collected from the neighbouring area. To the north west, around the site of the Dixon Street playing fields, lay the Wolverhampton Furnaces and Yards now owned by John Dixon. Further west, out towards what is now the Pond Lane area, Dixon owned the other large colliery in the area. The map also shows a collection of three small collieries north and south of the Birmingham canal, east of what is now Dixon Street. One is left to speculate as to which ones represent the 'Old' and 'New' collieries mentioned on the 1824 poster.

We get the first clear facts about the New Rough Hills Colliery in 1847 when it came up came up for sale by auction. Details of the property are provided in the 13 February 1847 edition of the Staffordshire Advertiser. The twelve-acre site is described as near the Wolverhampton Furnaces and nearly adjacent to the Birmingham canal. It goes on to say that there are twelve pit shafts exposing measures of coal and ironstone as well as 'an excellent mine of clay or brick earth'. The lease of the surface had 28 years remaining. The 'Old' and 'New' collieries of Rough Hills, named in the 1824 poster, are referred to again in Bakers's Practical survey of the geology, mineralogy, and historical events of the District of Dudley published in 1848. A court case reported in the Leeds Mercury of the 28 December 1850 refers to the owners as Messrs Hill and Dixon. When it came up for auction again in 1856, the sale details were similar with the addition of four cottages. Neither sale, unfortunately, gave any detail of the buyers.

During the 1840s and 50s, the distinction between the Rough Hills collieries in newspaper and trade articles is still obscure. For instance, an advert in the Wolverhampton Chronicle from January 1855 refers to the sale of boats by Mr James Dodd of Rough Hills colliery, while the records from the National Coalmining Museum of England in the same year and 'Memoirs of the Geological Survey of Great Britain' database for 1855 both list the owners at a Rough Hills colliery as Whitehouse and Poole, a fact corroborated by newspaper reports which describe the rioting by colliers in March 1855. A revealing insight into the ownership of the collieries at Rough Hills is provided by Perry's Bankrupt Gazette of 27 September 1856 which refers to a partnership at New Rough Hills Colliery being dissolved between James Cadman, James Dodd and Thomas Ramsell, following Ramsell's death. 'Memoirs of the Geological Survey of Great Britain' had listed one colliery only at Rough Hills in 1855 but the 1857 edition actually lists three: one of which is owned by Isaiah Aston and William Corns, another by James Cadman and Dodd and the last by Edward Poole. If one assumes, correctly or otherwise, that Cadman and Dodd owned the 'New' colliery, one is left to speculate on the owner(s) of the 'Old' colliery and the owner(s) and location of the third, or even the accuracy of the list. By the end of the decade, we have a court case in the Wolverhampton Chronicle of January 1859 which confirms that Aston and Corns owned one of the Rough Hills collieries, probably the Old Rough Hills Colliery, near Green Lane. Another court case came up in August of the same year which adds to the confusion over the number and ownership of these collieries. The trial reported in the Wolverhampton Chronicle reveals that the plaintiff, a butty miner at Rough Hills colliery, formerly worked for the trustees of Edward Poole until the colliery changed owners and the defendants, Aston and Corns became lessees. In all probability Aston and Corns, at the start of 1860, owned the Old Rough Hills colliery as well as Cockshutts Colliery and the Wolverhampton Ironworks and Colliery.

Up to 1865 the New Rough Hills Colliery was being run by Cadman, Dodd and Benjamin Francis but in March of that year the London Gazette announced that the partnership has been dissolved leaving Cadman and Francis to operate the business. Then in May 1865, the Wolverhampton Chronicle reported that this latest partnership has already been dissolved, leaving James Cadman, a timber merchant, in charge. A year later, the Staffordshire Advertiser of the 8 September 1866 reveals the sale by auction of Rough Hills Colliery, Green Lane, run by Isaiah Aston. Included in the same sale incidentally were The Wolverhampton Furnaces and Colliery. While the later issues of the newspaper provided no further information about the outcome of the sale, the auction details listed a comprehensive array of plant equipment including fifteen iron and wood canal boats, four steam engines and gearing with four large steam boilers and fittings, one winding gin, frame and chains, thirty iron pump trees as well as two machine houses.

As the decade came to a close, the 'Collieries of the UK at Work' database for 1869 still lists two collieries at Rough Hills: one owned by Aston and Shaw and another by Cadman. By 1871 two collieries were still operating, one owned by Aston and the other by James Cadman but significant changes were about to happen. In January 1873, the London Gazette announced that the partnership between Isaiah Aston and Enoch Cooper at the Old Wolverhampton (Rough Hills?) Colliery had been dissolved in the previous December. The colliery would now operate under the ownership of E. Cooper and Co. The Birmingham Daily Post edition of 9 October 1874 announced the sale of the New Rough Hills Colliery by James Cadman of Priestfield, Wolverhampton. Due to ill-health, Cadman was selling the lease of the colliery, describing it as having 20 acres of 2ft 4inch coal, 6 acres of ironstone, as well as other coal minerals and sufficient plant to work the mines. This sale was going through despite the fact that the lease was about to expire. Not for the first time, information about the buyer has not been found.

By now, one suspects that intensive mining at Rough Hills was in terminal decline. The historical documents increasingly record the sale and purchase of land on and around the Rough Hills collieries, with coalmasters left to exploit the remaining underground resources. The Birmingham Daily Post of 23 July 1875 reports on an incident at the (Old?) Rough Hills Colliery, owned by Enoch Cooper. Although it is not included in the Coal Mining History Resource Centre list of South Staffordshire collieries for 1880, the National Coalmining Museum of England lists Joseph Baugh (Bough?) as an owner. An article in the London Gazette of 1882 names Rough Hills colliery as belonging to and occupied by William Fenn. To confuse matters even further, an article on the mines drainage rates in the 1 July 1882 edition of the Staffordshire Advertiser lists two collieries at Rough Hills: one owned by Mr. B. Southan, the other by Messrs Johnson and Powis. The National Coalmining Museum of England records show that the Rough Hills collieries closed in 1885 with the last owners being Isaac Armstrong and R. Bailey. This may not have been the case as a report from 1896 by W. Beattie Scott, H.M. Inspector for the South Stafford District, lists two mines in the Rough Hills area. One was owned by J. Bough and the other by Cooper and Company. At each colliery, three workers were employed underground and two on the surface, suggesting that they were rudimentary enterprises: basic gin pits or maybe nothing more than bell pits. No further records of mining appear after that date.

Figure 10: Thompson Avenue - the old bus terminal and the site of Cockshutts Colliery in the 1800s.

Cockshutts Colliery

The Cockshutts Colliery area covered about 30 acres of land belonging to the Duke of Cleveland. It was centred on the junction of what is now Thompson Avenue and Parkfield Road, on the edge of the Parkfields Estate.

44

Coal and ironstone mining at Cockshutts was well established before 1810 with the first colliery run by Gibbons and Bickley. At the time of rioting in 1832, it was run by Bishton and Underhill. The article about the riots and the death of a worker in the 7 January 1832 edition of the Staffordshire Advertiser newspaper provides a useful description of the colliery. It appears that it was made up of several pits some of which shared a windlass, or whimsey, used to carry men and equipment up and down and minerals up the shaft. Its pits were 'under the care' of individuals such as Benjamin Butler and John Morris. In 1836, George and William Bishton were declared bankrupt. Their shares and interests in Cockshutts Colliery, one of the ten mines and ironworks in which they had a financial involvement, were put up for auction in February of that year. Research, so far, has not divulged who bought up their shares.

The 1842 Tithe map reveals that while the leaseholder of the 'main' colliery was now John Underhill, two other collieries to the west, Big and Little Cockshutt, were run by John Dixon and partners. The map also establishes that the colliery grounds were surrounded by a number of small enclosures described as 'House and Garden' or 'Garden'. At that time the settlement at Cockshutts was larger than the one at Rough Hills, made up of 40 houses with a population of 242. It was clearly another mining community with 60 miners recorded on the census and 29 of those 40 dwellings housing at least one miner. As well as coal, the colliery mined for ironstone and many of the miners are recorded on the census as stone miners.

As we saw with the Rough Hills Colliery, the Cockshutts Colliery went through a succession of owners but, just as before, the timeline has often been difficult to establish. We have to wait until 1857 when 'Memoirs of the Geological Survey of Great Britain' shows the colliery was now owned by the Parkfield Company. By 1858, ownership had passed to Isaiah Aston and William Corns. When Corns retired in March 1860 a new firm of Isaiah Aston and Co. was formed. By 1861, it was owned by Isaiah Aston and Richard Shaw. Perry's Bankrupt Gazette of 6 October 1866 announced that the partnership had been dissolved in July of that year, following the collapse of their Wolverhampton Furnaces and Colliery firm. Nevertheless, the 'Collieries of the UK at Work' database for 1869 still lists the colliery as operating under Aston and Shaw, despite Aston's temporary bankruptcy in January 1868. It was still under Isaiah Aston's ownership in 1874. A Birmingham Daily Post article on the 11 September of that year discloses that Edward Aston, probably a brother of Isaiah, is not to be involved in any financial transaction involving Cockshutts Colliery Company. The mine seems to have closed about 1875, but once again there are inconsistencies in the records and the National Coalmining Museum of England shows it was owned by Isaac Onions in 1900 and operating in 1915 under the ownership of John Carter.

Wolverhampton Colliery and Ironworks

Evidence of ironmaking in this part of the town goes back to at least 1788, with the Godson map of that year showing a 'furnace' marked in the area. It is not known how long this enterprise lasted and it does not make an appearance on the Lord Dudley 1812 map of mines. The same map does show, to the north west of the Rough Hills Colliery, another colliery belonging to Thomas Timmins and Company. This developed into the Wolverhampton Colliery Estate and was made up initially of coal and ironstone mines. The company, of which Joseph

Tarratt was a member, erected a single blast furnace during 1825 and produced 1,800 tons of iron in that year. In contrast, the three blast furnaces at Rough Hills produced 5,200 tons. By 1830, another blast furnace had been erected on the Wolverhampton estate and iron production had almost doubled. Joseph Tarratt continued to be a partner of Thomas Timmins in the company until the partnership was dissolved in 1835. At some point the ownership passed onto Dixon, Neve and Co., and Thorneycroft until the partnership was dissolved in February 1841 and Thorneycroft left. The ironworks are clearly marked on the 1842 tithe map, lying near to where the Dixon Street playing fields are located and in 1843 the Wolverhampton Chronicle reported that Dixon, Neve and Hill were working two of their three furnaces, producing 160 tons per week.

As we found with Cockshutts Colliery, there is another significant gap in the records after the 1842 Tithe map was drawn up. We have to wait until the 1855 edition of 'Memoirs of the Geological Survey of Great Britain' to find Whitehouse and Edward Poole listed as its owners. The 1857 version lists only Poole. It seems he was still the owner a year later when the inquest into the death of a miner, James Cane, was reported in the 14 July edition of the Wolverhampton Chronicle. In the article, Wolverhampton Ironworks Colliery is referred to as Poole's Colliery. This ownership is corroborated in the 1858 edition of 'Memoirs of the Geological Survey of Great Britain'. Edward Poole died around August 1859 and it would appear the trustees of his estate sold not only the Rough Hills Colliery to Isaiah Aston and William Corns but also Wolverhampton Ironworks and Colliery. Certainly by late 1859 newspaper articles in the Wolverhampton Chronicle identify Aston and Corns as the owners of both enterprises.

The Birmingham Daily Gazette of 30 July 1866 reported that July 'had been the most memorable month of disasters for the iron trade of these districts ever witnessed'. The newspaper referred to a drop in orders from home and abroad, with a dire warning that something must be done or 'half the ironworks of the Black Country will be closed and tens of thousands of iron workers without employment or means of sustenance'. The article announced that one of the many casualties were Messrs Aston and Shaw of Wolverhampton Furnaces, in debt to the sum of £30,000. The newspaper described Shaw as 'a gentleman of good family and position' who had brought £15,000 in hard cash into the concern. Isaiah Aston also received a glowing character reference and both partners were considered to have 'acted with prudence and economy'.

As described earlier, the Wolverhampton Furnaces and Colliery came up for sale by auction in September 1866 but there are no records that a buyer was found for the furnaces. Although production at the ironworks is believed to have stopped in 1866, the Collieries of the UK at Work records for 1869 indicate that the colliery was still operational, under the ownership of Isaiah Aston. The Staffordshire Advertiser of 28 July 1877 refers to 'the mines of William Fenn, known as the Wolverhampton Colliery, at Rough Hills'. Mr Fenn gained exemption from paying rates to cover the cost of draining mines in the Bilston area. Incidentally, an earlier newspaper article on the same topic gives the address as Green Lane.

The last reference to the colliery that I have found appears in the Birmingham Daily Post on 29 March 1888. The owner, George Arnold, is fined a total of £5. 7s for twelve breaches of the Mines Regulation Act.

Monmore Green Colliery

Close to the north and east of Rough Hills were the mining settlements of Monmore Green, Chillington and Portobello. The 1812 map shows Monmore Green Colliery straddling both sides of the Birmingham canal south of the road to Bilston.

By 1822 it was under the ownership of John Turton Fereday. The Wolverhampton Chronicle edition of the 24 September 1834 advertises the sale at the 'old' Monmore Green Colliery of plant equipment including five winding gins. The effects were described as the property of the late Mr W. Turner, presumably the owner until his death. At the time of the 1842 Tithe map, Monmore Green was by far the biggest of the three mining communities. 64 dwellings were listed on the census housing 361 occupants, of which 70 were miners. Records in the Memoirs of the Geological Survey of Great Britain for 1857 disclose three collieries owned by Corbett and Hartshorne, Cadman and Dodd and by Dimmack and Company. A year later, the colliery owned by Dimmack and Company had closed. By 1869, the 'Collieries of the UK at Work' database for 1869 records only one colliery, owned by Corbett and Hartshorne. This is believed to have operated until at least 1870, after which no further information has been found.

1875 and Beyond

Once we reach the early 1870s, it is evident that the heyday of mining and ironmaking in and around Rough Hills was over. By 1875 the leasehold on land occupied by the New Rough Hills Colliery had expired and other neighbouring collieries may well have experienced similar leasehold terminations. Coalmining in

South Staffordshire was now becoming dominated by the large pits around Cannock Chase. The centre of iron and steel manufacturing in the country was shifting to the north east in towns like Middlesbrough. For at least 70 years, Rough Hills had contributed towards of the growth and impact of coalmining and iron production in South Staffordshire and the Black Country. By the end of the century, only the pit mounds and disused pit shafts would be left to remind visitors of this significant involvement.

8

THE MINING COMMUNITIES IN AND AROUND ROUGH HILLS

Detailed information about the mining communities on Rough Hills and Cockshutts, as well as neighbouring settlements like Monmore Green has been obtained by attempting to analyse the census returns. Without a precise indication of these 'parish' boundaries, it is difficult to give accurate figures for houses, occupiers and occupations. Nevertheless, one is left in no doubt about the mining background of the three areas and the people who lived there.

The records for the 1841 census revealed how mining communities had become established around each of these collieries. The census records from 1851 reveal that the Cockshutts mining community had changed very little with the same number of houses, 40, and a population of 244, almost identical to ten years ago. The Rough Hills community had become significantly smaller with only 20 homes housing 99 inhabitants. These were still genuine mining communities and most homes included at least one person working as a miner of coal or stone. Around Cockshutts colliery, 35 of the 40 homes included at least one person working in the mining industry. While most wives stayed at home, some of the daughters were working as banks women or girls, the 'pitbonk wenches'.

Working Conditions

The working conditions of miners in the nineteenth century are well documented. In the first half of the century a day's shift could be as long as 13 hours, with the only day of rest being Sunday. Work was extremely strenuous and associated with a number of occupational injuries and diseases. Coalminers aged early with many unfit for work by the time they reached 40. Life expectancy was low and even in South Staffordshire, where working conditions were comparatively favourable, few men were said to reach their fifty-first year.

Despite the lifetime exertions by a miner, the general public held mixed views about mining communities. While they had little sympathy for the men, perceived as wild, hard drinkers lacking morals and education, they were horrified by the stories of the women and children spending long, strenuous hours underground in cramped and dangerous conditions. Pressure was put on Parliament for more information and a Royal Commission on the Employment of Children in Mines was set up in 1842. Commissioners were appointed to examine the conditions in the coalfields of the country, to take evidence from collieries and mining communities and to report back to

Parliament. The Commissioners covered Scotland, Wales and Ireland as well as sixteen regions of England including South Staffordshire. I have made the assumption, rightly or wrongly, that the report on the coal and iron mines of South Staffordshire gives an insight into the management structure of a typical coalmine in the Rough Hills area.

It reveals that most of the proprietors (landlords) of the coalmines in the country let them to tenants on stringent conditions, the chief of which was the payment of a royalty in proportion to the coal raised. In order that the landlord did not suffer from the tenant neglecting to work with "sufficient energy", there was a stipulation that the tenant brought up a certain amount every year. If he failed to do so, he was still expected to pay the same royalty as if he had. As well as discouraging negligence by the tenant, the terms also stopped him from retaining possession of the mine and land after the coals were exhausted. The landlord would employ a person, the ground bailiff, to watch the progress of the mines and ensure the landlord was gaining the maximum financial benefit from his property.

The tenant who took the lease of a coalmine was usually an ironmaster, a manufacturer of iron who dug the coal for his own use, or a coalmaster, who intended to raise the coal for domestic heating in a town or to sell it to the ironmasters.

The contractors who did the work on behalf of the landlord or tenant in South Staffordshire were usually called 'butties' and operated a 'butty' system. A butty was generally a dependable man, who had risen from being a common workman by his good behaviour and work rate. Under this system the butty agreed to supply coal to the landlord or tenant of the mine at a set price and employed a small group of men to dig out the coal and minerals. The average payment made to the butty was from 2s. 6d to 3s. 6d. for every ton, but it could be higher if the pit was problematic. The 'butty' system continued until the Coal Mines Act of 1872 made it illegal.

The work in the pit and on the bank was carried out by men, women and children with clearly defined roles. The holers (hewers) dug the coal and were considered the most important men in the pits, being employed at work which required the greatest strength and skill. The pikeman broke up and brought down the 'top coal' in the gallery with a long pikestaff. This was another skilled job, albeit dangerous, and pikemen were some of the best paid miners in a pit. The man who was stationed at the bottom of the shaft to hook and unhook the skips of coals was the onsetter or hooker-on. He had charge of all ascending skips. The banksman was positioned at the bank, the top of the pit, and in charge of all descending skips carrying men, boys, tools, horses etc.

Miners were rewarded with good wages because contractors found it difficult to obtain enough suitable labour. It was an occupation only suitable for men who were strong and in a good state of health. Many potential workers were deterred by the harsh conditions and the probability of being injured, disabled or even killed. Hence many preferred to work in other branches of industry even if they earned considerably less. However, mining was not the only unappealing employment available to men in the Black Country and a trade such as brass casting had a reputation that was as bad, if not worse. The fumes from the zinc were excessively noxious and likely to reduce life expectancy. Workers were compensated by earnings that were equal to or even greater than the wages in the collieries.

The mining which took place was based around rigorous geological surveys that took place in the 1800s. A series of publications titled 'Memoirs of the Geological Survey of Great Britain' covered coalfields including that of South Staffordshire. The 1859 edition by Mr J. Beete Jukes describes the ground in the vicinity of Monmore Green, Rough Hills, Cockshutts and Parkfield as having 'complicated faults and contortions' creating 'a very broken and disturbed district of Coal-measures'. Over much of this area, shafts down to 300 feet or more were dug to reach the coal, ironstone and limestone seams, and men and machinery were employed to extract the

Figure 11: Coal pickers at Rough Hills (Photograph reproduced with the permission of Wolverhampton Archives and Local Studies).

mineral resources and remove the water which inevitably collected at the bottom of these mines. Elsewhere, the 'thin' seam was often very near the surface and in some instances the coal could be extracted relatively quickly and cheaply using less intensive methods. As recently as the 1930s there are photographs of men 'hand mining' the surface coal seam.

Initially the landscape was probably dominated by opencast mining with numerous, shallow, ill-equipped pits. Some of these will have been simple bell pits, in which a central shaft was dug down to the coal seams and widened at the bottom as the minerals were removed. As much coal as possible was removed until the roof showed signs of collapse, at which point the pit would be abandoned, and a replacement dug nearby. The bell pits had a windlass, also referred to as a whimsey, wound by workers to pull or lower skips up or down the shaft and as few as two men could operate such pits. In contrast, the 'gin pits' had gins, horse-driven winding gear, at the top of the shaft. They were more robust constructions, consisting of a large wooden horizontal drum around which the rope was wound, and turned by means of a beam to which the horse was attached. The horse walked in a circle, working a wheel that wound up or let down various loads into the pit. The gin-driver's job was to keep the horse going around and round, sometimes requiring the use of a whip. This work would be done by young boys and girls. Frequently there would be a simple

Figure 12: Gin pits from the Parkfields area (Photograph reproduced with the permission of Wolverhampton Archives and Local Studies).

shelter, the hovel, with a good fire at the side of the horse-track where the gin-driver could keep warm in bad weather while pelting the horse with small stones or coals to keep him going. Boys, girls and young women were also employed on the banks of the pits with some helping to empty the skips of coal after they were brought up. The skip was drawn up to just above the level of the ground. A slide was then pushed forward over the mouth of the pit, the skip lowered down upon it, then rolled forward on wheels and emptied of its contents. The empty skip was hooked on, and the slide withdrawn to let it go down. The death in 1855 of William Morgan from falling down a pit at Rough Hills colliery during one of these manoeuvres led to George Jones from Springvale Ironworks sending a letter to the Wolverhampton Chronicle. He feared that similar accidents would take place until the procedure was improved and announced that he had patented a 'landing machine', promising that it would prevent any further deaths. It is not known whether George's device was ever adopted.

Another task carried out by boys on the bank was to go to the local blacksmith with picks sent up the shaft to be mended. A little boy of seven or eight might carry half a dozen picks and as he grew stronger he was expected to carry a dozen or more. Many boys and young men worked in the mines as apprentices. According to the evidence of witnesses interviewed by the Commissioners, boys between the ages of eight and nine would start working at a mine on a trial basis. They were usually orphans and paupers sent from the local workhouse. It was said that this practice was more common in South Staffordshire than anywhere else. If they proved to be good workers, they were taken on at nine on a 12 year 'apprenticeship', despite the general belief that there was nothing significant for them to learn. The pay was poor and the main motive for this long 'training programme' was seen to be profit for all concerned from butty up to landowner.

Where you had deeper pits, and accident reports tell of shafts in the Rough Hills area going down 300 feet or more, an additional problem for the mine owners was flooding. To combat this, engine houses were built alongside the pit to accommodate a boiler and steam driven pump for removing the water. The presence of such structures and equipment in the sale by auction of Rough Hills Colliery and Ironwork in 1824 and Wolverhampton Colliery and Rough Hills Colliery in 1866 dispels the assumption that mining in the area was solely based on bell pits and simple gin pits. The additional data from geological surveys, mining accidents and the census records supports the likelihood that the Rough Hills and Cockshutts landscape comprised of not only bell pits but also deep gin pits of varying complexity, utilising a diverse range of plant equipment and mining occupations.

Living Conditions

The harsh working conditions of the miner were matched by the conditions in which they lived. The Rawlinson Report of 1848 to the General Board of Health contains a reference to the mining communities around Monmore Green and Rough Hills. He says, 'To the eastward, in the mining district, there is not much attention paid to agriculture, and drainage would not be of much avail, as the whole surface is disturbed by the mining operations carried on; when the coal and iron-stone has been removed, vast areas of the ground sink in, shaking and fracturing houses and buildings of all descriptions.' Houses in these mining communities were usually small single storey dwellings, with one or two rooms and tiny windows providing little or no ventilation. The interiors were invariably dark and damp, despite the cheap abundance of coal. An article in the 4 August 1858 edition of the Wolverhampton Chronicle suggests that tenants would have been paying an annual rent of about £1.

Despite the struggles associated with their harsh lives, a report in the Staffordshire Advertiser of 16 June 1855 illustrates how some residents in these mining communities were not readily defeated by them. The first show of the year organised by the Wolverhampton Floral and Horticultural Society at Oaks

Crescent, Merridale was described in detail and included the prize winners in the various categories. These included Mr Griffiths from Cockshutts Colliery in the amateur section. The newspaper highlights his circumstances as follows: 'The garden of the latter, let it be remembered to his praise, is situated in the midst of the Cockshutts Colliery; yet amid the smoke of furnaces and coke hearths this indefatigable man can grow succession cucumbers of unrivalled flavour, roses, geraniums, fuchsias &c.'

Compared to the wages of many other workers, those of miners were quite good, an acknowledgement of the arduous nature of their job. The weekly budget of a miner with a wife and two children earning 18/-d (90 pence) a week in 1850 would look something like this:

Item	Cost
Rent	3s. 0d
Food	9s. 0d
Shoes and Clothing	1s. 6d.
Household durables	1s. 6d.
Miscellaneous (education, medicine, newspaper, subscriptions, pocket money)	2s. 0d.
Services (travel, postage, entertainment)	1s. 6d

Other 'essentials' like drink, tobacco, savings for old age, emergencies and holidays are not accounted for.

Wages were based on a 'piece rate' basis with miners given a 'stent' or fixed amount of work to do each day or week. The 'stent' was determined by the landowner, tenant or the butty. Miners were not necessarily paid weekly or even regularly. Every two weeks was the norm but it would often depend on the output from the mine. In some cases, miners were the unwilling victims of the truck or "tommy" system whereby the butty paid wages not in cash but in the form of a voucher exchangeable for goods from the colliery owner's shop. This wage practice spread rapidly in Staffordshire in the 1790s. It became illegal for some trades in the 1830s, but a lack of enforcement meant it continued in many areas until the Truck Act of 1887. A South Staffordshire delegate at the National Conference of Miners, held in Glasgow in 1844, describes how the miners in his area were 'already bound, neck and heel, by the truck system'. The 1851 census records list a 'Tommy Shop' at Rough Hills.

The state of the mining industry was influenced by national and global issues. Communities had suffered badly when the Napoleonic Wars ended in 1815. This created a slump in iron production which in turn led to a fall in coal production. Even where mines remained open, workers' hours or wages were reduced and unrest grew amongst the men. Probably some miners from Rough Hills and Cockshutts will have taken part in the 'Colliers' March' of 1816 in which waggons of coal were pulled from South Staffordshire to London in an unsuccessful attempt to publicise their plight and persuade the Prince Regent to bring about improvements to their employment rights.

Dissent among workers continued for many years and inevitably it led to incidents across the country, including Wolverhampton. The Wolverhampton Chronicle reported on a serious confrontation which took place in April 1822. Striking miners arrived at the Monmore Green colliery of John Turton Fereday to intimidate working miners and stop production. A group of militia was already in place to protect the miners but in the fracas that ensued, shots were fired and John Robson was fatally wounded. Seven strikers were arrested for assaulting working miners. A few days later William Firmstone the manager at Rough Hills Furnaces suffered an alarming experience when colliers invaded the mines and manhandled him. The local Coal and Ironmasters met in Walsall in early May to discuss the incidents. It was unanimously resolved 'that the sole and entire cause of the disturbances has been a refusal of the workmen to work at the rate of the wages which have been offered them, which exceed those given in other Mining Districts, and, not as has been industriously propagated, the payment of wages otherwise than in money'. They went on to say that the refusal on the part of the workmen to accept the rate of wages was 'injudicious, unreasonable and unwarrantable'. The coal and ironmasters were not prepared to meet the demands of the miners even if the consequence was 'to produce the ruin and starvation of the workmen and their families'.

Discontent was to flare up again in the early 1830s when large numbers of miners across the country went on strike for a rise in wages. Once again groups targeted the collieries of Rough Hills, Cockshutts and Parkfield. Newspaper reports, such as the one in the 7 January 1832 edition of the Staffordshire Advertiser, describe strikers 'armed with bludgeons and other weapons' forcing colliers out of pits from their work and throwing them into water holes and throwing the pit ropes off their pullies. The eyewitness gives a graphic account of the violent scenes. At Cockshutts Colliery the strikers attacked John Morris, who ran one of the pits, as well as his son and daughter. At Parkfields Colliery, John Rowe, an ironstone 'getter', was forced out of a pit, pushed into the water hole and held under. He was eventually helped out of the water by a woman but died at his home a few days later.

It was not until the 1840s that trade unions began to emerge and in 1844 a National Conference of Miners took place with delegates representing miners from England, Scotland and

Ireland assembled in Glasgow. The 1850s saw the establishment of miners' unions operating throughout the coalfields and the beginnings of the formation of a national miners' union. Hostility between miners and coalmasters persisted and a strike in 1855 led to further rioting in South Staffordshire. The Staffordshire Advertiser edition of 31 March 1855 reported that 'a mob of 200 men assembled in the neighbourhood of the Rough Hills and, led by a man of the name of Donnelly, visited several of the collieries in that neighbourhood, intimidating those who were employed at them and attempting to do serious damage to the machinery'. During an incident at the Rough Hills colliery, owned by Messrs Whitehouse and Poole, an engine was damaged and the crowd pursued Mr Poole, throwing stones at him.

The legal and economic odds, however, were stacked against the employees. The Derby Times of January 1861 reported: 'Some of the coalmasters in the Wolverhampton district have given notices to the men in the thin coal collieries to increase their "stents", and to reduce the wages of the men paid by the day.' The report went on to say: 'The masters generally are leaving the butties to fight the battle with the men. In some cases, notice has been given to the butties who have the charge of stone-pits that they must get their stone at 6d per ton less than hitherto, without at the same time any notice being given to the butties of coal pits. The butties of stone-pits were compelled to require the men to do an increased quantity of work without an increase of wages; and the colliery butties, availing themselves of the opportunity, require their men to submit to a similar arrangement.'

While conflicts involving miners and their coalmasters were

to continue long after 1861, some coalmasters at the time demonstrated compelling empathy with their workers. The Wolverhampton Chronicle edition of 4 January 1860 reports that 'upwards of one hundred workmen of Messrs Aston and Corns of the Rough Hills and Cockshut [sic] collieries were entertained by their employers at dinner, on Monday night, at the house of Mr William Corns (the son), the Fox Inn, Dudley Road'. The following day the same employers provided a similar evening for 130 workmen from the Wolverhampton Colliery and Furnaces. The newspaper article emphasised the genuine mutual respect between the 'masters and their workmen'. Mr Sankey, representing the workmen, congratulated the firm and the workmen 'upon the good feeling that existed between them'. This appears to have become a regular event as The Birmingham Daily Post edition of the 31 December 1862 includes a letter to the editor informing the paper of an extraordinary Christmas service on the 19 December in one of the coal-pits on the Cockshutts Colliery belonging to Isaiah Aston and Co. He writes of 40 men and boys plus two of the coalmasters attending a morning service comprising a reading from the bible, a hymn and a prayer. Moreover, the same coalmasters entertained almost one hundred workers on Christmas Eve with a meal of roast beef followed by plum pudding.

The census records are particularly informative as they bring to life the families who were part of the Cockshutts and Rough Hills mining communities. One such family were the Hodgetts who lived in one of the dwellings on Cockshutts. George Hodgetts is recorded in the 1841 census as a 15-year-old boy living at Cockshutts with his parents and two brothers. By 1851 the census identifies him working as a coalminer and living on Cockshutts with his wife, Ann, and two daughters, Martha and Susannah. Ten years later, the census records show that George's family now numbers seven children. By 1871, George is still living on Cockshutts and working as a coalminer. One of his sons John, aged 18, is now a coalminer, living with his parents. The 1881 census records show George and his family now living on Parkfield Road. Another of his sons, James, is now working as a miner. John has married, moved to Rough Hills and continues to work as a coalminer. By 1891, George now aged 64 has moved back to a house on Cockshutts but, despite his age, he is still working as a miner. One more of his sons, George who in 1871 was working as a labourer in a furnace is now a coal dealer. There is no record of John; his wife Eliza is recorded as a widow. Whether he died of natural causes or a mining accident is not known.

9

MINING ACCIDENTS

Mining was notoriously dangerous and accidents affected communities across the country. The mines around Rough Hills were no exception. As early as 1806 the Staffordshire Advertiser reported the death of Thos Love, an eight-year-old lad, who fell down one of the ironstone pits at Rough Hills belonging to Samuel Fereday. In 1825, the Birmingham Chronicle described two separate accidents at Rough Hills Colliery, within two months of each other, which each led to the death of a miner. In 1830, a lad of about ten, Joseph Smart, was crushed by a carriage full of ironstone while working at Cockshutts Colliery. Perhaps the most tragic incident in the Rough Hills area occurred in May 1834 at the colliery owned by Timmins and Tarratt. While newspapers referred to the accident occurring at the Rough Hills Colliery, it is more likely it took place at the neighbouring Wolverhampton Colliery. The event, widely reported in regional newspapers, occurred when the chain carrying five miners up the pit shaft suddenly broke: all died. At the inquest it was revealed that the colliers had frequently spoken to the charter master about the condition of the chain. Despite his neglect, a verdict of 'accidental death' was given. Four of the men were married and the tragedy left a total of fifteen children without a father.

Accidents such as this and the appalling conditions in which women and children worked led to the 1842 Mines and Collieries Act. This banned all women and girls, and boys under 10 from working underground and introduced the appointment of inspectors of mines. The Act did not have a significant effect on the women employed in the coal mining industry in Wolverhampton, as work practices were different and very few worked below ground. Instead they were employed on the pit banks sorting coal, loading canal boats and fulfilling other surface activities. Even so, working on the surface near the mouth of the shaft was still dangerous for all concerned and many accidents ensued. Before 1850 there had been no systematic recording of mining accidents and deaths. In November 1850, the 'Act to Provide for the Inspection of Coal Mines' was passed in response to public concern about the number of mining accidents. For the first time, the names of all workers who died or were injured were formally recorded in the Mines Inspectors Reports. This information, in the table below, has been meticulously collated by Ian Winstanley and made available on a national database found on the Coalmining History Resource Centre web site. It clearly shows the dramatic impact of the 1850 Act on the official accident figures.

Year Range	Total No. of Deaths and Injuries
1700-1750	93
1750-1800	267
1800-1850	3,486
1850-1900	59,580

When William Morgan, a collier, died at Rough Hills colliery in February 1855, the Morning Chronicle edition of the 10 March reported on the inquest at the Builders Arms in Green Lane. A verdict of manslaughter was returned against Henry Devey, an engineer deemed responsible for the incident. Devey was committed for trial at the next assizes but was found not guilty.

Although the life span of the 1850 Act was to be only five years, a similar Act was passed in 1855 to extend its powers for another five years. Additional inspectors were appointed including Lionel Brough who briefly took responsibility in 1856 for South Staffordshire and Worcestershire before handing over a year later to Henry George Longridge. In 1859, the Birmingham Daily Post reported that James Dodd had infringed the law at Rough Hills Colliery by employing a 10-year-old boy, Thomas Simmons, 'in lowering and taking up men from a coal pit'. Although it was clear that Thomas was carrying out this task without adequate supervision, courts seemed reluctant to allot blame and the case against Dodd was dismissed on a technicality.

In the period 1850-1914 the same national database reveals over 90,000 entries for mining accidents. Eleven, including at least three deaths, took place at the **Rough Hills** Colliery between 1855 and 1875. Francis Humphries, for example, was killed when a brick fell out of the shaft. John Mills was killed under similar circumstances from a fall of rock.

Name	Date	Age	Occupation	Owner
William Morgan	23/2/1855	?	Collier	Whitehouse and Poole
David Turner	9/6/1856	?	?	Henry Hill
T. Tranter	25/7/1856	40	Butty	Cadman and Dodd
M. McHale	22/2/1858	36	Loader	Corns and Aston
Francis Humphries	11/8/1858	24	Onsetter	Corns and Aston
William Rogers	22/7/1859	?	?	Cadman and Dodd
S. Preston	10/9/1863	54	Pikeman	Cadman and Dodd
?. Wooley	9/12/1863	?	Butty	Aston and Shaw
J. Wallet	17/8/1864	?	Sinker	J. Cadman and Co.
John Mills	26/4/1870	40	Bondsman	J. Cadman
James Greenfield	6/3/1875	28	Timberer	William and Enoch Fenn

Seven accidents, including at least three deaths, are recorded in the **Cockshutts** Colliery between 1859 and 1866. The Birmingham Daily Post on 7 July 1862 reported the death of Enos Glover from a fall of dirt.

Name	Date	Age	Occupation	Owner
J. Smith	14/4/1859	25		Aston and Corns
E. Leadbetter	16/2/1861	18	Loader	Aston and Shaw
W. Vickers	16/4/1862	22	Pikeman	Aston and Shaw
Enos Glover	2/7/1862	17	Horse driver	Aston and Shaw
E. Hartshorne	6/8/1862	30	Pikeman	Aston and Shaw
J. Ashton	7/8/1862	42	Pikeman	Aston and Shaw
S. Chirm	24/1/1866	13	Gin driver	Aston and Shaw

A number of accidents was also recorded for **Wolverhampton** Colliery. Two were killed in the January 1861 accident when a steam boiler burst in the pumping engine. The two men who died were engine tenters, a term which referred to someone in charge of machinery.

Name	Date	Age	Occupation	Owner
J. Dickin	8/1/1851			Dixon and Hill
R. Larry	20/10/1853			Whitehouse and Poole
E. Garrett	28/12/1854			Whitehouse and Poole
W. Robinson	9/11/1854			Whitehouse and Poole
A. Bailey	29/1/1855			Whitehouse and Co.
W. Jones	22/2/1855			Whitehouse and Co
R. Amos	26/1/1859	35		Edward Poole
J. Legge	22/1/1861		Engine Tenter	Aston and Shaw
J. Elwell	22/1/1861		Engine Tenter	Aston and Shaw
G. Smith	19/4/1862	22	Engineer	Aston and Shaw
R. Williams	27/6/1863	25	Hooker-on	Aston and Shaw
W. Beaman	6/8/1870	16	Hanger-on	T. Aston
J. Foreday	2/9/1874	52	Foreman	W. and E. Fenn

A death was also recorded at **Monmore Green** Colliery in 1857.

Name	Date	Age	Occupation	Owner
Mary Swift	21/11/1857	21	Bankswoman	Corbett and Co.

Mary died when 'stretching out her arms to hang the horse-net to the foot-hook she fell down the shaft, the night being dark and slippery'. The shaft in question was 100 feet deep.

Not all mining accidents involved workers. It was not unusual for old and unused pit shafts to be left uncovered, even when they were close to footpaths. On the night of 4 November 1845 Abraham Wise fell into such a pit at Cockshutts Colliery on his way home. The colliery grounds also attracted trespassers at night. At Cockshutts Colliery in 1859, Joseph Smith, having wandered onto the land, 'jumped onto the dolly chain which broke on descending and falling to the bottom of the shaft was killed'.

The Coal Mines Inspection Act of 1860 followed on from the earlier Mines Act and increased the number of mines' inspectors and prohibited boys below the age of 12 from working underground. It set out 'special rules for the conduct and guidance of persons acting in the management of collieries and of all persons employed in or about the same in the South Staffordshire district'. The new Act did not immediately lead to safer practices by mine owners. As if to emphasise that point two mining tragedies in the Rough Hills area occurred within ten days of each other. The 18 January edition in 1861 of 'The Engineer' reported the death of a carter transporting goods on a horse and cart:

'On Monday afternoon last a boiler explosion occurred at the Cockshutt Colliery, near Wolverhampton, the property of Messrs. Aston and Co., and which was unfortunately attended with fatal consequences. The accident happened between three and four o'clock, and at the time it occurred a carter named John Yates, who lived in Wolverhampton, was passing within a few feet of the engine house. Some of the debris struck him, and he was so severely injured that it was deemed necessary to remove him to the South Staffordshire Hospital; but he died shortly after his admission. The engine driver had a miraculous escape. At the time the explosion took place, he was oiling the gearing immediately over the boiler. Some of the scalding water struck him in the face and on the right arm, and he fell to the ground a distance of 12 ft. or 14 ft. When discovered by his fellow workmen he was partly suspended over the pit shaft, and had it not been for the firm hold he had managed to maintain, be must unquestionably have fallen into the mine. As it was, he was comparatively unhurt, and in all probability he will be able to resume his employment in the course of a few days.'

Sadly, the Morning Post reported on another tragic boiler explosion on the 23 January at Rough Hills colliery. On this occasion two men, John Legge and Joseph Elwell, were killed. The 2 February 1861 edition of the paper described it as 'the second fatal boiler explosion at the same colliery within a few days' which contradicts the location of the explosion reported by The Engineer. To confuse matters even further, Ian Winstanley's database on the Coalmining History Resource centre website lists the accidents at Wolverhampton Colliery. Nevertheless, Aston and Shaw were named as the owners in both incidents and Thomas Elwell, the head engineer who died in the second incident, was heavily involved in the first one, being called during the inquest to answer questions on the safety of the boiler. The report includes a reference to the Government Inspector of Mines who attended the inquest and made safety recommendations to the mine owners in his district.

Such cases were now being followed up with more intent. The 5 April 1861 edition of The Engineer reported two cases of coalmasters from the Black Country being fined at Wolverhampton Petty Sessions for infringing the Mines Inspection Act. One of these involved the owners of the Cockshutt Colliery, Messrs. Aston and Shaw. The article does not make it clear whether these court appearances follow on from the boiler explosions in January of the same year. These men were summoned by Mr. Baker, Inspector of Mines for South Staffordshire and East Worcestershire, on three cases: the first for having a boiler without a steam gauge, the second for a similar offence, and the third for having winding gear without a brake. All the defendants pleaded guilty, and were fined forty shillings and costs for each offence.

In his 1865 Report on Mines and Mining in South Staffordshire, Baker covered not only the numerous accidents, deaths and incidents in the preceding twelve months, but also drew attention to the continued employment of children under the age of 12. The Inspection Act of 1860 only allowed boys aged 10 to 12 to be employed in coal and ironstone mines provided there was a formal certificate stating they could read and write or regularly attended school for a fixed period each week. Baker expressed his exasperation that he had not met a single case where a boy under 12 was working under such conditions.

The Coal Mines Regulating Act of 1872 attempted to tighten regulations even further, making it compulsory for Managers in mines to be properly trained and to have gained a state certification. It also insisted on the introduction of safety methods such as fan ventilators, stronger timber supports, wire ropes, improved winding gear and better safety lamps. It was not until the Mines Regulation Act, passed in 1881, that the Home Secretary was empowered to hold inquiries into the causes of mine accidents. It remained clear, however, that there were many aspects of mining that required further intervention and regulation. By this time, mining to all intents and purposes had ceased at the collieries around Rough Hills and Cockshutts.

10

THE RAILWAYS

The appearance of pit workings and furnaces had changed the rural landscape of Rough Hills and the surrounding area beyond all recognition. It underwent another significant change in the mid-1800s with the arrival of the railways to Wolverhampton.

In the 1840s Great Britain entered an era of 'railway mania' and like many manufacturing towns, Wolverhampton became heavily involved. Local manufacturers, merchants and traders foresaw its potential commercial benefits. In 1845, ironmasters like John Dixon, John Parsons Firmstone and George Thorneycroft became members of a provisional committee backing a proposed railway, the South Staffordshire Junction Railway, planned to connect Wolverhampton with Derby and the north midland counties. Between 1837 and 1854, four stations were built in the town. The building of the third station, the High Level, led to bitter disputes between two railway companies, the Shrewsbury and Birmingham Railway and the London & North Western Railway (LNWR), who were struggling for supremacy. The rivalry was fought out in a series of legal battles which initially failed to resolve the situation. Ill feeling persisted and resulted in fierce fighting between their workmen in July 1850 requiring the intervention of the police and army and the reading of the Riot Act. Problems continued and the opening of the High Level station on 1 December 1851 was marred by a series of violent incidents. The departure of the Shrewsbury and Birmingham Railway train to Birmingham was blocked outside the station by a LNWR locomotive. Further down the line another train was derailed and a section of track vandalised. The railway itself, known as the Stour Valley Line, eventually opened on 1 February 1852, but for LNWR goods only. On 1 July the railway opened for LNWR passenger services, and in a further attempt to keep the Shrewsbury & Birmingham at bay, they started a half hourly service on 1 May

Figure 13: A Virgin train makes its way across the canal bridge near D'Urberville Road.

1853, claiming that it would be dangerous to have any additional trains running at the same time.

From the High Level station, the Stour Valley Line to Birmingham bisected the settlements of Rough Hills and Monmore Green, running alongside the collieries and in close proximity to the Wolverhampton to Birmingham canal. Near to what is now D'Urberville Road, the railway line crossed the canal by way of a low bridge.

The Stour Valley name was used because the LNWR company intended to build a line from Smethwick through the valley to Stourbridge; this branch never materialised. Once the Stour Valley line was opened, additional stations were opened. The Ettingshall Road & Bilston station, located near to the junction of Ettingshall Road and Parkfield Road, opened in 1852. Another at Monmore Green opened on 1 December 1863.

The last of the Wolverhampton stations, the Low Level Station, was opened in November 1854 when the Great Western Railway (GWR) line from Birmingham to Wolverhampton was completed. The line travelled north of the Stour Valley line through Monmore Green. It was initially called Wolverhampton Joint station to serve the Shrewsbury and Birmingham Railway, the Oxford, Worcester and Wolverhampton Railway and the Birmingham, Wolverhampton and Dudley Railway. In April 1856 it was renamed Wolverhampton Low Level. The nearest station to Rough Hills on the GWR line was at Priestfield in Bilston.

This represented the last significant railway development in the town, despite an application in November 1882 by the Midland, Birmingham, Wolverhampton, and Milford Junction Railway to expand the railway network from Craven Arms beyond Wolverhampton to Willenhall. The new line was planned to link the Welsh seaports of Swansea and Milford Haven with the Black Country and improve the transport of raw materials and products associated with the coal and iron industries. The railway would have approached Wolverhampton via Shropshire and South Staffordshire, travelling through Blakenhall and across the disused Rough Hills Colliery land towards Bilston. As well as the main line, five branch lines were proposed. One of these would have diverted at Rough Hills to join with the Stour Valley line at the bridge on Dixon Street. However, the main line would have passed through rural villages like Worfield, Claverley and Trysull. This led to objections from The Commons' Preservation Society, now known as The Open Spaces Society, and local freeholders from other affected areas such as Penn. These protests proved to be decisive and the plan for the railway line never left the drawing board and alternative arrangements had to be made by the railway companies. What effect this railway line would have had on the landscape and long-term development of Rough Hills is open to conjecture.

Trainspotting

When we were old enough to wander away from Cheviot Road, without causing too much consternation for our parents, our interest in trainspotting took hold. Sometimes we might stop at the railway bridge in Dixon Street just beyond Miller's Bridge but more often than not we were happy to hang around the London Midland Scottish (LMS) line alongside D'Urberville Road. Not only could we do our trainspotting there but the canal running beneath the railway bridge provided extra scope for adventure. A gap in the boards allowed us to make our way up the embankment onto the railway line with an excellent view down to the signals near Ettingshall station and in the opposite direction towards town. When the signal dropped, we called out 'train from Etto' or 'train from Wolvo' and waited in anticipation for the trail of smoke from the oncoming train. As it got closer, we backed off to catch a good view of the name and number. The bridge was on a long straight section of track and the signals in both directions were in clear view. Despite dire warnings from our parents about the obvious danger, the temptation to wander across the railway line to get to the canal was too great. The other 'dare' was to shelter in the box girder that lay over the bridge separating the two railway lines, while a train passed by at over 50 mph. This 'rite of passage' had passed down the generations, remembered for example by George Paddock in the 1930s. Unlike George, we also used the opportunity to drop pebbles through a gap in the box girder onto any unsuspecting bargeman passing below. There was a 'wish list' for every trainspotter and on Rough Hills we dreamed of seeing a Coronation class or 'Semi' pass by, even a Princess class but our wishes did not materialise. The story circulated that if you travelled on a Sunday to the railway line at Milford, near Cannock Chase, these iconic steam locomotives would be seen but that journey to this trainspotting nirvana never took place.

A trainspotting club started up in earnest in my last year at All Saints School. At the end of the school day, we ran along Steelhouse Lane and down Cable Street to the bridge at the bottom. This time it was not to endure a lunchtime meal at Monmore Green School but to enjoy the sight of the London Glasgow steam train travelling along the London Midland Scottish (LMS) line that crossed Cable Street. Once the train's number and name had been 'copped', we wandered over

Bilston Road onto the bridge overlooking the Great Western Railway (GWR) line near to Monmore Green Stadium. The aim was to get there by 5 o'clock for 'The Cornishmen'. Sometimes we would hang around for an extra session of trainspotting or meet up later and spend a couple of hours by the GWR line until it was time to go home. Trainspotting had its rituals. So long as you saw the train, you could say you had 'copped ' it and were entitled to put the number in your note book. There was the odd person who would claim to have seen a 'semi' earlier in the day but cheating was frowned upon. Although the trains on the LMS line were visible from the Monmore Green bridge, they were too far away to see the numbers or names. If there was someone with a bike and the signals went up for the next train on the LMS line, their job was to cycle down the road from the bridge, write down the number and return the prized information to us. All numbers were recorded in a rough note pad.

While we waited for the signals to indicate the next train was due, boredom was easily relieved by endless adventure opportunities. There was time to get on a bike and ride no-handed or refine your 'broadside' or 'wheelie' skills.

Figure 14: The GWR bridge at Monmore Green with the gas pipe alongside.

Dave Simpson who lived opposite Dugmore's shop on Bilston Road took 'adventure' to a new level by walking across the gas pipe that ran across the outside of the bridge, risking a long drop onto the railway lines below.

At that age, you did not worry. Anyway, someone saw me doing this and on the Monday reported it to the Headmaster at my school. I was summoned to the Head's office where he had a good go at me. He said he was going to report me to the police or I could have the cane. No problems, I had the cane.

Once home, you took out your Ian Allen train books and with best pen and ruler, underlined the train number. The books were kept in pristine condition in a safe place and were never taken out on trainspotting expeditions.

Fortunately, our parents seemed to turn a blind eye to our trainspotting exploits. I cannot recall any unannounced visits to take us back to the relative safety of Cheviot Road. One could argue you had less chance of being hit by a train than you did by the No.30 bus making its rapid progress down the road. Accidents however had happened on that railway line.

As far back as 1863, Abraham Parker, a labourer from Rough Hills, was killed by a passing train as he crossed the track on a Friday evening. The incident was reported in the Staffordshire Advertiser on 20 June, the following day. The newspaper article included graphic detail of the man's injuries and used the death as an opportunity to warn trespassers on railways of the obvious dangers.

Figure 15: The Dixon Street LMS bridge - the site of much trainspotting in the 1950s and a railway tragedy in 1969.

Barry Marchant who lived in Whittaker Street at the time remembers the tragedy in 1943 involving Derek Lunn, a young lad from Myrtle Street. His foot got trapped between the lines on the bridge over the canal near to what is now D'Urberville Road. Despite attempts to contact the signal box man, he was killed by a train coming from the Coseley direction.

Shirley Morris remembers another railway tragedy that took place in 1969 when a freight train was struck head-on by a passenger train which accidentally passed a signal at danger: two were killed and 30 injured.

One very vivid memory from my childhood in the area is of a train crash on the Dixon Street bridge. I'm not sure what year it was, but I think it could have been about 1967 – 69 [Tuesday April 8 1969]. I remember it was a bank holiday and I'd gone to the chemist at Fighting Cocks with my sister, to collect a prescription for my dad who was poorly. As we walked back along Parkfield Road, we heard the loudest bang, followed by seeing a massive plume of black smoke. We were really scared and kept thinking it was our house that had blown up. As we got nearer, we realised it was behind our house, so we kept following the smoke (forgetting our dad was waiting for his medicine). Eventually we got to the canal bridge, but were stopped by police from going any further. There was quite a crowd along with fire, police and ambulances. Two trains had crashed and one had rolled down the embankment. I believe the two train drivers were killed, but quite a few were injured. My lasting memory was feeling very sad when I saw policemen carrying burnt luggage from the trains. It was holiday time and I just thought how sad it was that people's holidays had been spoilt.'

After the canal incident with Ronnie Bagnall, trainspotting on the estate was never to be the same. The canal was now out of bounds and we looked for other places. We continued trainspotting on Dixon Street, below Miller's Bridge, but someone discovered Sun Street near the town centre. It was not the easiest destination to reach but it was worth the long journey. It involved a considerable walk along the canal towpath from Dixon Street towards town. Near the town centre, we came off the canal at Corn Hill walked past the Great Western pub and just beyond there was a low wall, ideal for sitting and spectating. Behind us and above us ran the LMS line next to the High Level station. Below we had a view into the Low Level station for identifying trains arriving and departing on the GWR line. This was a superb place for a trainspotter. When we sat there during the football season, we could hear the roar of the crowd from Molineux, distinguish the noise generated by a home or an away goal and return home around 5 o'clock, confident that we knew the final score.

Our infatuation with trainspotting disappeared almost as quickly as it started. On reflection it was the sight, smell and sounds of the steam trains that attracted us and as soon as their numbers declined so did our interest. Even at the height of our enthusiasm for trainspotting, we greeted an oncoming diesel train with disdain. By the autumn of 1960 I had left primary school; the railway was no longer on my doorstep after school and other interests took over. Although the two tracks were unaffected by the Beeching closures, visits to Monmore Green or Dixon Street stopped. News of an 'interesting' steam train passing along the LMS line might reawaken the old passion temporarily but trainspotting had lost its magic. The last steam locomotive had been built in 1960 and train services were increasingly run by diesel trains. Electrification of the West Coast Main Line from London to Scotland commenced in the mid-60s and Ettingshall station closed in 1964. Trainspotting turned out to be a 'passing phase' that one recalls with affection but also a tinge of embarrassment. In later years, when discussing this fleeting childhood obsession, one still feels required to qualify your involvement by stressing that it was "only in the days of steam". At the time, it was far more than that.

11

THE DECLINE OF MINING AND IRONMAKING IN ROUGH HILLS AND COCKSHUTTS

Following its unsuccessful sale in 1866, it is likely that the furnaces at the Wolverhampton Ironworks had already closed by 1867. Those local furnaces which were still making wrought iron were increasingly being supplied by iron ore from outside the area and by 1883 the Earl of Dudley was said to be the only ironmaster using Black Country ore. Wrought iron itself was being superseded by steel, made using the Bessemer process, and major centres of steel production were developing elsewhere in the country in towns like Middlesborough. By 1872, even Edwin Dixon, the son of John Dixon who had been owner of Wolverhampton Ironworks in the 1840s, was investing outside the Black Country. He had become a director of the newly established Lincolnshire Iron Smelting Company, formed for the purpose of 'erecting and working blast furnaces of the most approved construction for the manufacturing of pig iron from the ironstone obtained on the Lincolnshire estate of Mr Winn in Frodingham, Lincs'. The company's board of directors also included H.O. Firmstone, a relative of the brothers John Parsons and William Firmstone who had bought the Rough Hills colliery in 1817. This new company was proposing to erect three blast furnaces, capable of producing 30,000 tons per annum, way in excess of the quantities ever produced at either the Wolverhampton or Rough Hills furnaces.

When Queen Victoria arrived in Wolverhampton on 30 November 1866 to unveil the Prince Albert statue, she was greeted by an impressively large arch made entirely of coal. Unfortunately, the town's prominent involvement in the industry was already in decline. The mining of ironstone and coal in the Black Country had peaked around 1860 and reserves of both iron ore and coal were now diminishing. The minerals had been exploited in an extremely wasteful and haphazard manner with small, shallow pits rarely more than 300 yards apart. Faced by prohibitive drainage costs as well as stricter health and safety regulations, some coalmasters judged it was easier and cheaper to sink new shafts than to drain the existing ones. The local mining industry was now becoming dominated by large scale operations such as those near Cannock Chase where reserves, deep underground, were being exploited. The scale of this decline in mining can be seen by examining the census records during the second half of the 19th century.

		Year of Census		
		1851	1861	1871
No. of Homes	Cockshutts	40	43	42
	Rough Hills	20	34	32
No. of Occupants	Cockshutts	242	206	198
	Rough Hills	99	134	134
% of homes with at least one occupant involved in mining	Cockshutts	85	71	57
	Rough Hills	70	50	31

While both settlements had maintained some stability in terms of its housing and its population, the percentage of dwellings which housed at least one miner was steadily going down.

The collapse of the mining industry in the Rough Hills and Cockshutts areas would have had a devastating effect on local employment. My second great grandfather Thomas Boddis had worked as a miner in the Rough Hills' collieries from the 1840s right up to the 1870s. By 1881 the census does not record him living locally with his family in Cable Street and it is possible that he had found mining employment away from his family home. This was certainly the case with his son James, also a coalminer, who is recorded on the 1881 census living as a boarder in Walsall.

This is not to say that mining activity ceased completely and we have seen earlier that records compiled from government publications confirm that collieries at Rough Hills existed spasmodically up to the end of the century. The nature of mining during this period is summed up in a report of the Select Committee on Coal of 1873. James Philip Baker, inspector of coalmines for South Staffordshire and East Worcestershire, makes the following point in his evidence to the Committee:

'... Some of the small collieries in my district appear and

disappear so suddenly and their duration is so uncertain, that they may be said to spring up very much like mushrooms; they are here today and gone tomorrow: working in some cases a few weeks, or months at most, and then remain idle for the rest of the year; and in many instances all trace of colliery plant (except the pit shafts) removed. The mines were small, easily opened, and mined also iron, limestone and fireclay.'

At the same time that coal and iron production on Rough Hills, Cockshutts and Monmore Green went into decline, several significant transactions were taking place on land in the area. For example, in May 1872 a mortgage was taken out on four pieces of land, namely the Green Lane Piece, Poultney's Field, Evans Piece, Cockshutts Piece and Colliery ground. These parcels of land were located near what is now the junction of Birmingham Road and Thompson Avenue. Those named on the mortgage document were:

1. William Fenn and Enoch Fenn of Wolverhampton, coal merchants,

2. Samuel Fenn, coalmaster.

In Jan 1874 a mortgage on a plot of land further south, belonging to William and Enoch Fenn, was sold to Edwin Dixon for £2,890. Edwin, a landowner and industrialist from Wolverhampton was the son of John Dixon a prominent owner of land, including Wolverhampton Ironworks, in the 1840s. The land is described as 'enclosed out of Winfield, two pieces of land in Wolverhampton in Parkfield Road, next to the Cockshutts Colliery, several closes called the Long Acres in Wolverhampton and Bilston part of the Rough Hills Colliery with the Red Lion Public House standing on another part, two parcels at Hell Lanes, Bilston, two closes called Hembirch in Bilston and two closes called the Long Acres in Wolverhampton'.

The Fenn family played a prominent role in the history of coalmining in and around Rough Hills during the second half of the 19th century. Samuel, born around 1817 in Bilston, had started work as a stone miner in Bilston and by 1871 he was a coalmaster employing 20 men and 4 boys. William and Enoch Fenn were two of his four sons. They also started as miners and by 1875 were running a colliery at Rough Hills. A family dispute led to their partnership being legally dissolved in April 1875. Samuel died in July 1878 and the mortgage originally arranged in 1872 was transferred to his four sons and Joseph Crowther Smith, a solicitor and ex-mayor of Wolverhampton. William Fenn was involved in further land transactions which continued into the late 1870s and early 1880s involving Wolverhampton and Staffordshire Banking Company, Joseph Crowther Smith and Edwin Dixon. It was the trustees of Joseph Crowther Smith who were to play a major role in the development on the Parkfield Estate.

For families on Rough Hills and Cockshutts, mining was no longer the inevitable employment for father, son and daughter. The 1881 census records show a more diverse range of employment among the residents of Rough Hills reflecting the variety of local factories and workshops that had become established in the last three decades. Men were now seeking employment at brick, iron and galvanising works, the gas tube and edge tool factories or the railway. Men could now make the short journey to Bayliss, Jones and Bayliss, Edwin Lewis's gas tube factory, Frost and Sons Galvanising Works or travel a little further to Eagle Works, Phoenix Brick Works or Springvale Furnaces, Ltd.

If this paints a rosy picture of employment and living conditions, it is far from the truth. In 1865, the iron trade and related activities had provided the highest single source of unemployment in the town. Fast forward to 1874 and all parts of the country were in the grip of a 'Great Depression' which continued up to around 1890. Wolverhampton was not immune to rising unemployment and during this period many of the major ironworks in the town closed: in 1877 Colonel Thomas Thorneycroft closed the Shrubbery Ironworks while the Chillington Ironworks closed in 1885. The Wolverhampton Relief Committee was set up in 1877 to address the social problems being created by high levels of unemployment. The London Daily News edition of 29 January 1879 reported that three thousand loaves and a thousand packets of oatmeal had been distributed in Wolverhampton, a larger distribution than ever before. As well as food hand-outs and soup kitchens the Relief Committee set up labouring work for unemployed men in return for small payments. Sites in and around Rough Hills were utilised for this work with many reports in the newspapers of the time referring to men employed at the Rough Hills relief works. Activities included breaking cinders, and preparing the ground for the proposed drainage work to be carried out by the Corporation on land at Rough Hills belonging to Mr Edwin Dixon. In 1885, men were paid by a fixed daily rate of 1 shilling(s) or a 'piece' rate of 1 shilling(s) 3 pence (d) per cubic metre of broken metalling. The landowner of Cockshutts Colliery, the Duke of Cleveland, also made effective use of the situation, donating £50 to the town's relief fund and offering employment to men who would level the pit banks on his land.

Donations from individuals and businesses such as Messrs Butler and Co. of the Springfield Brewery paid for food and wages.

Census returns from 1881 showed that the settlement of Rough Hills had grown to 55 houses and was sufficiently established to be shown on the 1887 Ordnance Survey map. It comprised of irregular house enclosures connected by sinuous roads, a layout characteristic of a squatter settlement, constructed quickly and legally by migrating labourers seeking work in the mines and factories nearby. Cockshutts was also shown, although the settlement appears to have contracted in size and population. Some of its houses and enclosures were set along Parkfield Road but the majority were arranged in a haphazard fashion with no adjoining roads, in contrast to the situation at Rough Hills. By 1890, the Borough Council had produced a map titled Rough Hills Estate which showed the boundary of the land. Whether this suggested that a short or long-term plan for the area was already being prepared, one can only speculate.

12

INDUSTRY

While the mines and furnaces that had provided work for much of the 1800s were disappearing, new industries were appearing on the outskirts of Rough Hills. The proximity of the Birmingham canal created an important transport artery for raw materials and goods and encouraged a corridor of industrial development which extended from Cleveland Road down Bilston Road and Steelhouse Lane beyond to Monmore Green, Ettingshall and Rough Hills. The pattern of manufacturing in the town was changing. The 'cottage industry' approach that Wolverhampton had adopted so successfully in the 1700s and the early part of the 1800s had been replaced by one based around companies running factories employing a large number of workers with diverse skills.

In Eagle Street adjoining Steelhouse Lane and Bilston Road,

the Mitre Iron Works backed onto the Birmingham canal and in close proximity was the Eagle Works, the home of the Eagle Edge Tool Company. This company, set up around 1871, produced a range of items including shovels, picks, hammers, plantation hoes, horse shoes, wheelbarrows for mining and railway contractors. It became a well-established firm, a contractor to Her Majesty's Government, supplying the chief dockyards with its requisite tools.

Adjoining Eagle Edge Tool Company to the south was Monmore Ironworks founded by Mr. E.T. Wright and Mr. David North to produce high quality iron plates and sheets. On the opposite side of the canal to the Monmore Ironworks was located the Imperial Tube Works, founded in 1861 by John Brotherton, where tubes and fittings for water, gas and steam were manufactured.

Monmore Ironworks extended south to Cable Street. On the opposite side of Cable Street was the Victoria Works established in 1826 by William Bayliss. His father was a blacksmith with a shop at the junction of Bilston Road and Ettingshall Lane. Blacksmiths were an indispensable member of the mining community and his smithy served the nearby miners, sharpening their picks and shoeing their horses. William dreaded working the night shift by himself. His apprehension was fully justified: the area was notorious, a hotbed of criminal activity and closely linked with the aftermath of the rioting at Rough Hills Furnaces in 1822. Following this incident, the military were determined to capture the men involved in the incident. A troop of soldiers led by Lieutenant Colonel Littleton and a force of special constables led by Captain Musgrave along with two local magistrates made their way early on a Saturday morning in May 1822 to Ettingshall Lane, known locally as 'Hell Lane', where most of the rioters lived. The houses of the culprits were surrounded and seven men were arrested and committed to Stafford Assizes for punishment.

William was a natural businessman and gradually took over from his father. He kept tight control of the bills and introduced a 'pay on the nail' system which saved his father from making the Saturday journey around the public houses to collect payments from their customers. By 1826, while still in his early twenties, he had saved sufficient money to buy a large plot of wasteland, formerly part of a colliery, in Cable Street and set up the Victoria Works factory. This manufactured a wide range of items including sheep hurdles, railings, gates, stable fittings, ornamental ironwork and chains for mining and shipping. Eventually his brother Moses, a nut and bolt maker at Providence Works, Darlaston, joined him in the venture. The two firms were amalgamated as W. & M. Bayliss of Victoria Works, Monmoor (?) Green and Providence Works, Darlaston, with a London office in Eastcheap. In 1859 they were joined by Edwin Jones, an iron trader from South Wales who had married William's daughter, Jane. The partnership then became Bayliss, Jones and Bayliss. By 1871, the company was well established.

The 1887/88 Ordnance Survey map shows that only the eastern side of the existing site had been developed as the Victoria Iron Works with the original section of Major Street forming the western boundary of the works. The Monmore Iron Works, on the opposite side of Cable Street had also become well established and in 1896 it was purchased by Bayliss, Jones and Bayliss. Following its amalgamation, the Monmore Iron Works expanded, occupying more space to the west and north.

Major Street was named after an industrialist, John Clarkson Major, who set up the first tar distillery in Wolverhampton, Major and Company, in 1857 with his partner E.L Turner. It was located south of the Victoria Iron Works close to the canal and next to the road which by 1877 carried his name. The company was one of the first British tar distillers, manufacturing a range of products including creosote, solvents and disinfectants from tar supplied as a by-product of the town's gas works. On the 1881 Ordnance Survey map, the tar distillery works are adjacent to the Edwin Lewis' gas tube factory. Edwin Lewis produced a wide range of tubes for boilers used in trains, ships and buildings. At a later date his factory closed and the whole site eventually became occupied by Midland Tar Distillers Ltd.

Following Major's death in 1896, his son John Lewis Major took over. Production continued at Rough Hills but the company's Head Office moved to Hull. There was always a high risk of accidents at the factory because of the volatile nature of its raw materials and products. In March 1901 a fire occurred at the Rough Hills site when one of the vessels used for distilling chemicals sprung a leak. The fumes found their way into a flue and a loud explosion followed. A large quantity of brickwork blew out and flames spread in every direction. Great effort was made by workmen to cope with the outbreak but it was not until the Wolverhampton Fire Brigade had been at work for some time that the flames were suppressed. In 1923 the company became part of Midland Tar Distillers Ltd.

Maps up to 1894 showed that Major Street did not originally start at the end of Steelhouse Lane but at a junction about half way along Cable Street. Steelhouse Lane itself petered out just beyond Cable Street. By 1899, maps show the layout of Major Street had significantly changed. As it made its way from Dixon Street towards the Victoria Works factory, it now veered off left to join up with Steelhouse Lane. By 1902 the original stretch of Major Street from Cable Street had closed and become incorporated into the grounds of the Victoria Works factory.

Dixon Street was named after the Dixon family who played a prominent role in the town in the 19th century. John Dixon lived in Merridale Grove near Chapel Ash and as early as 1824 he is reported as owning a brass foundry in the town. By the 1840s he was well established in the financial world and was appointed as a treasurer to the Royal Bank of Ireland when the Agricultural and Commercial Bank of Ireland ran into difficulty. The 1842 tithe registry shows him listed as one of the major landowners in the town with 57 acres in his possession including a large swathe of land from the Birmingham canal in the east across to Pond Lane in the west. This incorporated the Wolverhampton Iron Works, built on the site of the Dixon Street playing fields, and the Little Rough Hills colliery built on land to the west, in the area of what is now Pond Lane. His skills extended beyond finance matters and the Worcester Journal of 9 May 1844 announced that he had taken out a patent for improvements in heating air for blast furnaces and for other uses. By 1845, he was extending his business portfolio to include the emerging railway industry. His son Edwin, born in 1823, inherited his father's business acumen: by 1854 he was running Wolverhampton Tube Works and by 1858 was a director of the Wolverhampton and Staffordshire Banking Company.

Edwin became heavily involved in supporting local institutions such as the South Staffordshire General Hospital, known later as the 'The Royal' and he was listed in 1862 as one of the subscribers to a proposed memorial to the late Prince Consort, 'The Man on the Horse', which was to become the town's most renowned landmark. In January 1865, Edwin is listed as a director of the proposed Wolverhampton and Walsall Railway. Not all his financial ventures were successful and the British Steam Cooperage and Cask Company, set up in 1865 under his chairmanship, was wound up one year later. Having taken over the ownership of his father's property, he became involved in a string of land transactions involving the land around Rough Hills during the 1870s and 80s. He died in 1896. The family legacy is sustained in the naming of the road which runs from Bilston Road to Thompson Avenue and the recreation field that has provided pleasure and leisure for local youngsters like myself.

13

RELIGION

Rough Hills Methodist Church

The first church for the Rough Hills community is believed to be Rough Hills Methodist Church, to the east of the settlement. It was set up near to Parkfield Road by the Rough Hills Primitive Methodist Society and opened as a chapel on 16 September 1860. Primitive Methodism had started in England in the early 1800s in an attempt to restore what its followers believed were the true principles of Methodism begun under John Wesley. A similar church had been built in 1849 further up Parkfield Road near to Fighting Cocks. In October 1873 the church members of Rough Hills raised £40 to purchase land to build a new larger chapel. In 1875, £230 was paid to the builder, William Pritchard, with a further £175 in 1876. The official opening services were held over several days on 7, 12, 19 and 26 March 1876. Noted for a musicians' gallery said to be large enough to hold an orchestra, further structural changes were made in 1896 and over the years the church became known as Parkfield Road Methodist Church.

All Saints Church of England

Not far from the collieries of Rough Hills, Monmore Green and Cockshutts lay Steelhouse Lane. Much of this area belonged to the Duke of Cleveland estate and in the 1830s there were only two prominent buildings in this part of the town. One was Cleveland House with its impressive gardens and a long drive leading to a lodge at Steelhouse Lane. Cleveland House was the residence of the perpetual curate for the surrounding area. The other was the new workhouse built in 1837 on the south side of Bilston Road to accommodate over 600 inmates.

In 1865 the Reverend Henry Hampton, the Vicar of St. John's Church in the town established a Mission church and a schoolroom in Steelhouse Lane, on the site of a disused pigsty, to serve the growing population of the area. A resolute man of forthright opinions, he described the temporary construction, built at a cost of £300 and capable of accommodating 300 worshippers, as 'essentially a poor man's church to provide for the miners and grimy iron-workers of Steelhouse Lane, Monmore Green and part of Rough Hills'. He later recalled when 'it was not really decent for a woman with any sense of propriety to walk down Steelhouse Lane. The Lane used to be full of dog-fighters, pigeon flyers and other rough characters'. On one occasion Henry Hampton claimed that he 'had had to go into the midst of a gang of impudent fellows, and threaten that if they did not disperse he would use his stick to them'.

In 1862, Hampton had moved to St. John's Church from London. He had left under a cloud: long-standing disagreements with the Bishop of London and unsubstantiated claims that money had been misappropriated had put his professional and private life under close scrutiny by the newspapers. Controversy followed him to Wolverhampton, and within a few weeks of starting at St. John's, he had sacked the organist, Mr Allen. This ultimately led to a court case in which Rev. Hampton sought damages of £2,000 against Mr. Allen, claiming Allen had spoken and published malicious comments about his character. The Islington Gazette of 21 March 1863 seemed to draw much satisfaction when the jury found in favour of The Rev. Henry Hampton, but awarded damages of only one farthing!

Before too long the congregation at the Mission church had risen to around 120 and Rev. Hampton was calling for its replacement by a permanent building. A design in the early gothic style by London architects T. Taylor Smith & G. F. Roper was approved in 1876 and built by Messrs Higham between 1877 and 1879. Despite accumulating debts of around £1000, mainly as a result of litigation, it was consecrated as a Church of England place of worship by the Bishop of Lichfield, Dr. Maclagan, on All Saints' Day 1 November 1879: an event that was reported in the 5 November edition of the Wolverhampton Chronicle. Despite the ceremony taking place on a Saturday, the consecration was well attended by local dignitaries including the mayor, John Clarkson Major, and representatives from many of the town's parish churches. Following the service, a luncheon, supplied by Reynolds and Sons of Queen Square, took place in the old schoolroom adjoining the church. The church eventually gained its independence as a parish church in July 1881 when All Saints became a separate ecclesiastical parish. The Reverend Henry Hampton was unable to celebrate this landmark, having died in 1880. He is commemorated at St. John's church with two windows and a marble tablet. His contribution to the All Saints community is immeasurable.

In 1891, an appeal was made to raise £2000 to build a chancel and this was picked up by The Lichfield Mercury of 3 July 1891 which reported that 'through the poverty of the congregation the church has remained over 14 years in its present incomplete state'. By 1892 new plans had been submitted by local architect Frederick Beck to add a chancel, vestry, sacristy and side chapel, 34 feet long by 22 feet wide. These were approved and constructed during 1892-93 by Willcock & Co. of Wolverhampton and consecrated on All Saints' Day 1892, prior to full completion in 1895.

My great grandfather, Isaac Anderton Taylor married Mary Ann Boddice at All Saints Church in October 1892. At the time of his marriage, he was a sheet iron worker, living in Gordon Street, while Mary Ann lived nearby in Cable Street. Following their marriage, they moved to Cable Street as neighbours of Mary Ann's parents. It was in Cable Street that my grandmother, Phoebe, was born in 1893.

St Martin's Church of England

The need for a church in the area around the new Parkfield (Rough Hills) council estate had been raised as far back as 1932 by the Archdeacon of Stafford (Ven. Hugh Bright, M.A.) on a visit to Wolverhampton. In the Tamworth Herald edition of the 23 April, he refers to the a fine (church) building that had been erected in Oxley and declares that 'a similar building is required in the Rough Hills district of Wolverhampton to serve, probably, both a section of St Luke's and the two adjacent parishes'.

In 1939 St. Martin's Church, at the top of Dixon Street near the junction with Thompson Avenue, was completed at a cost of approximately £20,000. A significant amount was contributed by way of bequests in the wills of a brother and sister, Henry and Sarah Marson from Tettenhall. Designed by the architects Lavender and Twentyman in the 'Power Station' style, it was built to serve the new Rough Hills (Parkfield) Estate.

Figure 16: St Martin's church on Dixon Street.

A report in 'The Architect and Building News' journal at the time of its construction includes a description of the civil engineering challenge that the area posed for builders: 'The site is on an old pit mound and the ground is composed of slag to a depth of 8 to 10 feet; old mine workings were suspected at a shallow depth underneath. The foundations of the church are of reinforced concrete down to a depth of 10 to 12 feet, where they rest on good clay, and are designed to act as a bridge across any weak spot over mine workings.' The eight feet high statue of the patron saint, above the west door, was made by Mr Donald Potter, who went on to become a distinguished sculptor, wood carver and potter. In 1960 he carved the granite statue of Robert Baden Powell which stands outside the Scout headquarters in London. Potter died in 2004; he is credited with influencing several generations of designers, architects and designers including Sir Terence Conran.

The church, built to seat 515 people, was finally consecrated on Friday 21 July 1939. Despite a thunderstorm which caused the procession around the outside of the church to be abandoned, over 500 people attended the ceremony carried out by the Bishop of Lichfield.

During WW2 it was to play an important role for many in the community. In October 1943 the church started to produce its own monthly magazine, The Broken Sword, a title which celebrated the broken sword of St Martin at the front of the church. This home produced news sheet included the events calendar for the month, the vicar's letter and a notice board announcing baptisms, marriages and burials. A limited number of adverts for local businesses such as Thomas the Chemist, at 652 Parkfield Road helped to finance the newsletter, keeping the cost down to 2d per issue for subscribers. The newsletter proved popular in the community and the January 1944 issue, reference is made to an increase in the number of subscribers to 240.

14

SCHOOLING

The Influence of the Church

Prior to 1800, education for poorer children was limited to isolated charity schools. One such charity school existed in the 1700s in the High Green part of Wolverhampton. In the early 1800s, churches of all denominations began to provide education for the poor.

In 1811 The National Society (for Promoting Religious Education) was founded as a Church of England body in England and Wales for the promotion of church schools and Christian education. Its aim was that 'the National Religion should be made the foundation of National Education, and should be the first and chief thing taught to the poor, according to the excellent Liturgy and Catechism provided by our

Church'. Such Church of England schools like All Saints were usually built adjacent to the parish church, and named after it.

The first school in the Rough Hills neighbourhood appears to have been set up in the 1850s in Parkfield Road by another church organisation, the Rough Hills Primitive Methodist Society, referred to in the previous chapter. A letter sent to the editor of the Birmingham Post and published on 10 August 1860 provides a fascinating insight into the establishment of this 'Sabbath School'. The letter, composed by George Cooper an engineer, refers to 'a little cottage village, designated Rough Hills, and a very populous place for its locality, was void of a Sabbath School or any place wherein the poor children of this neighbourhood could be collected in for education'. It describes how 'a few good men of Primitive Methodist Connexion of this locality rented an upper room, a place apparently little calculated to offer much advantage but which, however, has done much good in this place'. George Cooper acknowledged that 'a proper edifice for Sabbath Instruction was much desired and very needful'. He goes on to say how some money had been raised but 'when driven to their wit's end for money', a gentleman, J. Aston Esq, an ironmaster, has come to their aid and donated £20 followed by a loan of £7 which will make up the first payment to the builder. Whether this 'Sabbath School' focused entirely on religious instruction or covered the skills of reading, writing and arithmetic is not clear from the letter.

All Saints School

Further north of Parkfield Road, on Steelhouse Lane, All Saints' Mixed Infants School opened as a Church of England school in a converted barn on 4 February 1865. The school log book reveals that the 73 children, boys and girls aged between two and twelve, who attended on that first day 'were in a shocking state of ignorance, ten only being able to read'. As well as the mistress, Miss Best, two teachers were engaged: Mary Ann Doran and Lucy Evans. These will have been pupil teachers in their early teens. Unfortunately, Lucy Evans lasted only one month before she was 'dismissed for her inability to teach'. Schooling was not free and attendance was affected not only by the weather but more crucially by the employment situation in the neighbourhood. Very soon after the school opened there was a dramatic drop in attendance when workers in the iron trade came out on strike. In August of 1865, the school logbook reported: 'three of the most regular scholars left this week, the Wainwrights; they gave as the reason: poverty.'

The school was inspected each year by a representative of the local church. The report for 1866 makes somewhat unexpected reading: 'The situation of this school is good, the children are supplied with country air and the playground is good.' The presence of clean 'country' air suggests that the developing industrialisation of the All Saints and Monmore Green areas had not yet made an impact. It goes on to say that, 'The children have been very fairly taught; the order is pretty good.' The log book shows that the pupils were taught a curriculum based on the 3 R's: reading, writing and arithmetic. Grammar was also assessed. The school soon ran into administrative problems: the 1868 report stated: 'The school has increased in numbers. The children are very intelligent and well behaved. ... The children in the upper standards did not pass a good examination and cannot be well taught in a room among so many infants. ... A school which comprises so many children above the age for which Infant School methods are adopted can no longer be regarded as an Infant School.' As a result, the grant to the school was reduced by a tenth.

By 1873, the log books include an annual report by a Diocesan Inspector. In line with its Church of England ethos, the school examined pupils on scripture, catechism and liturgy. It was not only the children who were examined. Pupil teachers, many of whom were in their early teens, were tested each year as they worked over five years towards their qualification as fully fledged teachers. One such pupil teacher, Mary Edwards completed her 'apprenticeship' in 1874 and was presented with a writing desk paid for by her generous colleagues.

Inspectors continued to praise the achievements of the younger children while expressing concern about the performance of the older scholars. This led to recommendations in later reports that the older boys should go to one of the Central Schools and separate departments for infants and girls should be established. By 1875, 'several big boys left and had gone to the new Board School at Monmore Green'. The report for 1877 makes a passing reference to 'approaching reformation of the premises'. In a similar understated manner, the HM Inspector's report for 1881 announces: 'There is a separate department for girls' and subsequently the logbook records only focussed on the Girls department. The good work at All Saints was recognised in 1882 when the Mistress, Miss Mary Perry, received a certificate for two good reports from the Staffordshire Board of Education. The logbooks include a valuable insight into the health and welfare of the community. In July 1883, for example, the school received notice from the Sanitary Department that Jessie Shaw will not be able to attend school; her mother having been taken to the Workhouse with smallpox. In the winter of 1891, the school was closed for seven weeks to control an outbreak of measles in the area.

By 1888 the school had moved to a building next to the Church; the 1888 OS map showing the building designated for Girls and Infants. Despite this significant milestone in the school's history, no mention is made in the logbook. These buildings were soon superseded by new school buildings. The HM report for 1893 had criticised several aspects of the school building, stating, 'The classroom of the Girls' school is below the size required by the Building Rules. My Lords may be unable to continue their recognition of this room unless it is enlarged.' The report released to the school in December of that year appears to have had an immediate effect. By 21 September 1894, the logbook records 'furniture moved from old room to new room'. Three days later, the vicar is reported to have opened the (new?) school. This is confirmed by the HM report of November 1894 which states: 'The new premises in which the school will in future be conducted are excellent ... A good year's work has been done in the old buildings.' In that year, the school staff consisted of: Mary Perry, the Mistress, three Assistants, Elizabeth Weston, Elizabeth Stubbs and Annie Roden and one Teacher, Louise Thomas, designated as Article 68 and one Pupil Teacher, Jessie Hudson. The average attendance was now over 230 and the grant earned by scholars and pupil teacher totalled £260.5s 0d.

In the absence of any further help from the school's logbooks about the new buildings, Kelly's Directory for Staffordshire for 1896 provides useful additional information. In its section on Wolverhampton schools, we are told the new buildings for All Saints National School, Steelhouse Lane were

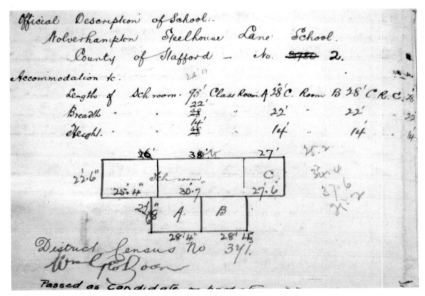

Figure 17: Plan of the new Boys School. (Photograph reproduced with the permission of Wolverhampton Archives and Local Studies)

completed in 1894 at a cost of £3,500. The school would provide an education for up to 320 boys, 320 girls and 400 infants. Miss Mary Perry was Mistress for the Girls department, while the Infants section was run by Miss Sarah Perry.

The new building for boys was opened at 9 am on 7 January 1895 and school life for the 108 pupils began with an address by the Rev. J. Warner on manners, neatness and punctuality. Mr Andrew Tyler had been appointed as Headmaster with George Wade as his Assistant teacher. George Lawrence, a probationary teacher, was the other member of staff. The pupils were organised into six standards with most of the intake starting at i (58 boys) and ii (24 boys). Mr Tyler had previous Headship experience. During the first week he concentrated on the three R's, created a school motto for the first year: 'Whatever is worth doing at all is worth doing well', and introduced a trial timetable. Mr Tyler was soon imposing his authority on the school which, by the start of February, numbered 136 pupils. Two boys were sent home to clean their boots and Thomas Emery, a boy with 'history' from his previous school was severely punished for threatening to throttle Mr Charles Baker: a baptism of fire for the probationary teacher who had started one week earlier. The first report by Her Majesty Inspector (HMI) states: 'The school has made an exceedingly promising beginning.' The log book shows the layout of the school with three classrooms and a school room. It is not clear how the teaching was distributed across these three classrooms.

By 1900, My Tyler had left, replaced by Mr William George Boon. It is not clear whether he was able to maintain the high standards set by his predecessor as the HMI reports became increasingly focussed on the fabric of the school. Indeed, the 1908 report made no reference to academic progress, concentrating instead on its failings in the provision of heating, ventilation and hygiene.

The Influence of The State

Even where schools existed, there was dissatisfaction. Speakers at an education conference in Wolverhampton in June 1870, reported in the Birmingham Daily Post, expressed many of the frustrations experienced by teachers, inspectors and clergymen. The conference heard that even those children who attended school were taken away at twelve 'just when they were beginning to understand what they were being taught'. Mr Horton, a master at a local school, St Peters, is quoted as saying that 'the parents were indifferent, the children were indifferent and the number of teachers was insufficient to affect much good'.

Concerned about industrial and economic competition from countries like Germany and America, the government had begun to take more interest in the education of this group of children. Following on from the campaign begun in 1869 by the National Education League for free, compulsory and non-religious education for all children, Parliament introduced the Elementary Education Act in August 1870 whereby "public school accommodation" would be made available for all children. The key aims of these "elementary schools" were:

- to cater for all children up to 14;

- to provide education for the working-class;

- to provide a restricted curriculum with the emphasis almost exclusively on the '3Rs' (reading, writing and 'rithmetic);

- to ban religious teaching which was distinctive of any particular denomination;

- to pursue other, less clearly defined, aims including social-disciplinary objectives (acceptance of the teacher's authority, the need for punctuality, obedience, conformity etc.);

- to operate the 'monitorial' system, whereby a teacher supervised a large class with assistance from a team of monitors (usually older pupils).

The Act established locally elected and interdenominationally representative School Boards to oversee and complete the network of schools. The Act did not provide free education, except in proven cases of poverty, and while it gave School Boards the power to create byelaws making attendance at school compulsory for children between the ages of five and thirteen, it did not require them to do so. It was not until the Elementary Education Act of 1880 that school attendance was made compulsory, and not till 1891 that elementary education became free.

Wolverhampton was one of the first boroughs to adopt the provisions of the Act. The elections to the School Board, contested between the Conservatives and the Church of England on one side and the Liberals and the Non-conformists on the other, resulted in a slight majority for the Liberals. One of the first Board Schools to open in the area was Dudley Road School on 9 June 1873 with 29 pupils. More detail about the school is provided in the next chapter.

15

THE BEST DAYS OF OUR LIFE

It is a debatable point as to whether those ten or more years at school actually represent the best years of our life. If they do, maybe we have conveniently forgotten the stress of starting a new school year, summer exams, failing to make the school team and the odd bit of bullying. Despite these experiences, and many others like them, we all remember our time at school, and many of us still do so with affection.

Joan Underhill started at All Saints in 1930 aged 5. She describes the teachers as 'the salt of the earth, they were strict but kind'. The school was in a state of disrepair and if there was heavy rain, the roof was liable to leak and classes were sent home. Toilets for both boys and girls were outside.

She has fond memories of the Infant School. The two Brown sisters, 'Little' Miss Brown and 'Big' Miss Brown, were particularly kind and at Christmas ensured that every child had a present to take home and open on Christmas morning. May Day was enjoyed by all with the May Day Queen taking centre stage. Joan suspects that the election of the Queen was 'rigged' by the staff as it always seemed to be someone from the All Saints/ Vicarage Road area with a Mom who would be good at sewing to adjust the dress to the correct size. Children from the new Parkfields estate like Joan were considered the 'poor relations' to those from the All Saints/ Vicarage Road area.

The Headmistress of the Junior School, Miss Jemmett, is warmly remembered. Life there, however, was not always so agreeable. Punishments could be severe with boys caned on their bare backsides in front of the class and girls caned on the hands. If someone did not own up to a particular misbehaviour, the teacher would line up the whole class and cane them one by one. In winter, coal fires were lit to warm the classrooms. If you were returning to school from an illness, the teachers would allow you to sit at a desk near the fire.

Towards the end of her time at their Junior School, pupils took the General Exam, an '11 Plus' type exam in two parts. The first part was taken at the school, while the second part was taken at Graiseley School. Joan did well enough to go to the High School in Tettenhall Road but her parents would not have been able to pay for the uniform and sports kit. Instead she went to the Intermediate School in Old Hall Street where she stayed until she was 15.

I turned 5 years of age in August 1954, and a week later on 6 September I was one of 29 children admitted to All Saints School. It was the nearest school to where we lived and I presume that my parents were happy with the arrangement. My parents had completed a conventional schooling, experienced by millions of working-class children, and left at 14, the school leaving age in the 1930s. I have no idea what educational aspirations they had for me.

The school had recently undergone a successful HM Inspection but I suspect the report would have been received with indifference by any parents about to send their child there. It was described as a school which 'serves an area of industrial housing in the south east of the town centre.'... 'and consists of a room for the Headmistress, two cloakrooms and six classrooms; one of the last-named is used as a hall and for dining purposes .... Heating is by open fires, is reasonably satisfactory in the two rooms where it is augmented by gas fires, but inefficient elsewhere.'

The report makes disheartening references to the perceived shortcomings of the school's pupil intake. It regrets the deficiencies in the lavatory and sanitary facilities 'in view of the overwhelming need for good social training in the area from which the pupils are drawn ... Standards of work in the school have to assessed against ... the problem presented to the school by the poor home background and lack of ability of many of the children.' It also expresses concern over the rising number of children going to the school and the impact of the new Rough Hills Estate. 'There are at present 200 children on roll, organised in five classes. The incidence of a new estate may account for a heavy intake of 45 children this first term. Admissions cannot continue at this rate.'

The school itself was going through a significant transition. An Educational Development Plan written in 1957 proposed that the Infant and Junior Schools should be demolished and rebuilt on a site across the road occupied by St Joseph's RC School. Miss JM Wood had recently retired after 38 years at the school. A new head had been appointed two years earlier and another two long established teachers were about to retire. The new teachers were relatively inexperienced. In the concluding part of the report it stresses that the 'school's most striking point is, indeed, the care and sympathy expended on the children.'

Grandad stayed over after the weekend and on my first morning we walked to All Saints School. Bearing in mind it was over half a mile away, getting to my destination was no mean achievement. I do not remember recognising the building. It was not on the bus route (there was none) and I had no recollection of attending an induction day. I have a vague recollection of being introduced to Mrs Sutton, the Headmistress of the Infant

School, a pleasant lady who did her best to put me at ease. Grandad reassured me that he would collect me at lunchtime and off I went to my class teacher.

Figure 18: All Saints Junior School building in 2002.

I have no happy memories of that first day or week. It seemed like most of the class had already started in the previous two terms and there were no familiar faces. The school drew mainly from the numerous streets of terraced houses stretching from Cleveland Road across to Dixon Street. The immediate area around the school and church made up a thriving community. They went to the same schools, worked at the same factories and worshipped and married in the same church. In contrast, Rough Hills Estate was in its infancy with friendships still to be forged. When the mid-morning bell went, everyone else already seemed familiar with the school's routines and escaped to the playground. This small area, enclosed by metal railings, extended both front and back of the Infant school. Alongside was a larger building, the Junior School, for the older pupils and in front the tarmac playground with an alarming Jungle Jim, a climbing construction made out of metal tubing that would challenge today's Health and Safety regulations.

The photograph on the previous page shows the school and church in 2002. The end of the playground, where the Jungle Jim stood, has been landscaped. The playground at the back included the outside toilets and coal store, heaped high in preparation for the winter fires in the classrooms. We had no grass, changing rooms or even any indoor toilets; we would have to wait several years for them. I survived the first week with my dignity intact, went home and expressed relief that my school career had now been completed. My mother halted my short-lived joy by breaking the dreadful news that I would be returning to school after the weekend. I clearly remember the despair.

Resigned to life at school, I turned up each day, signed up for school lunches and got used to eating strange combinations of foods, prepared in advance, delivered to school and heated up by the school cooks. Mom was a good cook, conservative with her recipes and I pestered her to allow me to eat lunch at home but she was having none of it. Every morning we had our bottle of free school milk. I found to my pleasant surprise that I enjoyed milk for the first time in my life, failing to comprehend why the milk we had at home was so dreadful in comparison. I was to realise later that like so many other people in the Black Country we bought *sterilised milk; a drink that tasted foul but stayed fresh for several days and proved ideal for a family in the days before fridges became an accepted part of everyone's home.*

I have few clear memories of the Infant school and remember none of the teacher's names apart from Mrs Sutton. Whether that is a reflection of their personalities and teaching qualities, it would be unfair to judge. For some ex-pupils their infant school teachers made a lasting impression.

Margaret Carroll attended the Infants School from 1937 to 1940 and remembers Miss Lucy Smith, the Headmistress and four teachers: 'Little' Miss Brown, 'Big' Miss Brown, Miss Overton and Miss Ford.

'I seem to remember there were around 40 children in each class. The Reception class was overseen by Little Miss Brown, and after a while we went into Miss Overton's class, then we were divided into Big Miss Brown's class and the top (6-7 yrs.) were in Miss Ford's class. I am not sure whether the Misses Brown were sisters, one was short and chubby and the other taller and slimmer, but everyone seems to remember them. I remember in Miss Ford's class we were taught to knit and I learned with two meat skewers and some string!'

Junior School was the building which, when looking from All Saints Rd, was on your left. The front of that school was the boys' playground and the area at the back of the Infants School was the girls' playground. The area at the front of the Infants' School was for the Infants. As Miss Smith's (Head Mistress) office overlooked this area, she was able to keep an eye on things.

Colin Jackson (along with his future wife) was a pupil from 1945 to 1951 and remembers some teachers at the

116

> *infants like 'little' Miss Brown and 'big' Miss Brown, as well as Miss Kirby who played the violin (and was presumably the same Miss Kirby who was to be my class teacher in Year 3 of the Juniors).*

Carole Bridgen who attended All Saints from 1949 to 1955 has mixed memories of her time in the Infant School.

> *'My memories were all good from that school except for Miss Brown (big or little?) in the infant's because my eldest brother kicked her for some reason when he was in her class, so when my eldest sister and then I went into her class she always picked on us.'*

Shirley Morris who attended All Saints from 1964 to 1969 cannot remember the early teachers' names, but in the last year of the infants she was taught by Mrs Baugh (not sure of spelling or if she was married).

> *'She was a little frightening, although I did like her. My lasting memory of her class was when, being left handed, I was asked to sit at the teacher's desk, with other children around me. I was asked to try to write with my right hand, which I couldn't do and all the children were laughing at me – things were very different and politically incorrect in the 60's!'*

May Day

In the 1930s, Margaret Carroll (nee Williams) remembers two celebrations taking place each May. On 24 May, the school celebrated Empire Day and girls were allowed to wear their

Brownie uniforms which 'made us feel very important'. Far more important, however, were the May Day celebrations. She thinks this particular photograph was taken in May 1939.

Figure 19:

Top row: Sidney Dear, Rita Pittaway, Tommy Taggart, Joan Walton, Roy Hammond, Beryl Davies, Donald Davies

Bottom Row: Olive Round, Reg Turner, Doreen Welsby, Stanley Bryan, Margaret Williams, Alan Griffiths,?, ?, Rita Anderson.

The May Queen event, however, was the real highlight of the year. The May Queen and her attendants would be chosen ahead of the day. The climax of the event was the procession around the playground of the May Queen and her attendants followed by pupils dancing around the May pole.

Many of the May Day celebrations in the 1950s were well documented. A photograph from 1951 shows a large crowd of parents, relatives and friends attending the crowning of Sandra Bickley as the May Queen. Leading the May Queen procession is Peter Philips, his head unfortunately hidden at that precise moment by the flowers.

Figure 20: May Queen procession, 1951.

Formal photographs of the event, such as this one below, from 1953, were taken. The school group has assembled in the main hall of St Joseph's R.C. School on the opposite side of All Saints Road, presumably to avoid the rain.

My own memories of the annual May Day celebrations in the mid-50s, one of the highlights of the school year and a clearly a lasting memory for many ex-pupils, are vague to say the least. Maybe, as a member of the second stream, we did not play a particularly significant part in the event. I have no recollection of wearing a white shirt and participating in a procession. It is very, very unlikely that I danced around a maypole: my school career at All Saints revealed a complete lack of appreciation of my dancing skills by the teachers. I certainly have no photographic record showing my participation. Maybe I stayed at home, read from my extensive collection of comics and ate jam sandwiches.

Figure 21: May Day celebrations from 1953.

In contrast, Shirley Morris (nee Burt) has fond memories of her May Days in the early 60s.

'We all took part in the 'big' May Day celebrations. I think it was in the early infants that we performed The Elves & The Shoemaker's Wife on the back playground of the Junior School, where I was the Shoemaker's Wife. In another class I danced around the maypole and played an instrument in a band.

Figure 22:

Back Row: Paul Simpkiss(?), ??, ??, ??, Carol Pugh, Kenneth Edwards, Julie Morgan, Lorraine Hodson, ??, Carol Lever, Janet ?, Neil Pitt.

3rd Row: ?? ,?? ,??, ??, ??, Alan Stokes, ??, Clive Pendrell, ??, ??.

2nd Row: Lynn Gibbons, ??, Victoria ?, ??, Vashanti (Spelling?) Patel, Debra Jones, Susan Bastable, Carol Meanley, Shirley Burt.

Front Row: ??, ??, ??, Robert Gill, Gaylene Powell, ??, ??, Ian Foxall, Robert Wycherley

Figure 23:

Back Standing: Alan Lewis(?), Jane Beaman, Olga Ferguson, Clive Pendrell, Kenneth Edwards, Robert Gill.

Middle Seated: ??, Robert Whicherley, Christopher Cunningham, Paul Simpkiss, Vashanti(spelling????)Patel, ??, Shirley Burt, ??, Alan Stokes.

Front floor: ??, ??, ??

Everything took place in the playground. There was always a May Queen and attendants. This must have been done for years, as my sister, 6 years older than me, also took part in similar celebrations. I took part in the final May Day celebration. My mum had commented to my teacher that it was a shame they were not going to do this in the future, but again, things being very politically incorrect, she told my mum that there were so many 'foreign' children coming into the school and they could only 'dress up'. She said they couldn't understand May Day/ plays/ dance steps etc – she would have been sacked these days for saying such things!'

121

One of my first happy memories at All Saints was the day that the Rough Hills bus service started. Grandad stayed over. We boarded the bus at the bottom of Cheviot Road. As we got to each bus stop, there was loud cheering from inside and outside the bus. By the time the bus approached the school, it was probably well over its permitted capacity. We turned off Steelhouse Lane into All Saints Road to an ecstatic reception. A welcome party of teachers and pupils had already assembled in great numbers and we were greeted with smiles and more cheering. Once it had emptied, a few mothers stayed on as it continued its way to Wolverhampton town centre. No more trudging along Dixon Street to the bus stops on Bilston Road or Thompson Avenue. The number 30 was to provide a social lifeline for everyone on Rough Hills.

If starting at the Infant School tested my fortitude, it paled into insignificance compared to my first day at the Junior School. It may have been across the playground but it was a whole new world. By the time my two years at Infant School had finished, I was feeling fairly settled. I knew my place in the class, knew the alphabet, could hold a pencil or crayon, knew how to add and subtract (despite a dodgy lesson at home from Mom) and had made friends. The Junior School had streamed classes: an 'A' class, a 'B' class and an 'R' class with which everyone else avoided contact. As a late starter, I had progressed through the Infant School in the 'B' stream. It did not particularly bother me but we were all aware of the privileged few in the top stream.

We assembled in the Infant School and were escorted across to our new classrooms in the Junior School block. So far, so good but having arrived at the classroom for 1B, it appeared that a mistake had been made and I was taken next door to join the rest of 1A. The reality of streaming was that anyone from a lower class was a social outcast. I recognised faces but witnessed no signs of friendship. There were three or four from the estate including two girls from further up Cheviot Road, but no one I knew well. Mercifully, the mid-morning break came around and I looked for companionship from my old classmates. Unfortunately, six weeks' separation during the summer holidays and promotion to 1A meant that my old classmates were now ex-mates; time to start again.

Matters got worse. The Junior School had no dining area and meals were provided about half a mile away, at Monmore Green School on the Bilston Road. By now, walking such a distance was no longer a big deal and supervised by a teacher we marched in procession along Steelhouse Lane and down Cable Street. I emphasise the word 'down'. The walk to Monmore Green should have been easy with the incentive of a stodgy school dinner to keep us going, the return journey a chance to walk off the meal. Unfortunately, for my seven-year-old legs, the walk up Cable Street took on the challenge of a mountain assault. It was steep and I struggled with the daily climb. My pestering of Mother was more productive this time and after a few weeks I was allowed to go home for lunch. It was probably longer than walking to Monmore Green but I no longer had to face the ascent of Cable Street.

At home I became a big fan of comics with fond memories of the Beano and Dandy. There would be an anxious wait by the letterbox for their weekly delivery, a quick perusal to check on the latest Bash Street Kids or Desperate Dan storyline before settling down with a glass of pop and a jam sandwich to read it from cover to cover. A lovely elderly couple from two doors down, the Leach's, were kind enough to buy an additional comic for me each week. I progressed onto The Lion with Paddy

Payne - Fighter Ace, The Tiger with Roy of the Rovers and the adventure comics like The Hotspur or The Rover with Alf Tupper - "Tough of the Track". Both Roy and Alf provided valuable sporting instruction that was to prove useful in years to come. Fortunately, I never had to reproduce the heroics of Paddy. The comics were also invaluable for the adverts for buying gadgets like magnifying glasses and for buying stamps which became another big passion. One of their annuals became a regular Christmas present. Mom was into her women's magazines and Dad was an avid reader of the newspapers (Daily Mirror in the week and The People on a Sunday). I remember no novels in the house but I did have an encyclopaedia, a Christmas present, which I could dip into if I needed to know the length of the River Amazon or the inventor of the jet engine.

In the mid-50s my parents bought our first TV, made in Britain by Pye. In the 50s you were happy to buy British: Bush radios, Triumph motorbikes and, if you were wealthy, cars made by Austin, Morris or even Jaguar. Foreign goods were not widely available and their quality was viewed with some suspicion: British goods, on the other hand, still retained a good reputation. Dad was a big sports fan and was sold on the prospect of watching the FA Cup Final and Test cricket on its 12-inch screen. His decision was vindicated when he left work early to watch Jim Laker complete his 19 wicket demolition of the Australians in 1956.

When we bought our TV, the only channel was the BBC. Broadcasts were restricted to children's programmes in the late afternoon then evening programmes which finished around 10.30pm, followed by the National Anthem and 'the disappearing spot' on the screen. For the rest of the time, TV coverage consisted of the Test Card and Interludes featuring short films such as The Potter's Wheel. Such was the novelty of TV that even an Interlude film was enough to drag us off the street to watch these gap fillers. The radio was still an important part of our lives. By the time I woke up for school, the morning news would be on, unless the closing overs of the latest Ashes Test were being broadcast from Australia on the Third Programme. By the time I got home from Junior School at lunchtime 'Workers Playtime' would be on the Light Programme. Dad would arrive from work soon afterwards and at one o'clock he always switched over to the Home Service to listen to the national news. In the afternoon, Mom would have the place to herself and listen to 'Mrs Dale's Diary' and 'Woman's Hour' in peace. Over time, the TV schedules expanded, ITV started up and introduced us to the pleasures of commercial breaks, and we listened to the radio less and less. There were still longstanding routines. During the football season, we listened on Saturday afternoons to the football commentary (second half only) of a key game in Division One, followed by Sports Report with its iconic theme music leading up to the eagerly awaited full time scores. On Sunday it was Billy Cotton's Band show ('Hey, you down there - you with the glasses!') or Beyond our Ken while we ate our dinner.

I hated my first year in the Junior School and have no recollection of my class teacher. It was not completely unproductive. I learned how to cut paper in a straight line with scissors, how to cheat at tests and how to mime in Music lessons. I disliked anything to do with Music: singing, playing or dancing to it. Unfortunately, the school was famous across the borough for performances by the choir, for recorder playing and for folk dancing. Each year the musical elite from the school would be taken in the summer to the prestigious Leamington Music Festival, returning with a hoard of trophies for folk dancing and singing. A school needs an inspirational teacher to gain such a reputation. In the case of All Saints Junior School, it was Mr Lancaster. This particular teacher, originally from the north east, had arrived as Headmaster in 1949. Even in the 1950s when schools still had a well-deserved reputation for strict discipline, Mr Lancaster, was tough, if not very tough. He was a dark man in all respects; hair, moustache, and spectacle frames. He was also tall and predictably his nickname was 'Lanky', a word you would only utter in the safety of your home.

Mr Lancaster ensured that Music played a prominent part of our curriculum. Apart from the 3 'Rs' and Art and Craft, the whole week sometimes seemed devoted to Music in one form or another. If we were not singing to it, performing it with a recorder or dancing to it, we were listening to it. It would often be a classical piece like The Sorcerer's Apprentice. We marched off to the Civic Hall in the town centre one morning to listen to a lunchtime performance by the City of Birmingham Symphony Orchestra. In his quieter, less combative moments, we would sit in absolute silence while he played a gramophone record of Kathleen Ferrier singing "Blow the Wind Southerly". Her death from cancer at a young age had been a great shock to the musical world and I suspect a particular shock to Mr Lancaster.

Music was not restricted to the classroom. All Saints was a Church of England school, the church a 'High Church' establishment with a vicar we addressed as Father Shannon. Religion played a big role in the school. Each week we learned by rote sections of the catechism, only to forget them by the following week. Each year, leading up to Easter, we visited the church and learned about the 'Stations of the Cross'. When we were not practising traditional folk songs, we spent time rehearsing hymns.

The school needed little encouragement to celebrate a Christian festival or Saints day in the church. The highlight for the school was the service on 1 November to celebrate All Saints Day. It was classed as a school holiday but we were first required to attend a morning service. The service would finish with a rendition of the hymn, "For All the Saints", the school's unofficial anthem. Encouraged to raise the roof, we duly obliged. Since leaving All Saints, I have never heard it sung with the same gusto as it was in Steelhouse Lane. Once the service was over we trooped out of the church to enjoy the rest of the winter's day.

We rarely had games or PE lessons. The slightest shower seemed sufficient to deter the teachers from organising rounders on the playground or football, initially on Pond Lane Rec, and later on the Dixon Street playing fields. Despite its complacent attitude towards providing exercise for its pupils, the school took the fortunes of its football and cricket teams very seriously. The photograph of the school cricket team, courtesy of Peter Phillips, was taken in 1955. Mr Lancaster and Mr. Henning stand proudly at the back. Four years after leading out the May Queen procession, Peter takes up his captain's position at the middle of the second row.

Knowing far less about sport than music did not deter Mr Lancaster from giving robust support to school teams. He provided home advantage by virtue of his brooding presence and booming voice on the touchline. In the days before the Alex Ferguson 'hair dryer' team talk, we always gave that mythical '110%' to avoid any contribution from him to the half time pep talk.

Figure 24: All Saints' cricket team of 1955.

Figure 25: All Saints' football team of 1959/60.

In my last year at the school, both the football team and cricket team had very successful seasons and we won two trophies. The photograph, taken in 1960, shows the football team proudly showing off the Wolverhampton Primary School cup with the author proudly sitting next to Mr Henning on the right of the middle row. This achievement culminated in a presentation evening at the Wolverhampton Technical College, later to become the University, in Wulfruna Street. Our two trophies were presented by none other than the legendary manager of Wolverhampton Wanderers, Stan Cullis. Wolves had recently won the FA Cup and narrowly missed out on the double, finishing a close second in the First Division to Burnley. An opportunity to shake hands just once with Stan at this point in the club's history was wonderful; to shake hands with him twice, as some of us were privileged to do, was beyond our wildest dreams.

Dad had nurtured my passion for sport and we followed it avidly through programmes on TV like Sportsview with Peter Dimmock. While football was our main obsession, our sporting interests in the summer happily switched to athletics, Test cricket and Wimbledon tennis. Our involvement was restricted to watching the big events on TV but on one occasion I was taken to Edgbaston to watch the South Africans play Warwickshire. Regular visits were made to Molineux to watch reserve and youth matches. Dad was first and foremost a Wolves fan but admired all the top professionals, whichever club or country they played for. Convinced, wisely in retrospect, that I was too small to see anything, it was a while before he took me to my first Division 1 game (won 2-0, vs Newcastle) at Molineux to show me the skills of their inside forward, George Eastham.

I discovered how important sport would be to me during the rest of my school days. Becoming part of the school sports teams created new friendships. By the time that my four years at the Junior School came to a close, my singing voice was still out of tune, I was still unable to play a musical instrument and my two left feet for dancing were still intact but there was genuine disappointment that it was all to end. Each year had provided a stepping stone on that traumatic journey of growing up. After the distresses of Year 1, I had been lucky enough to be taught by outstanding teachers like Mr Henning my class teacher in Year 2 who was also in charge of the boys' sports teams. Mr Henning's particular claim to fame was his 'bubble' car, a 1950s motoring phenomenon which chugged into the playground each morning. More conventional transport was used by Miss Kirby our lovely class teacher in Year 3 and Mr Tod, our excellent class teacher in Year 4 who both arrived by bus along with most of the other teachers. In contrast, Mr Lancaster lived nearby in lodgings in Vicarage Road. He ruled by fear but his reputation meant that punishments existed more in theory than reality.

The last session on a Friday afternoon would usually start with an informal spelling test organised by Mr Tod and a good performance by the class was rewarded with the teacher reading out a children's classic by someone like Robert Louis Stevenson. It was not unusual for Mr Lancaster to make an appearance, turn the test into something far more formal and set a higher score before we could get our book reading reward. However, once the target was achieved, he relaxed and was known to hand out a prize of 6d (2 pence) to the best day's speller; enough in those days to buy a good stash of sweets on the way home. Mr Lancaster, firm but fair, was feared but respected by all.

It may well be that the summer of 1960 was a watershed for All Saints School and its environment. An Inspector's Report for November 1962 noted that the 'area in which the school is set appears to have changed considerably since the last inspection nine years ago'. It noted that many houses had been demolished, many families had been rehoused with some vacated houses occupied by immigrant families: 19 immigrant children now attended the school. At a Governors' meeting a year earlier, Mr Lancaster had stressed the difficulties experienced with the intake of Indian children who were unable to speak English. Another inspection followed in January 1964 and although it highlighted the improvements such as the new toilet block and central heating that had been made to the school's facilities since 1953, it conceded that 'the staff are facing considerable difficulties many of which stem from the drab environment in which many of the pupils live'. I wonder which leafy suburbs these inspectors went home to?

Mr Alfred William Lancaster resigned as headmaster of All Saints Junior School on 31 December 1964 to take up a new post in North Shields, Northumberland. He had been Headmaster since 1949. As Sylvia Enefer, a pupil from 1946 until 1952, said, "We all wanted to do our best for Mr. Lancaster."

By the time that Shirley Morris moved to the Junior school in the early 60s, Mr Lancaster had left.

'I moved into the big Junior School next door and the Headmaster was Mr Werry, who had recently replaced Mr

Lancaster. My sister had said Mr Lancaster was very strict and scary. He was apparently often seen with his cane. Mr Werry seemed a very nice man, although I can't remember seeing him about much in school. (I did once see him at Kinver, sledging with his family and I though it hilarious to see him in a woolly hat). We couldn't use the staircase at the front of the building as it came out by his office and we may have disturbed him. On the rare occasion we did use it (possibly for fire drills) we felt very important and I just remember it being very dark and scary. In the Junior School I was first taught by Miss Austin, who was really lovely and she used to bring her guitar into class and we would sing Puff the Magic Dragon. I remember being told that she had left to go to teach deaf children. I then went into the 2nd year and was taught by Mr Patel who was very gentle and kind. I seem to remember part of that year I was also taught by a lady teacher too. It was in this class I first remember loving to write stories. In the 3rd year we felt very grown up, when we moved upstairs into Mr Bayliss' class. These classes joined the next classroom by a door, which fascinated me. Mr Bayliss was a young teacher with a beard and we used to wait for him in a morning by the railings, because he used to be dropped off by his wife and they would have a goodbye kiss, which made us young girls giggle. He was good friends with the other male teacher – Mr Sexton who taught next door.

My final year was in Mrs Clark's class and she was very scary indeed. Looking back, she was a very good teacher and certainly helped me pass my 11 plus. We were set out in groups, with top tables for the brighter kids and then down in levels. There was no hiding the fact that we were being judged like this and I was proud to be on top table. I think schools are far more discrete with their grading now. Mrs Clark started my interest in what turned out to be a lifelong hobby of patchwork, when she picked only me to take up this craft. This was also the only class where I can remember one little girl being put across the teacher's knee and having her bottom smacked! I never stayed to school dinner. My poor mum always fetched me at lunchtime and took me back, which must have been difficult time wise, living in Rough Hills. I can very clearly remember the horrible smell of school dinners in the church hall which was used for PE and school dinners. The children who stayed for lunch said that they had to lie down after their dinner, to try to have a little sleep, but I don't know if that was true. I can also remember other 'random smells' that take me back to All Saints – the smell of the little milk bottles, the wooden number bricks we used in maths and the smell of the pump cage, which had all the rubber based pumps in, which we used for PE. These were provided by the school and we all used to wear each other's pumps.

Occasionally we used to go to church, next door, especially for All Saints Day. We went swimming in the upper years to Wolverhampton Baths. We had to go by coach which was exciting. I can't remember going on many school trips, but I can remember one outing to the children's theatre in Birmingham and my mum came with us as a helper. I can remember my mum being so angry one Christmas when my sister was in the early juniors. Apparently, one of the senior teachers (Miss Trubshaw) popped into the class to wish them a Happy Christmas, but as she left, she said 'Oh and I hope none of you still believe in Father Christmas'. There were so many upset children that Christmas, not to mention angry parents! Another of my sister's teachers was Mr

Davies, who was a very popular, nice, kind man. He retired before I reached his year (4 year I think), but I did have to go into his class once when I was too ill to go swimming and I learned the words to 'The big ship sails ....'. My sister was also in a group of children who used to go to Leamington to dance in competitions. They did lots of rehearsing and the mums made the girls dresses.

Not everyone went to All Saints. My big friend from four doors down, Ronnie Bagnall (of canal fame), went to St Luke's Junior School, having moved to Cheviot Road from Blakenhall. Other children we met on the playing fields went to Dudley Road School. This had opened in 1873 as one of the original Wolverhampton Board schools. By the 1920s, the Boys' school had acquired a motto:

The use of the word "Quit" rather than 'acquit' lends some ambiguity to the strong message it is trying to make. While the message is undoubtedly commendable, to explain it in the context of a war between the Philistines and Israelites would not be appropriate in today's political climate.

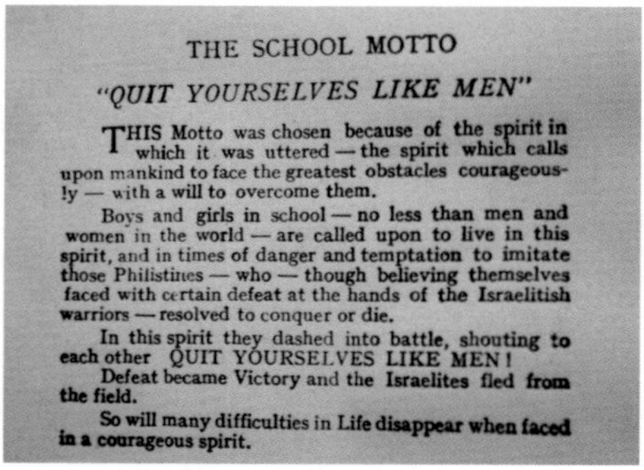

THE SCHOOL MOTTO

"QUIT YOURSELVES LIKE MEN"

THIS Motto was chosen because of the spirit in which it was uttered — the spirit which calls upon mankind to face the greatest obstacles courageously — with a will to overcome them.

Boys and girls in school — no less than men and women in the world — are called upon to live in this spirit, and in times of danger and temptation to imitate those Philistines — who — though believing themselves faced with certain defeat at the hands of the Israelitish warriors — resolved to conquer or die.

In this spirit they dashed into battle, shouting to each other QUIT YOURSELVES LIKE MEN! Defeat became Victory and the Israelites fled from the field.

So will many difficulties in Life disappear when faced in a courageous spirit.

Figure 26: The motto of Dudley Road school. (by Kind Permission of Wolverhampton Archives and Local History).

By 1926, the motto had been set to music with credit given to Miss Ethel Sneyd for the music and someone with the initials HDJ for the lyrics of the four verses. It was first sung by the school on 1 July 1926 and one can imagine the passion with which the words of the chorus were belted out by the pupils and staff.

Both the Boys' and Girls' schools closed in 1931. The log book of the Boys' school finishes with the following emotional farewell, written on 1 April 1931 in red ink:

'Here endeth the record of Dudley Road Boys School – opened June 9 1873 with 207 scholars – closed with 427 on Reg'r.

6813 scholars have passed thro' school.

On reopening the block will contain Infants – Mixed Junior and Mixed Senior.'

My father, Roland Mills, was one of the 427 pupils at the school when it closed. On 13 April he transferred to All Saints Junior School.

Figure 27: The school song. (by Kind Permission of Wolverhampton Archives and Local History).

As planned the school reopened later that year as Dudley Road Senior Mixed School with many of the new students coming from Dudley Road, All Saints and St Luke's Schools.

My father was again caught up in the reorganisation and one year later on 29 August 1932, he re-joined Dudley Road School, this time as a member of the Senior School. He left on 2 August 1934 shortly before his fourteenth birthday with grades of Good, Good, Fair for Character, Industry and Ability respectively to start work at Gibbons Lock factory in Church

Lane. Considering the disruptions to his education, it was a very commendable achievement.

At the same time, the Girls school became Dudley Road Junior Mixed, then Dudley Road Junior and Infant Schools in 1961. The Senior Mixed School had a short life, closing in 1938.

Derek Shorthouse from Parkfield Road went to Dudley Road School during the war years.

'In 1939 after a period when we were taught in private houses (because the school's air raid shelters had not been completed) we transferred to Dudley Road School. The bus fare from Thompson Avenue to Derry Street was one halfpenny.

There Miss Williams was Headmistress and Miss Nicholas, Miss Bullock and Miss Hamer taught me. Miss Hamer, small but terrifying, was a very effective teacher and I was thrilled to be awarded a scholarship in 1943.'

Brian Hall grew up in Parkfield Grove from 1942 to 1964. He started Bowen Street Infants in 1944 aged 5, before moving onto Dudley Road Juniors. He also remembers Miss Hamer.

First day at Dudley Road Juniors was great as my best friend, Gregory, a year older than me, showed me the ropes and looked after me as he had already been there for a year. Our form teacher was Miss Worby, a pleasant, good looking young lady in her twenties. We sat in old fashioned double desks with cast iron frames and wooden tops and seats which folded up. In the top of the desk was an inkwell each. This was the first time I'd seen inkwells as we only had pencils in the infants. Next to me was a lovely girl named Betty Mullinder, who made me giggle with her jokes and, of course, quite a few of my friends from Bowen St. infants were there as well. The head mistress was Miss Williams and the other teachers I recall were Miss Cox, Mr Williams(Art), Miss Birch, Mr Breeze and Miss Hamer who would be my form teacher in the following years. The boys' playground was separate from the girls with a door between and at the bottom of our playground was a steel tin roofed large shed which we could go under if the weather was bad. One of the first things I noted was there was no sleep in the afternoon as we had in the infants and most of us got to and from school without our mothers. I have no particularly bad memories of the teachers, of course I was quickly aware that you couldn't mess about with some teachers but mostly they were OK. Miss Hamer would rap my knuckles and prod me in the head if I made silly mistakes in English but I wasn't caned until the last year there, by the new headmaster, Mr Tuffley and I did deserve it.

At All Saints we were part of a school with large classes sizes and relatively few resources. It did not have as strong an academic record as schools on the west side of the town and we followed an eclectic curriculum which was probably less focussed on passing the 11 plus. Even so, our sporting success that year was mirrored by examination success. While neither of my parents could be described as scholarly, they strongly believed in the importance of education, expressed confidence in Mr Lancaster and his staff and showed restrained interest and encouragement for me during my time at the school. Even so, I suspect they were as surprised as I was when, with great apprehension, the results letter was opened to reveal that not only had I passed the fearsome 11 plus but I had won a place at the prestigious Wolverhampton Grammar School. I was one of five who had won places to go there. In previous years no more than one or two had been successful. As well as the five going to the Grammar School, several more pupils had gained entry to the Municipal Grammar School and the Technical High School. Moreover, two pupils who were leaving the Wolverhampton area had gained places at the grammar schools in Wednesfield and Sedgley. We did not know it at the time but we were probably the school's 'golden generation', its most successful in terms of academic, music and sporting achievement. All Saints was a school that I remember with great affection.

Not everyone passed the 11 plus and in fact the majority of the pupils at All Saints would fail the exam each year. I do not have the figures for my year but one year earlier, in 1959, 70 out of the 89 pupils who took the exam were unsuccessful. This infamous exam was created as part of the 1944 Butler Education Act and presumed that different skills required different schooling. Pupils were directed towards a grammar or technical school if they passed and a vocational (secondary modern) school if they failed. Even in the 'A' stream, no more than 33% of the pupils at All Saints would pass each year. A 'failure' meant in theory four years at one of the town's secondary modern schools. The main destinations for children on Rough Hills Estate were St Peters, Graiseley and Eastfield. There was some in-built flexibility in the system and if it was clear that misjudgements had been made at 11, these 'late developers' could in theory transfer across to a grammar or technical school at the age of 13. Such transfers were few and far between. It was not necessarily a good idea for pupils at some secondary modern schools to raise their heads above the parapet and demonstrate that an error had been made.

St Peters was supposedly for children who were regular churchgoers and applications to go there had to be supported by Mr Lancaster, a task he carried out conscientiously. Even so, a small number of families seemed to 'find religion' in the final year coming up to the 11 plus exam and ensured that their children became regular attenders at All Saints church. It was not difficult to see why: St Peters was considered to be the best secondary modern school in the town, pupils wore a uniform and many stayed on an extra year to take the prestigious GCE (General Certificate of Education) exams. Neither Graiseley nor Eastfield could boast of such a good reputation. Graiseley School was in Blakenhall near to the Penn Road and pupils were affectionately known as 'Graiseley Grubs'. Eastfield School was near the Willenhall Road. A number of friends had started at Graiseley a year earlier and their stories of life at the school filled me with concern. At the time it provided a real incentive to pass the 11 plus exam.

Brian Hall went to Graiseley in 1950 and has favourable memories of the school but adds that some of the more "sensual [sic]" or "delicate" lads in his time might tell you a different story.

'I started at Graiseley Secondary Modern School in September 1950. I was a bit apprehensive as I'd heard tales of what they did to new boys. One was that they put your head in the toilet and pulled the chain! Nevertheless, I was OK as my friend Gregory was there to look after me - again. I was sent to Mr. Grew's room to join Lower One - how lucky

we were, "Dickie" Grew was one of the best and nicest teachers ever. His subject was English which included drama and poetry; he also did French but that was not taught at Graiseley. He never used the cane or any physical punishment and we responded by being reasonably behaved.

The headmaster, Mr. Beddoes was another decent man who would rather give you a good "talking to" than punishment. Other teachers were not so predictable, Mr. (Killer) Morris, deputy head and woodwork, would hurl a chisel at any boy messing about.

Mr. (Froggy) Martin would fall asleep but if he awoke and found anyone not at their desk you were in trouble; it was said that he had been in Africa and been bitten by a tsetse fly, causing "sleeping sickness". Mr. Pettit the metalwork teacher was a large man in a gown who drove a Standard Eight car which we often had to push down the playground to get it going. He shot rabbits and pheasants which we saw on the car's back seat and he would often fettle up his gun on the lathe. "Daddy" Exley was a Yorkshire man from Wakefield, in his twenties, who took us for Social Studies (another word for Geography). Most of us loved him as we could have a bit of banter with him and answer him back. His classroom of at least forty boys was kept in order by his use of the windowpole, about ten feet long, used for the top windows which he would use to hit us on the head with. It had a hook on the end as well. He tried to teach us to play rugby and would often tackle us to the ground or "back heel" us but I think we sensed that he cared for us really. I had the cane once in the juniors and twice at Graiseley, the last time when I was fifteen just before I left in 1955.

Our football etc. was also played at Marsh Lane (by the airport) or Dunstall race course. Sports day was at

Beckminster or at the rear of the Grammar school and at the back of the Villiers factory. Don Everalls carried us in their oldest double deckers.'

Whether we hold any affection for our primary or secondary school is obviously a personal matter. However, what clearly comes over in these reminiscences is the deep regard for many of the teachers. While our time at school may not necessarily have been the best years of our lives, they were certainly not the worst.

16

SPORT AND LEISURE

The 1830 Beer Act was introduced to encourage the drinking of beer as a 'harmless' alternative to gin. Any householder who paid rates could apply, with a one-off payment of two guineas (roughly equal in value to £159 today), to sell beer or cider in their home (usually the front parlour) and even to brew their own on their premises. They were known as beer houses. The original Monkey House, the Moulders Arms, was one such beer house dating back to 1860 and, although its address was given as Steelhouse Lane, it was located on the site of the present pub in Kent Road.

Drinking at their local public house or 'pub' became the most popular leisure pursuit of many working-class men. Beer was comparable in price to tea and coffee and safer to drink than water or milk. If it was consumed in sufficient quantity, and it often was, it could dull the aches and pains of a day's work and boost morale. Moreover, the pub provided companionship as well as light, warmth and lavatories: features often lacking in their homes.

The 1887/88 Ordnance Survey map shows three more public houses in the vicinity of Rough Hills: The Red Lion on Parkfield Road near to the junction with Rooker Avenue, The Duke of York (later renamed as The New Inn) at the bottom of Dixon Street on Bilston Road and The Rough Hills Tavern alongside a track now occupied by Rooker Avenue.

Figure 28: The Pub Sign outside the Rough Hills Tavern.

The original Rough Hills Tavern dates back to at least 1851 and was also initially licensed as a beer house. Located near a tram road between Ettingshall Colliery and the old Wolverhampton furnaces, it was owned in 1871 by Edwin Dixon, a banker and a magistrate of the county. In 1877, he sold it to William Fenn, the coalmaster. Almost immediately, the land and premises were passed onto James Trevitt. In August 1877 his beer licence was renewed. However, the house was in a very poor condition owing to mining subsidence and it was pulled down. In August 1878 the licence was again renewed, despite the fact that the house had not been rebuilt. In the following twelve months, Trevitt neglected to complete the legal formalities and when the renewal came up in August 1879 it was refused. Despite this setback, Trevitt saw potential in the area and after an appeal it was granted in October 1879. Further confusion arose when the new Rough Hills Tavern was built on a new site about 60 yards away. Following another court case involving the legality of the licence, the ownership was transferred in March 1880 to John Edward Stephens. Under his ownership, the tenants changed on a regular basis:

- 1882 - Samuel Waters
- 1885 – Richard Bates
- 1888 – J. Benjamin Asbury
- 1891 – John Russell

It was not long before the pub was involved in another court case. In September 1882 Samuel Waters made an appearance in front of the magistrates at the Town Hall when he was convicted 'for unlawfully permitting gaming to wit bowl playing and card playing for money to be carried out on his licensed premises on 19 August 1882'. He was given the choice of a £5 fine and costs or a one-month imprisonment. The newspaper article does not make it clear which option he chose.

Pubs which originally had brewed their own beer increasingly began to buy it in from outside breweries. Springfield Brewery started up in 1873 near the town centre and was in full operation a year later. Banks's and Company started brewing at the Park Brewery near West Park in 1875. The Wolverhampton & Dudley Breweries, PLC was formed as a public company in 1890 by an amalgamation of three local businesses: Banks's and Company, George Thompson and Sons of the Dudley and Victoria Breweries, Dudley, and Charles Colonel Smith's brewery at the Fox Brewery, Wolverhampton. It was not long before breweries were not only supplying the beer but also owning the pubs that sold it. In 1892 ownership of the Rough Hills Tavern and surrounding land was transferred to Thomas Skidmore who in turn sold it to Wolverhampton and Dudley Breweries in 1900. The ownership of the Moulders Arms pub also passed to Wolverhampton and Dudley Breweries when Sherwood sold it in 1900.

At the beginning of the 19th century, leisure pursuits would also have included attending events such as cock and dog-fighting and baiting of bulls and bears. The Fighting Cocks pub at the junction of Parkfield Road and Goldthorn Hill was one of many to carry the name and remind later generations of a time when bloodsports were an established part of the British culture. Their brutality was said to reflect the harsh living and working conditions of the time but these 'sports' were practised and watched by men from all social and occupational groups and were slow to disappear despite the passing of the Cruelty to Animals Act in 1835. Another popular spectator sport deemed illegal was prize fighting. In December 1849 the Staffordshire Advertiser reported on a fight which took place at Rough Hills with a prize of £4. A crowd of several hundred had already enjoyed eighteen rounds of the contest between Richard Crockett and William Riddy when the police arrived to break it up and make arrests. Despite his obvious tiredness, Crockett was still fit enough to make an escape and was only caught after a long chase by the police.

During the second half of the century, men began to enjoy shorter working hours and more time could be spent watching or participating in leisure activities. Many of today's major sports like football, cricket, cycling and athletics built up their popularity amongst working men during this time. Another lesser known sport was quoits, but this game was surprisingly not restricted to the ruling classes. The 16 November 1897 edition of the Gloucestershire Echo reports on a match at the Central Quoit Ground, Wednesbury between the Midland champion, Joe Smith, and John Russell from Rough Hills. 'The pitching throughout was very accurate' with John Russell, the landlord of the Rough Hills Tavern, winning the £100 prize money. A minority sport, maybe, but certainly not minority earnings.

While the growth of sporting pursuits was more pronounced in the north of Staffordshire, there is considerable evidence that sporting events became established around Rough Hills. Next to Rough Hills Tavern on the 1887/88 Ordnance Survey map was located a prominent piece of land labelled as the Victoria Grounds. It continued to appear on Ordnance Survey and Town maps as late as 1934 and only disappeared when houses and shops were built on Rooker Crescent and along Rooker Avenue in the 1930s.

Research on the land initially proved elusive but a strong sporting connection slowly became apparent. The first confirmation of a sporting event at the Victoria Grounds turned up surprisingly in an American newspaper, The Spirit of the Times, in 1881. The article states:

'At this season of the year in America, sporting events are rare, and our tables of fixtures distressingly meagre. It is both interesting and instructive at such times to note what is going on in England, and compare the winter sports of the two countries.'

A long list of events in the newspaper's edition for 26 December 1881 included:

Pedestrianism: 100 yards handicap, 12L(£). 10s. Victoria Running Grounds, Rough Hills, near Wolverhampton;

Also T. Richards, of Wolverhampton, and J. Giles of Wednesfleld, run 120 yards, for 30L(£)., Rough Hill Grounds, Wolverhampton.

Pedestrianism was a 19th century form of competitive running and walking and a popular spectator sport in the British Isles. It was funded by income from betting and the top competitors, sometimes referred to in newspapers as 'peds', were rewarded with huge prize money. Pedestrianism events were becoming established in Wolverhampton as far back as 1862. In May of that year, the Wolverhampton Chronicle advertised a 'Grand Pedestrian and Athletics Gala' at Harthill Field, Dudley Road. The star event was to be a four-mile race between the celebrated Aboriginal Indian Chief, Deerfoot and six of England's finest runners. Described in the advert as the 'GRAND RACE for the CHAMPIONSHIP of the WORLD', it carried a prize of £50, equivalent to over £4,000 in today's money.

Pubs and beer houses were starting to compete for customers by providing better facilities and attractions. Many sporting arenas were built next to, or within, the grounds of the rural public houses and hotels, with landlords enclosing their grounds in order to benefit financially through charging entrance fees, providing drink and food and offering betting commissions. The Birmingham Daily Post edition on 28 August 1871 reported on a pedestrianism meeting at the Royal Oak grounds at Burnt Tree, Dudley Port where 'fifty pedestrians from the districts around assembled to contend the money prizes announced'. The betting started at 6 to 1 on the field.

The pedestrianism events at Victoria Running Grounds, Rough Hills had close links with the adjoining Rough Hills

Tavern. A report on a court case in the 12 September 1882 edition of the Birmingham Daily Post refers to a running track next to the Tavern. The 5 November 1884 edition of the Birmingham Daily Post mentions 'Samuel Walters, licensed victualler, of the Victoria Grounds and Tavern, Rough Hills'.

The June 1881 edition of the Sporting Life describes a crowd of 1,500, and many more watching for free outside, attending a race at Victoria Running Ground, Rough Hills between Thomas Richards and Mark Steward. In 1882, the October edition of the Sporting Life advertised forthcoming dog handicaps and bird shooting as well as pedestrian events at the venue. In 1885 it had become sufficiently well established and respected to attract an attempt by Harry Hutchins from Putney on the world records for 150 yards and 350 yards. On a fine day and before a 'fairly large company' and assisted by two pacemakers, Harry, described in the 21 September edition of the Morning Post as the champion sprint runner of the world, just failed to beat the record for 150 yards that had been held since 1851. For his attempt on the 350 yards record, held by G. Walsh since 1871, he again used the same two pacemakers and 'although he tired towards the finish, he nevertheless got home in 38 2/5 secs beating Walsh's time by 1 3/5 secs'.

One year later over 300 spectators attended the Inter-Club Championships between Walsall Harriers and Wolverhampton A.C. Despite its popularity as a sporting venue, a detailed description of the Grounds has not been found with reporters concentrating on the races themselves. The only exception to that is hidden away in the Birmingham Daily Post report (21 September) on the Harry Hutchins races where the track is described as being 'in first rate condition' and having a straight of nearly 200 yards.

The Victoria Grounds were not only used for pedestrianism. In 1884, the Express and Star on 8 September reported on

Figure 29: Rooker Crescent - built on the site of the Victoria Running Grounds.

cycling at the Victoria Running Grounds, Wolverhampton. In the article, it describes a 'fairly large assemblage of spectators at the Rough Hills Running Grounds on Saturday afternoon as a number of crack bicyclists were announced to compete in Mr. J. Barrett's one-mile handicap'. The results of 12 races are given. Most of the cyclists were from Wolverhampton, recognised at the time not only as one of the centres for bicycle racing but also for bicycle manufacturing. In the following year on 18 May 1885 the Express and Star reported on 'a small but very respectable sprinkling of people assembled at these grounds to witness the first rounds of Mr. R. Bates' one-mile professional bicycle handicap'. Richard Bates would have been the landlord of the Rough Hills Tavern at the time. The race was easily won by O. Farndon from Northampton, earning him the substantial prize of £10.

Both Bates and his predecessor Samuel Waters appear to have led a chequered life at Rough Hills, making spasmodic appearances at the local courts. Waters was charged at the Borough Police Court in August 1882 with permitting gambling on his licensed premises on three dates. The Birmingham Daily Post edition of the 12 September of that year reported that he was fined £5 on each of the three cases and his license was endorsed. According to the paper, Waters had taken out a mortgage on the property and by the end of 1884, his finances had deteriorated to such an extent that in November he was declared bankrupt. The same fate was to befall another ex-landlord, Benjamin Asbury, in 1896.

Betting at these meetings inevitably led to disputes which sometimes escalated into court appearances. The Birmingham Daily Post on the 10 February 1887 reported an assault on a bookmaker at the Rough Hills Running Ground. The case at the Wolverhampton Police Court was thrown out when the bookmaker admitted that he had told one of the competitors to run to lose. The same paper on 3 April 1887 reported an alleged breach of the Betting Act by Richard Bates, the landlord of the Rough Hills Tavern, who was charged with 'illegally permitting the use of an enclosure for betting purposes upon the occasion of certain foot races'. On a legal technicality, the case was adjourned.

The Victoria Ground was also an established football and cricket venue. A photograph in Alec Brew's Images of England book on Ettingshall and Monmore Green shows the Wolverhampton Early Closing Association Football team posing for a photograph before a match in the 1896-7 season. The Early Closing Association was formed in the 1840s to control the working hours in retail shops and to abolish Sunday trading and it is probable that the Associations in most major towns in the country will have set up sports teams. There are no details, unfortunately, of Wolverhampton's opponents or the longevity of the club. The 11 June 1904 edition of the Walsall Advertiser gives the score card for a match in the Wolverhampton and District Cricket League between Blakenhall and Walsall Centenary, held at the Victoria Grounds, Rough Hills. Blakenhall, presumably playing on their home ground, scored 73 runs and went on to win by 20 runs.

Both George Cartwright and Barry Marchant remember that an area of land near Mount Road was known by locals as 'The Runners'. They have no knowledge of the rich and diverse sporting history that has just been described but understand it was reputed to be the venue for whippet races. Newspaper reports show such events going back as far as 1882. A meeting organised by Mr John Russell in June 1903 attracted 55 of 'the speediest whippets in the Black Country'. There are also numerous reports of rabbit coursing events at the Victoria Running Grounds whereby dogs set off in pursuit of a rabbit or hare. The Gloucester Citizen edition of 21 February 1894 describes Mr John Russell's All England £10 Whippet Coursing Stakes held at the Victoria Grounds, Rough Hills. 'Open to All-England, 10s entrance each, one yard to pound, 60 yards' Law. The winner was a 'smart bitch' called Nettle belonging to Mr Hogg from Gloucester.

Rough Hills had also gained a national reputation for a less salubrious 'sport'. The Lancashire Evening Post of 25 May 1901 described the Rough Hills area as 'notorious' because of 'the prevalent practice of shooting birds', the birds in question being homing pigeons. In a later edition on 1 June two men, John Hodnett and William Rickhuss were prosecuted by the N.H.U., the National Homing Union. Hodnett who was described as 'an expert at avoiding detection, shot as many as 50 or 60 birds a day, and had actually a wager with another man as to the number of rings from pigeons that he could collect'. Both men were found guilty and fined heavily.

Pedestrianism races at the Victoria Grounds venue continued into the 1900s. The Express and Star edition of 1 June 1908 reports on a meeting in which 16 handicap races were run with most competitors from neighbouring Black Country towns. These meetings, somewhat surprisingly, were still taking place during WW1. At a meeting in November 1916, a one-hundred-yard race between two runners, Bradley and Hodgetts, ended in a 'dead heat' which led to a dispute between two of Bradley's relatives and Harry Timmins, the race referee and stakeholder. Bradley's relatives who predictably had put money on Bradley claimed the race referee had initially given the decision to Bradley and then changed his mind. Even more surprisingly the case went to court in Dudley and was reported in the Birmingham Daily Post of 12 January 1917. The verdict went in favour of Timmins.

No further newspaper reports of races have been found after this date, but there exists a tragic postscript to the history of this sporting venue. The Staffordshire Advertiser reported that six young men went to the running track on 13 July 1926 for their regular training session. As on previous occasions, they made use of an adjacent stable for changing. After the session, as they changed back into their normal clothing, the roof collapsed and John Fellows, aged 18, died later from his injuries. The owners, Wolverhampton and Dudley Breweries, stated that the landlord, Arthur Gascoyne, had not given permission for this changing arrangement. Although this was disputed by the runners, the jury found a verdict of accidental death.

Richard Bates and John Russell, landlords of the Rough Hills Tavern in the 1880s, 90s and early 1900s are closely associated with organising many of the sporting events at the adjacent Victoria Running Grounds. Another tavern owner and promoter in the town was McGregor, the proprietor of the famous Molineux Arms and Gardens. He started promoting bicycle races at his own establishment in 1869 after seeing the success of the first Wolverhampton races organized by manufacturers Forder and Traves at Vauxhall Gardens, near Cannock Road. In August 1870, nearly two thousand attended an event at Molineux Gardens starring international class racers like John Keen from London. In the early 1870s McGregor was responsible for building his establishment into one of the most important venues in the country, arguably making Wolverhampton the bicycle racing Mecca of England. On Boxing Day 1875, eighteen thousand spectators turned up to watch a race between Keen, Fred Cooper, James Moore and David Stanton, four of the top cyclists in the world. Such was the reputation of the town in cycling circles that the sport adopted a code of conduct referred to as the 'Wolverhampton rules' governing behaviour and fair play on the track. Riders, for example must 'pass each other on the outside, and be a clear length of the bicycle in front before taking the inside'. Molineux Grounds, however, were to take on even greater significance for the town before the 1800s finished.

Not far away, the early history of Wolverhampton Wanderers was unfolding. After starting as a schoolboy football team in 1877, it merged two years later with a local cricket team, Blakenhall Wanderers, and became known as Wolverhampton Wanderers. Matches were initially played in the Goldthorn Hill area near the Niphon Works in Lower Villiers Street, but by 1881 they were using a field off Dudley Road opposite the Fighting Cocks.

1888 - First ever fixture played in The Football League between Wolverhampton Wanderers and Aston Villa.

Figure 30: Wanderers Avenue, Blakenhall.

In 1889, they moved to Molineux Grounds, the town's leading cycling venue in the 1870s and 80s, but their origins in the Fighting Cocks area were not forgotten. Following the club's first FA Cup win in 1893 an enthusiastic developer who was building houses in the Dudley Road area celebrated the event by naming one of the streets Wanderers Avenue. Some of the houses were even named after members of the victorious team.

Allen Villas', for example, is named after Harry Allen, the team captain who scored the winning goal in their 1-0 victory over Everton and '1893' on the plaque marks the year of their first FA Cup success.

The century however was to end on a sour note for Wolves, losing 2-1 to The Wednesday in the FA Cup final at Crystal Palace on 18 April 1896.

Figure 31: Plaques on houses in Wanderers Avenue.

Figure 32: The plaque above the Allen Villas house in Wanderers Avenue.

17

WOLVERHAMPTON AND ROUGH HILLS FROM 1850 TO 1900

Health

The population of Wolverhampton continued to rise steadily throughout the second half of the 19th century. In 1861 it was 60,860 and by 1871 it had risen to 68,291. There were now 13,272 inhabited houses while the average number of persons per household was 5.2, a figure that had stayed fairly stable since 1811. In Griffith's 1873 Guide to the Iron Trade of Great Britain, he acknowledges that Wolverhampton 'cannot boast of street architecture to compare with that of New Street, Birmingham or Sackville Street, Dublin'. He does, however, draw attention to the 'architectural beauty and design' of particular churches and identifies public buildings such as the 'handsome' town hall and 'noble' infirmary. He also compliments the merchants, factors and tradesmen who 'are noted for punctuality in the payment of accounts'.

This description unfortunately masked health and housing

problems that Wolverhampton shared with other cities and towns in the country. In an eight-month period during 1863/64 over 1200 cases of smallpox were reported in the town and in 90 cases they were fatal. This was the town's second epidemic in seven years and badly affected parts of the town such a Monmore Green and Stafford Street. Another epidemic broke out in 1871 and while it was most severe around the notorious Stafford Street and Caribee Island areas, it extended to other parts of the town populated by tradespeople and professionals. The Birmingham Daily Post of 15 November 1871 reported that the annual rate of mortality in Wolverhampton had reached 36 per 1000 people, much higher than in major cities such as London, Bristol and Manchester. In January 1872, deeply concerned by this high incidence of smallpox and the excessive death rate from other causes, the Local Government Board (LGB) sent Dr Edward Ballard, an English physician, to the town. Ballard was best known for his reports on the unsanitary conditions in which most of Victorian England lived. Following his visit, he delivered a scathing report in 1874 on the living conditions and health of the town's inhabitants, entitled: 'Report to the Local Government Board on the Sanitary Condition of the Municipal Borough of Wolverhampton.'

Ballard stressed that despite some moderate improvements to the living conditions in the town, there were still significant problems, particularly in the older parts of the town. In his opinion, 'the poor and labouring population of Wolverhampton is lodged very unwholesomely'. He describes a town centre made up of numerous courts and alleys with small houses and courts with maze-like entries. Ballard's report is of particular interest owing to its graphic description of the community of Rough Hills. Although coal and iron production had more or less ceased, Ballard's report confirms that a distinct settlement still existed in the Rough Hills area.

'There is one part of the borough, on the outskirts of the coalfield known as the Rough Hills, where the land is very irregular partly from natural causes and partly from accumulations or heaps of refuse from coal pits (now abandoned). The depressions between them which are known as "swags" are partly caused by the subsidence over the land by the mines and, since the surface of the soil is clay, water accumulates in ponds and pools of various sizes. Upon this irregular land a few blocks of houses are erected but in addition a few huts isolated, or two or three together, each with its irregular plot of garden-ground. These plots belong to the occupiers who are generally colliers, who pay a few shillings annually as an acknowledgment for the use of the land.' He considered the cottages on Rough Hills and at Monmore Green as amongst the most unwholesome localities he visited describing them as places 'in which infectious diseases have been most prevalent and most fatal during the last four years'.

It is probable that one of these cottages was occupied by my second great grandfather, Thomas Boddice. A distant relative on my mother's side of the family tree, he had lived and worked as a collier on Rough Hills since at least 1851, raising eight children with his wife, Phoebe, between 1847 and 1872.

Ballard criticised at great length the unavailability of good quality drinking water in the town, associating polluted water with the spread of 'enteric fever, cholera, diarrhoeal diseases, and other maladies communicable through the evacuations of the sick'. Once again he drew specific attention to the situation at Rough Hills: '... the cottagers residing in the huts and dwellings on the Rough Hills just beyond Monmore Green, have no supply of water, and are under the necessity of taking what they require from a rill of impure water emanating from the railway embankment, and, probably, originally from the neighbouring canal, into which rill sewage matters are washed down from privies, pigsties, and all other sources of pollution. The inhabitants dignify this rill with the name of a "spring".' This may have been the same 'spring' that gained notoriety when difficulties with providing adequate quantities of water led the Wolverhampton Waterworks Company to supplement its supplies from the Rough Hills Collieries. One alderman in a Council debate complained about the quality of the Rough Hills water, saying that on adding the water to his glass of brandy the contents had turned as black as ink.

Epidemics continued to sweep through the crowded and insanitary houses, reinforcing Ballard's concerns. Between 1872 and 1884, 790 children died from scarlet fever, 353 from measles, 461 from smallpox (446 of these in the epidemic of 1872) and 1,120 from diarrhoea. In the 1880s infant mortality in the town ranged from a high of 188 per 1000 to a low of 156. In 1889 deaths from TB of children below the age of 5 were twelve times greater in the east in areas like Rough Hills and Monmore Green than in west Wolverhampton. In 1891 the Wolverhampton Medical Officer of Health reported 'mortality fearfully high' with the death rates the highest since 1875. Differences in the death rate between the east and the west of the town continued into the 1890s, as pronounced as ever, and when corrected for the fact that the Workhouse was in the east, gave the following:

Area of the town	Death rate per 1000 in 1893-98
East	25.4
West	18.1
Borough	21.5

An east-west social divide had existed in Wolverhampton for many decades. The electoral wards created in 1848 were arranged along a north-south plane with four wards in each half. By 1868, none of the borough's aldermen lived in any of the eastern wards. Although most councillors lived in the west of the town, many earned their living through manufacturing in the east and would have been aware of the severe health, environmental and social problems. In 1874, S.T. Mander, one such manufacturer, wrote to the Wolverhampton Chronicle describing the east as 'smoky, dreary and hard' and asked rhetorically whether any of the people from the west of Wolverhampton would like to live there.

The first major hospital to open in Wolverhampton was the South Staffordshire General in Cleveland Road in 1849, later known as the Wolverhampton and Staffordshire General Hospital and in my day as 'The Royal'. At the time of the outbreaks of smallpox, cholera and scarlet fever in the early 1870s, the 1871 census shows the hospital was staffed by one superintendent, one matron, just one surgeon and one physician, a team of four 'head' nurses and seven 'under' nurses with seven supporting staff including a cook and laundry maid. Ninety-seven patients were being treated on the day of the census. The hospital was disinclined to admit anyone with an infectious disease and reluctantly set up temporary smallpox accommodation in the basement of one of their wings, but only on the understanding that the corporation would build a separate hospital for infectious diseases. Apart from sending paupers with smallpox to the Union Workhouse, Wolverhampton's provision for people with infectious diseases depended upon the limited goodwill of the General Hospital.

It was not until 1881 that the Council voted to purchase land at Green Lane on the far edge of Rough Hills for the purpose of erecting an 'Infectious Hospital'. The 23 September 1882 edition of the Birmingham Daily Post reported that the Sanitary Committee had been given assurance that the place would be ready in about a fortnight to receive any cases of smallpox that might occur in the town. The timescale for completion was hopelessly inaccurate and the foundation stone was not laid until December 1883. The Borough Hospital, later to be renamed the Parkfield Isolation Hospital and known by locals as 'The Fever Hospital' finally opened in 1884, consisting of a pavilion with 12 beds plus a disinfecting station, a laundry, a mortuary and part of an administrative block. It was clear from the start that this provision would be inadequate with insufficient room for staff or patients and no quarantine ward. The Sanitary Committee had initially recommended that £8,000 would be required but this was reduced by the council to a figure of £3,250. When a significant outbreak of scarlet fever occurred in 1890, the Sanitary Committee provided £300 from its own funds for the construction of a temporary building to accommodate the patients. With renewed vigour the Sanitary Committee, passionately led by its chairman, Alderman Major, recommended that the Council apply for a loan, this time of £6,750, from the Local Government Board to pay for the necessary improvements. On this occasion the request was granted in full and the Christmas Eve edition of the Birmingham Daily Post in 1891 announced the formal opening of the new buildings on 23 December 1891. The additional buildings, built by Mr H. Lovatt, included a new entrance lodge, enlargement to the administrative block and a pavilion comprising two new wards. Recurring outbreaks of smallpox, diphtheria and measles justified its existence.

The Borough Hospital later catered for patients with tuberculosis (TB) and other infectious diseases like diphtheria and measles. In the 1940s and 50s, immunisation programmes for a wide range of infectious diseases like TB, polio, smallpox and measles were introduced. Adverts encouraging people to be immunised against diphtheria had already appeared by 1943 in local newspapers like the Express and Star and these medical advances accelerated the closure of the 'fever' hospitals across the country. When an 'infectious diseases' block was opened at New Cross Hospital in 1948 the days of 'The Fever Hospital' were numbered and its activities began to wind down. Even so it was 1984 before it finally closed its doors; the grounds are now occupied by a housing development.

Lying between Thompson Avenue and Pond Lane, the Borough Hospital was known to us in the 50s as the 'scarlet fever hospital'. This surprised us since scarlet fever was regarded by then as a mild childhood disease. However, in the 1800s and early 1900s, in the absence of antibiotics, the name of this childhood disease struck fear into the hearts of parents. Fatality rates were high and in the worst cases all the children of a family died in a matter of one or two weeks. Scarlet fever and other diseases like diphtheria were still prevalent in the 1920s and 30s when Parkfield Estate was being built.

Joan Underhill from Whittaker Street recalls the distress it created in the 1930s when the 'fever ambulance' from the Isolation hospital arrived to collect a sick child.

Almost every family in Myatt Avenue had someone who caught scarlet fever or diphtheria. My brother Victor contracted scarlet fever and I carried him down to the ambulance when it arrived. Although I expected to catch the disease, I did not. Victor was kept in the hospital for over 5 weeks. Visitors were not allowed into the premises. Miss Bertha Wilmot, one of their neighbours on the estate, would answer the main door to the hospital and accept presents for the patients.

Another serious disease feared by households was tuberculosis (TB). I remember a neighbour from Legge Street catching the disease and being sent to Prestwood Hospital near Stourbridge. Unable to pay the bus fares, the family would walk the 12 miles to the hospital to see their relative.

Like many children at the age of 10, I had my tonsils taken out at New Cross Hospital. I was admitted at 10 am and discharged at 4 pm.

Olwen Medlicott who lived in Rooker Crescent also caught scarlet fever as a young girl.

My mother was a nurse at the Fever Hospital and when I became ill, they said my Mum could look after me at home at first, but Mum thought it best if I was in hospital, so that she could keep an eye on me and all the other patients at the same time.

Housing

The council initially adopted a very defensive stance with regards to the Ballard report. On later reflection, it conceded that his criticisms were fundamentally correct. On Ballard's recommendation, it took on board the national legislation on housing and slum clearance introduced in the 1860s. The Artisans' and Labourers' Dwellings Act 1868 (Torrens) made the landlord responsible for maintaining his houses in a proper condition and facilitated the demolition of insanitary properties. This evolved into the Artisans' and Labourers' Dwellings Improvement Act of 1875, better known as the Cross Act, which addressed whole areas rather than individual houses and allowed towns and cities to carry out a more systematic clearance of slum property. These legislations provided the impetus for 'The Wolverhampton Street Improvement Scheme'. Following a public enquiry which began in April 1877, a loan of £207,330 was obtained to tackle these housing issues. The main focus of the scheme was to clear the worst area of the town, roughly between Queen Square, Berry Street and Stafford Road. This area which had been particularly affected by the smallpox outbreak of 1871 consisted of 846 properties. 704 of these were houses of which 632 were inhabited. 408 of these were old and dilapidated and 54 in ruins and condemned. The 632 inhabited houses had only 39 wc's and 366 privies between them. This area included the infamous Caribee Island, mentioned earlier. Land to the north of the town at Springfield was purchased for £5000 and a further £3500 spent on sewerage and laying out the streets. Despite this considerable outlay by the Corporation, the area did not prove attractive to private developers and it would eventually provide only 290 houses for 1,400 inhabitants.

Despite the concerns expressed in the Ballard Report, the area around Rough Hills and Cockshutts was not considered to be suitable for any similar improvements. Wolverhampton Borough Council produced a formal response to his 1874 report stating its reasons for not providing any sewerage at Rough

Hills. The statement painted a bleak image of the Rough Hills landscape and revealed the low regard held by the Council for the area and its residents.

'The land for the most part consists of old pit mounds and unsettled ground arising from mining operations. The few cottages to be found in this isolated district are mainly also isolated from each other, and occupied chiefly by squatters who gain access to them by no recognisable road, and who are liable at any time to be removed by owners of the land. When subsidence has ceased, the land will either be restored to agricultural usefulness or be laid out as a building site. When that time arrives, and then only can an efficient system of drainage be applied.'

Distressing details of these houses are revealed by way of a letter to the Birmingham Daily Post on 9 June 1870 by George Griffith. Deeply concerned about the education of the youngsters in Staffordshire, he visited the homes of colliers in Rough Hills. While his priority was to enquire about the reading and writing skills of the children, he observed the reality of their appalling living conditions. The first house he visited was occupied by a family of six who all slept in one room. The next cottage he visited had been built by the tenant. Here all eight members of the family slept in the same room. At another home there were eight children; four slept in one room while the other four slept with the two parents in another room.

It is worth noting that a few years earlier, in April 1866, a witness in a court case stated that he lived in Rough Hills which he proudly assured the magistrate "was a neighbourhood as rough as its name".

Steelhouse Lane and All Saints

In the 19th century, houses were privately owned and working-class families lived in rented accommodation belonging to landlords. This type of housing was found in and around Steelhouse Lane, originally part of the Duke of Cleveland's estate. An advert in The Wolverhampton Chronicle from August 1863 for the sale of a plot of land in Steelhouse Lane describes it as being situated in 'the midst of a populous and improving neighbourhood', a depiction which would not have been shared by Rev. Hampton. Indeed, a Birmingham Daily Gazette report from 24 September 1867 on a murder in Steelhouse Lane paints, in unappealing detail, a grim image of this area. Steelhouse Lane is described as 'a long lane which ends in a collection of "spoil-banks" and "cinder-heaps" which disfigure what are still called "fields" on the "Black Country" side of Wolverhampton'. It has a row of about eighty small four roomed tenements. Every eight or ten of these houses has a common yard at the back which is entered by a passage or "entry". Many of the yards have a pigeon-house. Flying pigeons, discussing their relative merits, and drinking and quarrelling over them, are the chief characteristics of Sundays thereabouts.

The depressing report, mentioned above, reveals upsetting information about distant relatives. It covers a hearing at the Borough Petty Sessions in Wolverhampton at which Thomas Neale was accused of murdering his wife, Naomi, in the yard behind their house at number 54, Steelhouse Lane. One of the witnesses called by the prosecution was William, the eldest son. At the time of the trial he was 15 years old and two years later he married Sarah Parker, my 2nd great aunt. At his trial at Stafford Assizes in December 1867, Thomas Neale was found not guilty of manslaughter.

A map of 1871 shows a similar layout of terraced housing on the opposite side of the road, immediately below the hospital site, in Portland Place and Sutherland Place.

The 1871 census showed that William Neale, now an engine driver at an ironworks, was living with his family at no.53, Steelhouse Lane, the house of his father-in-law John Parker, my second great-grandfather.

By 1891, a broad strip of land below Sutherland Place belonging to the Duke of Cleveland estate had been sold off and an extensive network of new roads and private housing developments was emerging. In February 1891, a tender of £1,477 was accepted from Mr Herbert Holloway for the construction of All Saints Road and a portion of Vicarage Road. Land for the All Saints Vicarage in Vicarage Road was donated by the Cleveland estate. To the north of All Saints Road, six new roads lying parallel to one another and extending up to Sutherland Place were constructed. The layout of roads and housing is clearly seen on the 1903 Ordnance Survey map. Cleveland House still lay isolated but it was now houses rather than fields that surrounded it. Its gardens had shrunk in size; the lodge at the Steelhouse Lane entrance and the long landscaped driveway to the house had both disappeared. Owned by private developers, most of the houses would have been rented out to workers employed at the numerous factories in the neighbourhood.

This model of housing for working-class families was soon to be challenged within a stone's throw of All Saints Road.

18

COUNCIL HOUSING IN WOLVERHAMPTON AND ROUGH HILLS FROM 1900 TO 1914

The Advent of Council Housing

The appalling sanitary conditions which existed in many rented dwellings, particularly in town centres, grew into an important political and social issue. A number of Acts were introduced in the second half of the 19th century to address the problem. Towards the end of the century the government intervened again and the Housing of the Working Classes Act of 1890 gave local authorities more responsibility for improving housing conditions, encouraging them to buy up available land and build houses for rent. The first 'council' housing in the country was built in 1896 by London City Council at Bethnal Green.

Council housing in Wolverhampton was launched around the same time and the first ones were built in 1902 in Green Lane (now Birmingham Road) and Cartwright Street. This land was also part of the Duke of Cleveland estate but following the death in 1891 of the 4th Duke, there were no legitimate offspring. The title became 'extinct' and a distant relative, Henry de Vere Vane, was declared the rightful heir with the title of Lord Barnard. 4,000 sq. yards of this land belonging to Lord Barnard was sold to Wolverhampton Corporation for £550 (£665 per acre) and the building contract was eventually given to G. Cave & Son at an enhanced price of £5,068.

Rough Hills and Cockshutts

Although Cockshutts Colliery was marked on the 1901 Ordnance Survey map, evidence from the Lists of Mines taken from either Government publications or trade publications such as the Colliery Guardian suggested that mining operations had ceased. On the same map, Rough Hills colliery was shown as disused and by now there was little doubt that formal mining operations had finished. A report sent in October 1908 by the Borough Engineer to the Local Government Board in Whitehall described the area thus:

'The Estate commonly known as the Rough Hills Estate … contains about 30 acres belonging to Lord Barnard and 47 acres belonging to the Trustees of the late J. Crowther Smith.

This land was formerly covered with Collieries and Ironworks, which were worked out many years ago. The contour of the land is very uneven and is covered chiefly with heaps of pit mound clay and cavities, from which slag and other materials have been taken out. The ground has also sunk considerably in places owing to the coal workings.

There are one or two cottages and a small portion of grazing land on the Estate, and some rough cart tracks and footpaths, but otherwise the land is entirely waste and unfenced, and not useful for any purpose until it is reclaimed. The pit mounds in some places are 15 to 20 feet higher than the general level of the surrounding land, and in parts the valleys or hollows are 15 to 20 feet below the level. There are small quantities of blast furnace slag over portions of the Estate which are still unworked.

Portions of the Estate, which have been sold some time ago, have been reclaimed and built upon, immediately fronting the Parkfield Road, adjoining the Bilston Urban District.'

No reference was made to the Relief Work which had taken place in the early 1880s. Rough Hills was still portrayed as an abandoned wasteland, in much the same way as it had been in the 1874 response by Wolverhampton Borough Council to the Ballard report. However, after decades of being overlooked, it was about to receive much needed attention, courtesy of the Local Government Board (LGB) based in Whitehall and the creation of two specific committees by Wolverhampton Borough Council: The Distress Committee and The Rough Hills Improvement Committee.

The Local Government Board and Distress Committee

The LGB was created by the Local Government Board Act of 1871 to supervise the laws relating to public health, the relief of the poor and local government. Headed by a president, generally a cabinet minister, the Board ran from 1871 to 1919.

The Unemployed Workmen Act was first passed by the Conservative Party (UK) in 1903 and renewed by the Liberal Party (UK) in 1905. It empowered the LGB to set up local

Distress Committees in boroughs and urban districts with a population of not less than 50,000. These committees had the power to distribute grants to businesses or local authorities to enable them to hire more workers. The aim was to reduce the number of unemployed people and prevent many from entering the Union workhouses. The members of the Distress Committees were drawn from the Councils, the Boards of Guardians (chosen from local gentry, clergy and major tradesmen to control the work of the Poor Law Union), and co-opted persons (one of whom at least had to be a woman).

Wolverhampton's Distress Committee was appointed on the 25 October 1905 and made up of individuals from the three separate backgrounds. The largest group consisted of 12 members from the Council itself:

Aldermen: Berrington, Craddock, Lewis,
John Marston and Thorne.

Councillors: Bantock, E. Evans, F. Evans, Frost,
Lamsdale, Sharrocks and Whittaker.

Eight members from the Board of Guardians, responsible
for administering the town workhouse, were appointed
by the Council:

Reverend J.J. Darmody, Messrs H.S. George, F.J. Gibson,
T. Jones, F. Lewis, W.H. Mason, W. Myring and T.H. Sawyers.

The remaining five members were individuals from the town experienced in the relief of distress. These were also appointed by the Council and would hold office until the 31 March 1907:

Reverends C.F. Bone, Alfred Charles Howell, (vicar of St Matthew's church), Miss Edridge, Mr C. Coley and Ensign Jeffs

Following the death of Mr. C. Coley, Mr S. Albiston was appointed to take his place.

Their first meeting took place on the 30th October 1905 and Councillor A. Baldwin Bantock was appointed chairman. On the 5th January 1906, Mr Benjamin Lamb was appointed as Investigations Officer to receive and investigate applications for work assistance.

During the next three years, schemes for unemployed workers were set up in a number of locations around the town:

1906

- Re-sewering Hunter Street and part of Newhampton Road.
- Repairs to Lea Road.

1907

- East Park - making a new embankment and re-puddling a portion of the lake for 240 men.
- Sewerage work at Horseley Fields and Blakenhall for 79 men.
- St. Peters Improvement Scheme – labouring, widening and re-making a portion of the street, and assisting paviors and other employees of the Streets Department for 106 men.
- Laying out the land around St. Peter's church.

1908

- Work for Water Committee (excavating trenches for pipes) at Codsall, Bilbrook, Kingswood and Penn Road.
- Construction of storm sewers in Compton Road and Richmond Road.

- Sewerage work at Gorsebrook Road, Pond Street and Stowheath.
- Re-ashing walks and other improvements at East Park.
- Double-digging at Barnhurst Sewage Works.
- Clearing snow from ice on West Park lake.

By now the work was providing employment for 975 men.

Wolves enjoyed another FA Cup win surprisingly beating Newcastle United 3–1 in the 1908 final.

It was on 26 September 1908, that Mr S. Albiston, in his role as Secretary of Wolverhampton Trades Council, sent a letter to the Distress Committee suggesting another seven schemes for the unemployed during the coming winter. Amongst this innocuous list of schemes, he recommended the creation of allotments on Rough Hills. This proposal was to have a profound and long lasting effect on the area.

19

THE (ORIGINAL) ROUGH HILLS ESTATE

Albiston's letter set in motion a series of events that would lift Rough Hills out of its obscurity. At a meeting of the Special Sub-Committee on 29 September 1908, the Mayor, in response to this letter, focussed on the desirability of acquiring and levelling land in the vicinity of the East Park and Rough Hills. In his opinion it would provide long-term employment for a large number of men and the land would then be utilised for allotments or other schemes. A discussion ensued and a resolution was made that a Special Sub-Committee consisting of the Mayor, Alderman Berrington and Rev. Howell together with the Borough Engineer would be appointed for the purpose of inspecting the land and establishing the cost. With impressive speed and commitment, the Mayor, by mid-October, had addressed the Distress Committee (2 October), Council (5

October) and held meetings with legal representatives of the owners of land at Cockshutts (6 October) and Rough Hills (16 October) regarding the terms required by them for its purchase.

At a meeting on the 20 October 1908, the Mayor reported that in accordance with the wishes of this Committee, he had, along with Alderman Berrington and Rev. Howell, inspected the land at Willenhall, Stowheath and Rough Hills. On balance they believed the land at Rough Hills would be more suitable for the purposes required. Once levelled, they suggested the land could be utilised for a range of schemes including a children's playground, allotments, a cemetery and building land. The Distress Committee-in-Committee meeting on the same day recommended that the Council purchase the land subject to the approval of the Local Government Board. The Mayor stressed that no time should be lost in bringing the matter to the Council and to the Local Government Board.

Accordingly, a letter was sent to the President of the Local Government Board in Whitehall on 24 October 1908 setting out the case for substantial aid from the Board towards the scheme. The following points were made:

■ The total number of unemployed was 510 and rising.

■ Under consideration was the purchase of land upon which work might be found for the unemployed.

■ The land covered 77½ acres and must first be levelled at a cost of £9,000.

■ Once levelled the land had the potential to be used for a recreation ground, allotments, a cemetery, a building site and new roads.

It went on to say that whilst the Council was very eager to purchase the land, it would be entirely conditional upon a substantial contribution being made by the Board towards the cost of labour to be employed in making the land suitable for future operations. A decision was requested by 30th October, the date of the next Council Meeting. This led to a series of frantic exchanges:

On the 29 October the Local Government Board replied, expressing doubt as to whether they would be in a position to provide a grant in excess of £750 to £1000. The following day the Mayor replied that he was afraid the Council would abandon the purchase of the land unless the grant towards levelling the ground was increased to £2000. The Local Government Board immediately came back to say they could not specify the amount of their grant at this moment in time but advised the Council not to abandon the scheme.

Despite the financial wavering from central government, the Council meeting held on the 30 October 1908 made the decision, on the recommendation of the General Purposes Committee and the Distress Committee, to go ahead with the scheme. They would purchase 77 acres of land at Rough Hills from Lord Barnard and the Trustees of Joseph Crowther Smith at the price of £50 per acre plus solicitor costs. The land followed the same boundary shown on the 1890 map referred to earlier and extended from the Borough Hospital at the top of Cockshutts Lane down to Parkfield Road, with Cockshutts Lane forming a western boundary, across to the Rough Hills settlement near the railway (LNMR) line in the east. Although the land was described as Rough Hills, it skirted the Rough Hills Tavern and Victoria Grounds and did not include the majority of the land that is now occupied by the Rough Hills Estate built in the 1950s.

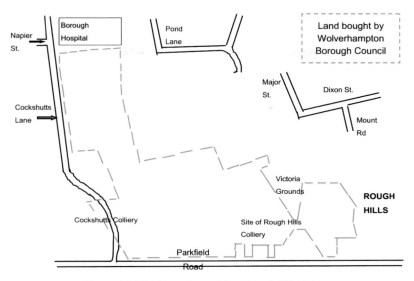

Figure 33: The Boundary of the 'Rough Hills' Estate.

The Rough Hills Improvement Committee

Matters continued to progress at speed. On 5 November 1908 representatives of the Council visited and inspected the whole of the Rough Hills estate which the Corporation was purchasing. Town Hall bureaucracy demanded a committee be set up to administer this project. At the Annual Meeting of the Town Council on 9 November, they appointed The Rough Hills Improvement Committee (RHIC) made up of:

The Mayor

Aldermen: Berrington, Craddock, Gibbons,
Jones, Marston, Plant,
Councillors: Bantock, Dickinson, Evans, George,
J. Jones, Sharrocks,

It was resolved that the RHIC would meet once a fortnight. At a later meeting on 18 November, Councillor Fred Evans was appointed Chairman. A report from the Borough Engineer's Office was read out to inform the Council that most of the existing tenants on Rough Hills had been notified that the land had been purchased. In his opinion, the first step should be to level the pit mound nearest to Parkfield Road and to continue Green Lane into Parkfield Road from the Borough Hospital end. He also proposed:

- the erection of a shed for use as a mess room, shelter, store and smithy.
- the purchase of tools to include 50 barrows, 100 picks and 100 shovels costing a total of approximately £160.
- the appointment of Mr Duffy as superintendent alongside two gangers.

Having listened to his report, the committee made decisions on:

- tenancies.
- site of first operation (requiring the purchase of land adjoining Parkfield Road from Lord Bernard).
- Commencement of work (23 November).
- Hours of labour (Mon>Fri 8 hours/day, Sat 5 hours).
- Numbers to be employed (250, in two turns of 125, on 3 days each).
- Rates of Pay (4½ pence/hour and 5 pence/hour for skilled navvies registered by the Distress Committee).
- Differentiation between applicants to be dealt with by the Distress Committee.

- ■ Purchase of tools to be dealt with by Borough Engineer.
- ■ Appointment of Superintendent in accordance with recommendations of Borough Engineer.
- ■ Funds – Mayor to issue appeal to inhabitants for funds to support project. Alderman Jones promised to contribute £100.

The Borough Engineer was to play a central role in this scheme and most meetings included his latest report on the progress that had been made. For example, at a meeting of the Committee on 4 December, the report announced that:

- ■ Work commenced on Monday 23 November 1908,
- ■ 125 men were put on for 3 days at a time,
- ■ The shed was erected as an office for Mr Duffy,
- ■ He had received a plan from the Town Clerk showing the land purchased from Lord Bernard and the trustees of the late J. Crowther Smith.

One can only admire the speed with which the wheels of bureaucracy had turned. A suggestion made less than two months earlier quickly led to discussions at local and national level and to financial agreements involving landowners and government funding agencies. It may well be that preliminary agreements with the landowners date back to 1890 but nevertheless one is left to marvel at how quickly a successful outcome was achieved.

Inevitably a dispute soon arose. Within a month the Wolverhampton Trades Council protested about the payment of 4½ pence per hour and proposed an increase to 5d. Despite support by the Distress Committee, this proposal was thrown out by the RHIC. It pointed out that the primary objective of purchasing the Rough Hills Estate was the provision of temporary work for unemployed men until they obtained regular work or other means of supporting themselves. An increase in their payments would potentially reduce the number of men engaged, exhaust the amount of money at their disposal more quickly or increase the amount to be drawn from the rates. They emphasised that work was provided for the most deserving of the unemployed, without any attempt to select those most physically fitted.

The next report from the Borough Engineer on 3 March 1909 said that up to the preceding Saturday,

- 12 acres of land had been levelled at a cost of £190.10s.7d per acre,
- An average of 147 men per day were employed,
- 17 days had been lost because of snow and other causes.

During the first part of 1909, other parcels of land at Rough Hills were bought by the Corporation.

Having paid a considerable amount of money to purchase the land, the Corporation was very reliant on grants from the Local Government Board (LGB) to help finance these work schemes. In February of that year the LGB had awarded Wolverhampton Council £500 to level sections of Rough Hills. At a meeting on 12 November 1909, a letter from the Distress Committee applying for a grant from the LGB was read out. It reminded the Board that the Council had purchased land at Rough Hills in order for work to be provided for the unemployed. Of those 80 acres, about 21 acres had now been levelled. £1195 had been raised by voluntary subscriptions of which £180 had not been spent. At the next meeting on 26

November 1909, they were shown the letter sent to the Town Clerk from the LGB. It was a disappointing response, informing the Council that the Board were not in a position to promise a grant to cover the whole or even a large proportion of the cost of the proposed work. It asked the Distress Committee to reconsider their proposal and endeavour to obtain some contribution from the Town Council and also to make an appeal for voluntary contributions.

Unfortunately, minutes for the meetings throughout 1910 and 1911 and especially those leading up to the outbreak of WW1 in 1914 were not recorded with the same diligence. One is left with a frustrating lack of information about the outcome of the response from the LGB and the future progress that was made. One is left to speculate on whether the remaining 56 acres of land were levelled after November 1909. If levelling had proceeded at the same rate that was achieved in the first 12 months, the scheme would probably have been completed by the Spring of 1912. The 1914 Ordnance Survey map indicates little change in the physical landscape but clear evidence that the industrial landscape was undergoing a transformation: many of the brickworks had disappeared from the map and several other manufacturing works such as Green Lane Cooperage, Mitre Iron Works, and Eagle Tool Works were now labelled as 'disused'.

In the preceding six years, Wolverhampton Corporation had invested a considerable amount of time, money and manpower into the venture. Abandoned land which carried the scars from decades of mining and ironmaking was now the property of Wolverhampton Corporation and some if not all of this acquired land had been prepared for the next stage of its development.

This is not say that all the old pit shafts in the area had been identified and made safe. Wandering across Rough Hills still carried an element of danger. The Staffordshire Sentinel of August 1912 reported the death of a horse which had been grazing near Dixon Street. The brick covering of an old shaft, hidden by grass and earth, collapsed following wet weather and the unfortunate horse dropped 100 yards to the bottom. When the mutilated body of a six-week baby was found near the Moulders Arms near Major Street in May 1915, the Evening Dispatch edition of the 20 May described the spot as 'very lonely, for the few roads across the heath are little used', and the area as 'a dreary waste of pit mounds'.

Nevertheless, Rough Hills could no longer be regarded as a forgotten corner of the Borough and legal, financial and physical foundations had been laid down for its future. When the Housing Committee in July 1914 proposed a housing scheme at Green Lane to provide workmen's dwellings, not all members of the council were happy about the location. The Birmingham Daily Post of 14 July reported on the reservations of council members such as Alderman Bantock who said he was sorry the committee did not try their initial experiment at Rough Hills.

In fact, an alternative, somewhat exciting scheme for Rough Hills had only recently been drafted by the Borough Engineer: a track for testing the new cars being made in Wolverhampton and the other two main manufacturing centres at Birmingham and Coventry. At the time, new vehicles were tested on existing roads and there was increasing concern about the roads becoming overcrowded with this additional traffic. The Sports Argus of 20 June 1914 reported on the proposal to construct a circular track, one mile in radius, at Rough Hills on land already

182

owned by the local authority. It would have two advantages: a reduction in public traffic and an opportunity for vehicles to reach the high speeds required for effective testing. There was strong support for the scheme, notably from Alderman John Marston, the owner of Sunbeam Motors, who believed that Rough Hills was a very suitable site. In his opinion the local authority should pay for the track, estimated to cost £5,000, and manufacturers should reimburse them with a lump sum and pay a fee for each car tested on the track. With WW1 less than two months away, this draft proposal did not progress. As with the proposed railway line mentioned earlier, one is left to ponder on the long-term impact such a test track would have had on the Rough Hills area and indeed on Wolverhampton itself.

20

WOLVERHAMPTON AND ROUGH HILLS FROM 1918 TO 1939

WW1 began in Europe on 4 August 1914.

By the start of WW1 in 1914, council housing still represented only 1% of the country's housing stock. The First World War was labelled as the "War fought to end all wars" and, when it finished, Lloyd George spoke at the Grand Theatre, Wolverhampton of "homes fit for heroes to live in". Many motives have been suggested for this policy. Some have claimed a return to the same poor and overcrowded conditions might have triggered a civil revolution by WWI soldiers. A more transparent reason was the government's concern about the nation's health, highlighted by the poor physical condition of many men who had joined the army. A housing poster of the period declared, 'you cannot expect to get an A1 population out of C3 homes.' At the beginning of the war, one tenth of the conscripts had to be barred from service because of poor health.

My grandfather, James Mills, was one such person. Within two weeks of Britain declaring war on Germany, he had enlisted. Having been passed as "fit" by the Medical Officer on the 17 August 1914, he was given his primary medical examination the following day and pronounced fit for service in the South Staffordshire Regiment. However, he was unable to cope with the training and 46 days later he was discharged from the army for "being medically unfit".

In order to carry out these ambitious promises the Housing and Town Planning Act of 1919, better known as the 'Addison Act', required each town to make a survey of housing needs and submit housing schemes to the Minister of Health. The 'Addison Act' gave local authorities financial subsidies to build council houses for working-class families. The costs for each house were therefore shared between tenants, local rate payers and the Government Treasury. This three–way approach to paying for council housing survived for more than sixty years

The Act came into force on 31 July 1919 with its aim to provide 500,000 'homes for heroes' within a three-year period. Wolverhampton Corporation lost no time in implementing it. Suitable sites had already been selected and acquired at Green Lane, Birches Barn, Oxley and Parkfield Road. In October of that year the Council approved an ambitious scheme in which 5,659 houses would be built at an approximate cost of £6M. The plan was to build 100 houses in 1919, then 750 houses each year from 1920 to 1926, with 409 houses in 1927 to reach their target.

The Green Lane Estate

Their impressive programme started at Green Lane, now known as Birmingham Road. Approval for the Green Lane Housing Scheme had originally been given in 1914 just prior to the outbreak of WW1 when a 3¼ acre site on Cartwright Street, adjacent to the first council houses built in 1902, was purchased. Housing activity had stopped during WW1 but in 1918 the scheme was resurrected and new plans for 60 houses were approved in October by the Council. Following discussions in early 1919 between the Borough Surveyor and an official from the Local Government Board, the Green Lane scheme gained backing for a government subsidy. In the revised plan, the number of houses was reduced to 50. This number was later reduced even further to 48 and in July 1919 a tender from Parkinson and Sons (Blackpool) Ltd of £33,848 was approved. On 6 November 1919, the Mayor of Wolverhampton, Mr. Alfred G. Jeffs, unlocked the first pair of houses erected on the Estate. At the ceremony, Councillor Hughes, the Acting Chairman of the Housing Committee, proudly announced that these were the first 'Addison Act' houses to be completed in England.

Prospective tenants of these council houses were invited to complete an application form and selection was based on a set of agreed criteria:

1. **Naval or Military Service.**
    a. men who had served in HM Forces.
    b. widows and children of men who had died on active service.
    c. wives and children of men serving in HM Forces.

d. mothers and unmarried brothers and sisters of men who had died on active service.

2. **Those living in overcrowded accommodation.**

3. **Those living in houses condemned as unfit for human habitation.**

As each new batch of houses was completed and made available, tenants were selected from the list of applicants. A small selection from the Housing Committee minutes is shown below.

Name	Address	No. in Family	Remarks
**	*, East Street	5	Husband killed in action – training for dressmaker. Overcrowded.
**	*, All Saints Road	3	No military service – over age. In apartments.
**	*, St Marks Road	5	Rejected twice. 4 sleeping in one bedroom – one boy very ill.

The Parkfield (Rough Hills) Estate

The Public Works Committee agreed to transfer a portion of the 77 acre Rough Hills Estate, purchased by the Council in 1908 from Lord Barnard and the Trustees of Joseph Crowther Smith, to the Housing Committee. This land, on the site of disused colliery land at Cockshutts and Rough Hills, would become the location of a housing development known as Parkfield Estate.

The Housing Commissioner on behalf of the Minister of Health inspected the site and agreed that 27.8 acres could be used for a housing development. One assumes that it represented land that had been successfully levelled under the auspices of the Rough Hills Improvement Committee between

1908 and 1914. Initially 226 houses were earmarked for the estate. The housing, built to relatively high standards based on the Tudor Walters Report of 1919, consisted of three bedroom dwellings with a living room and scullery referred to as Type A; the larger properties referred to as Type B also included a parlour. By November 1919, the tenders for the first phase had been awarded to Mr. Arthur Powell (6 houses) and Mr. Henry Gough (14 houses).

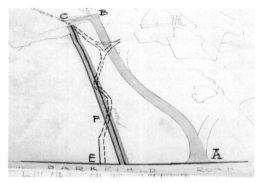

Figure 34: The Plan of the proposed Thompson Avenue. (Photograph reproduced with the permission of Wolverhampton Archives and Local Studies).

As part of this scheme, a new road named Thompson Avenue was built. Since 1908, there had been plans to extend Green Lane to Parkfield Road. The most obvious solution would have been to improve the existing Cockshutts Lane but for whatever reason a different route was adopted. Plans drawn up in February 1920 show the first section of Thompson Avenue marked A to B, 40 feet wide, running from Parkfield Road and roughly parallel to Cockshutts Lane. Once the new section of road was completed, the portion of Cockshutts Lane marked C to E would be closed to traffic.

The first major housing development of 70 houses commenced in April 1920. Of these 70 houses, 44 (shown in red on the plan) would be Type A, while the remaining 26 (shown in blue on the plan) would be the larger Type B. The layout for the new housing is shown opposite with new houses built mainly on Parkfield Road and a new road named as Parkfield Crescent. Parkfield Road would mark the southern edge of the housing development, sometimes confusingly referred to on housing plans as the Rough Hills Estate.

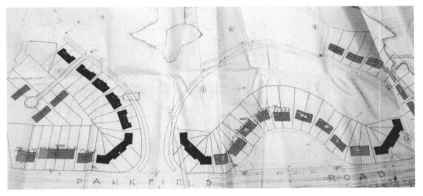

Figure 35: The First Section of the Parkfield Estate development. (Photograph reproduced with the permission of Wolverhampton Archives and Local Studies).

The house in the photograph is on the corner of Thompson Avenue near to its junction with Parkfield Road. The plaque on the front of the Type B house shows the town crest and the year 1920, in which it was built.

In January 1921, a report was submitted by the Chairman of the

Figure 36: One of the first houses to be built on the Parkfield Estate.

Housing committee on the progress made to the four council estates at Green Lane, Parkfield Road, Birches Barn and Barnhurst. At Parkfield Road where a total of 235 houses were to be built, 30 houses were completed and another 67 were scheduled to be ready by the end of July 1922. Rents had been set at 9/- (nine shillings) for Type A houses and 10/- (ten shillings) for the larger Type B houses.

In 1923 plans were approved for another 68 houses to be built at Parkfield. The Government would no longer provide a housing grant for the 3 bedroomed, Type B, houses with parlours so the new development was made up of 24 Type A houses and 44 Type C houses (smaller versions of the non-parlour Type A). The majority were built on Parkfield Crescent, and what is now Parkfield Grove and Legge Street with the remaining 16 houses on the west side of Thompson Avenue.

By 1924, Thompson Avenue had been extended back to the Borough Hospital and in October, plans were approved for 76 Type C houses to be built in the vicinity to take account of the demolition of houses in the Faulkland Street, Littles Lane area near the centre of the town. Known as the Faulkland Road Scheme, this was the first Wolverhampton clearance scheme since the late 1870s. Of these 76 houses, 40 were built on Thompson Avenue itself at its Borough Hospital boundary, 8 near its junction with what would become Dixon Street, 20 on Silver Birch Road and a further 8 on Legge Street, near Parkfield Crescent.

The infrastructure for the Parkfield/ Rough Hills estate continued to be put in place and in 1925 the Council acquired a narrow strip of land between Bilston Road and Thompson Avenue to extend Dixon Street up to Thompson Avenue.

Figure 37: Looking along Thompson Avenue towards Birmingham Road (the old Green Lane).

At the start of 1926, the second and third instalments of the Faulkland Road Scheme commenced and plans were approved to build additional Type C houses. 60 were to be built in Thompson Avenue, extending housing down to its junction with Dixon Street.

My father with his parents and siblings became one of the 200 or so families who moved into this development of new houses in 1926. They lived at number 79 on the west side of the road, part of the second instalment of the Faulkland Road Scheme. My Dad had been born in 1920 at 9 Court, Littles Lane in the Springfield area of the town, his parents having moved there from Bagnall Street around 1916.

Figure 38: 79, Thompson Avenue where my father spent part of his childhood.

This photograph taken in 2012 shows a section of the 1926 development in Thompson Avenue with my grandparent's house at number 79 still intact (although boarded up and offered for sale). In the third instalment, another 64 Type C houses were built north of Parkfield Crescent, extending the estate up to what would become Myatt Close and Myatt Avenue.

An aerial photograph taken in May 1927 clearly shows the progress that had been made at Parkfield, with the housing development in marked contrast to the derelict land extending beyond to the canal and railway line at Rough Hills. Further building on the Parkfield development took place during the remainder of the 1920s and in September 1928 Mr A. Powell was again given a contract to build 44 two bedroomed houses in Joan Street.

On the edge of this new 'Rough Hills Estate' being built at Parkfield, the A4123 Wolverhampton-Birmingham New Road opened on Wednesday 2 November 1927. Up to then the main link between Wolverhampton and Birmingham was Telford's A41 Holyhead Road which passed through the centre of towns such as West Bromwich and Wednesbury. The New Road was built at a cost of £600,000 to relieve traffic pressure on the A41 and deliberately bypassed all the town centres on its route, avoiding urban areas wherever possible. At the Wolverhampton end, the New Road connected to Thompson Avenue. The New Road was the first purpose-built inter-city highway of the twentieth century, opening seven years before the more celebrated A580 East Lancashire Road between Liverpool and Manchester. The ceremony was carried out by the H.R.H. Edward, Prince of Wales, later (but not for long) Edward VIII, starting at 1 pm at the Quinton end of the road. Following an official luncheon, a motor tour of the road commenced at 2.30 and at 4.40 he cut the tape at the Parkfield Road end. Many of the local schools were on their half term holiday but some schools such as Parkfield Road School, St. Bartholomew's, Penn and the Royal Orphanage were well represented in the crowds which lined the road.

After the opening Coseley UDC arranged for trees, dedicated to those from the area who had lost their lives in the First World War, to be planted on both sides of the road. Each tree had a plaque attached with the name of each victim. It was not long before the road came in for criticism. The Western Daily Press reported on a meeting of Worcester County Council on

12 December 1927 at which it was described as "a deathtrap" because 'it was badly lighted at night'.

On the Saturday of the same week, 5 November 1927, the first automatic traffic lights in the United Kingdom were installed in Princes Square, Wolverhampton. The lights, originally installed as a temporary experiment, were installed as a permanent feature in October 1928.

The 'east-west divide' in the town, highlighted earlier, persisted into the 1920s with industry mainly focussed in the east. One consequence of this was a reluctance by the Council to build council housing in the west. This policy was adopted to discourage workers travelling across the town to the industrial east. This constraint meant there were few suitable sites for housing developments within the borough and it was recognised that the main developments in the future would have to take place beyond the borders in Old Heath, Oxley, Low Hill and Bushbury with some building in the south-east, notably at Parkfield.

Council house developments took place in the 1920s against a backdrop of political instability. Between 1922 and 1924 no fewer than three general elections were held and despite the potential difficulties these events may have caused, council housing expanded across the country. Inevitably, housing policies reflected political leanings and when the 'Chamberlain Housing Act' was passed by the Tories in 1923, it sought to encourage private builders to provide most of the new working-class housing. This Act directed the local authority to pass the government subsidy onto the builder of a house, whether it was available for rent or for sale. The local authority could only build houses themselves if they were able to show that private builders were not meeting local needs: a challenging task. The election of the first Labour Government in 1924 saw another change in housing policy. One of the few left-wing Ministers in Ramsey McDonald's Government, John Wheatley, was made Minister of Health and took on responsibility for housing. The 'Wheatley Act' of 1924 passed by the new Labour Government re-established the local authority as the main provider of houses for rent. It introduced higher subsidies from central government for council housing and also allowed for a contribution to be made from the rates. It envisaged a 15-year programme of housing built by local authorities at rents affordable by the working classes. Within one year another Conservative government under Stanley Baldwin was elected and the party stayed in power for the next five years. Fortunately, the Wheatley Act was not repealed and in the three-year period from 1925 to 1927 the great pre-1939 estates in the town were virtually started and completed. This era represented the greatest programme of house building that Wolverhampton had ever known. By the end of 1927 there were 1,892 houses at Low Hill and Bushbury, 396 houses at Birches Barn, 374 in Old Heath and 186 at Parkfield. In all, more than 3,900 council houses were built across the borough but the ambitious target, set in 1919, of 5,659 new houses by 1927 was not achieved.

In 1929, the Ministry of Health requested that local authorities build houses that met the needs of lower paid workers. The Council looked for sites for building a smaller type of house with two bedrooms which would be available for a rent of 7/6d a week. In November 1929, the Borough Engineer in a report to the Housing Committee suggested that another 10-

acre piece of land at Rough Hills, reserved for the Health Committee, should be utilised for building 174 two bedroomed Type E houses. This land was part of the original 77 acre Rough Hills site that had been acquired by the Council in 1908. The contract was given to Joseph Hickin and work had commenced by March 1930.

By the end of May, 20 of the 174 type E houses were roofed and ready for plastering. Work proceeded throughout 1930 and on the 29 January 1931, it was announced that the last of the 174 houses were being handed over for tenancy. The rent was fixed at 8/3d per week. The total cost of this latest development was £48,648.

Joan Underhill was about five years old when she left Old Fallings in 1930 with her mother and sister to move to this new development in Whittaker Street. Her father had deserted the family, money was in very short supply and her memories of the 30s are sombre.

She recalls the poverty that was common in many of the households. Britain was entering the Great Depression as its world trade and industrial output plunged. Mass employment rose to 3.5 million with many more attempting to cope on part-time employment.

'There was no work and if they did manage to get a job, the wages were poor. Some mothers walked over Goldthorn Hill to Penn and did domestic work and washing for the better off. In summer many walked over the fields in Birmingham Road to Sedgley Beacon and worked in the potato fields for a few shillings.'

Aged six, she remembers being taken to the Police station in Red Lion Street and queuing for shoes from the 'Chief

Constables Boot and Shoe Fund'. Clothes came from jumble sales and were darned and mended over and over again. Food was basic and often consisted of sandwiches of jam or dripping. A lot of people had groceries 'on the strap' and paid when they could manage it or when they had been to the pawnshop on Monday. She looked forward to visiting her grandmother in Dudley who had a range on which she cooked hot nourishing meals such as stews. Families shared and it was not unusual to receive half a loaf from a neighbour. Family benefits were means tested and tightly administered and they would hide anything remotely expensive from the eyes of the 'Poor Law' man who visited the house. For some people on the estate the struggle became too much and they committed suicide by gassing themselves.

When Joan was nine, her mother had another child. It was February, the house was cold, the family was destitute and she was given 4d by a neighbour to travel to Dudley to get help from her grandmother.

The house became too small for the family and in 1937 they moved to Myatt Avenue. She disliked the house intensely. Although it had 3 bedrooms rather than 2, it was an older house than the one they had occupied in Whittaker Street. The toilet was outside. The coal store was in the kitchen. The window frames were metal and rusted. Heating was provided by a coal fire but they could barely afford the coal.

Kent Road had not yet been constructed and she walked to All Saints School across a path towards Major Street. She recalls local characters like Mr Marchant, the kind-hearted postman, who would give Joan and her friends a swing and

> *a sweet if he met them at the end of his round. There was 'Old Toddy' who dug up a large hole behind where the houses in Kent Road were built. 'Old Toddy' was a one-man mining company who collected ironstone from his pit and sold it to Bayliss, Jones and Bayliss'.*

At the same time, the Council was buying up a 9¼ acre site near All Saints church. This piece of land fronting All Saints Road, Vicarage Road and Steelhouse Lane was purchased for £2,800 from Lord Barnard for the purpose of building up to 268 houses 'in an area where the erection of working-class dwellings was desirable'. The housing development would include a new road from Derry Street down to Cable Street, a road which was later to be named as Caledonia Road.

At a national level, the General Election of 1929 returned a Labour Government. Their Greenwood Housing Act of 1930 was brought in to run in tandem with the Wheatley Act of 1924. While the Wheatley Act focussed on the building of houses for let, the Greenwood Act marked a turning point in housing policy and introduced a five-year programme of slum clearance, with designated Improvement Areas. It compelled local councils to clear properties that were unfit for human habitation or posed a danger to health and provided further subsidies for the local councils to re-house the tenants. This single Act led to the clearance of more slums than at any time previously, and the building of 700,000 new homes across the country. Since slum clearance was a matter for the Health Committee, the Housing Committee agreed to a target of 150 houses a year in addition to those built to replace slum clearance.

By November 1931, the 5,000th house had been built by the

Council. Despite proposals by the Housing Committee, no formal action was taken to celebrate or even recognise this milestone. The Annual Report of the Housing Committee showed that 48 houses had been let on the Green Lane estate, 102 on the All Saints estate and 630 on the Parkfield Road estate. Not all of the 5,107 houses had been let to council tenants. While 2,378 of the 2,476 houses built by the council at Low Hill in Bushbury were let to council tenants, 52 of the 53 houses built at Oxbarn in the west of the town were sold to private owners.

The Conservative Government elected in 1933 brought in a Housing Act which abolished the subsidies to local authorities for general housing created in the Wheatley Act. Nationally over half a million houses had been built under the Wheatley Act but local authorities were now required to concentrate their efforts on slum clearance and rehousing.

The last significant developments on the Parkfield estate took place in 1933. In November plans were approved for 24 'D' Type houses on the east side of Myatt Avenue, again as part of the 1923 Faulkland Street Area Improvement Scheme. Another development was approved in 1933 on the north side of Rooker Avenue. This side of the road had not been purchased by the Corporation in 1909, the land belonging instead to Wolverhampton and Dudley Breweries. In May of that year a Building Notice was presented by the Breweries architect to the Public Works Committee of Wolverhampton Corporation. It informed them of their plans to build 58 houses, set out as 7 blocks of 4 'cottages' and 5 blocks of 6 'cottages', along Rooker 'Road' extending into a new road, Rooker Crescent. The architect involved was A.T. and Bertram Butler of Dudley. The original layout shows the street labelled as Rooker "Road" but a pencil line has been drawn through 'Road' and 'Avenue' has been written in. By the end of November, the plans had been revised and another Building Notice was presented. The layout now consisted of 27 pairs of houses with the street still labelled as Rooker Road. Approval was given by the Public Works Committee on 18 December. Until recently, a walk along Rooker Avenue and Crescent would have shown that the revised layout was largely put into practice although houses were only built along one side of the Crescent and a block of 4 houses can be seen at the Dixon Street end of Rooker Avenue.

The Rooker Avenue Shops

As well as houses, their plans included a proposal to build a block of eight shops. Prior to the Rooker Avenue shops opening in 1934, the only place in the immediate area to buy food was on the wasteland opposite

Figure 39: The Rooker Road (Avenue) development in the 1930s.

Whittaker Street. Owned by Mr Williams from Steelhouse Lane, it took the form of a big tin shed from which he sold groceries.

When the development had been completed, this row of three storey buildings became a prominent landmark and until the building of the Rough Hills Estate, Carole Bridgen's sister was able to pick them out from the top of Sedgley Beacon.

Figure 40: The Rooker Avenue shops.

Barry Marchant who lived in Whittaker Street at the time remembers some of the original shops when they opened:

> *The General Store was owned by Noah Williams who had started his business near Whittaker Street in a tin shed,*
>
> *The Butchers was owned by AJ Stevens made up of three brothers, one of whom was Alf,*
>
> *The next two shops were the hairdressers and greengrocers,*
>
> *The Sweet shop was run by Mary Jones,*
>
> *Next was the shoe repair shop followed by the Handy Stores run by Dolly Chambers,*
>
> *The last of the eight shops was the Chippy run by a mother and daughter.*

Even in the 30s and 40s, shops such as those in Rooker Avenue and neighbouring areas like Steelhouse Lane and Parkfield Road did not have a monopoly. A number of household items could be obtained from deliveries by horse and cart.

Sylvia Enefer who lived in Pond Grove in the 40s remembers her Uncle and Aunt, Jimmy and Emmy Ellis, delivering vegetables by horse and cart. Mr Price delivered lovely bread to the area for many years. Jimmy Allen delivered milk by horse and cart until he started using an electric van. The family also got their coal delivered by horse and cart.

George Cartwright recalls the man who delivered watercress on a Sunday morning. His horse and cart came from the Monmore Green direction and made its way up Dixon Street.

Carole Bridgen lived behind the Chippy. By the early 50s, it was run by the Smiths. She also remembers Alan Sadler, the cobbler, Miss Beech who ran the Handy Stores and Tommy Cox, the barber. Williams ran the General Stores as well as the greengrocers. Alf Stevens was running the butchers.

Along with other families on the new estate, we made good use of the shops which catered for most of our household requirements. Walking (or running) from Cheviot Road, along the alley past the garages, over the 'patch' of wasteland alongside Rooker Crescent, the first shop we came to was the grocery shop run by Mr Turner. As our teatime diet seemed to be based around sandwiches containing boiled ham, I was often asked to get the weekend supply. I remember queuing, transfixed by the machine that produced the wafer thin slices.

You could also buy newspapers there but for some reason we had our papers delivered by a shop at the end of Myrtle Street. Next along was Alf the butcher. Without a fridge to keep the meat fresh, Mom would make a visit to Alf every day or so. Fresh vegetables and fruit were bought from a shop run by two ex RAF ladies, Rita and Winnie. Like most families in the country, we ate to a routine. On Sunday we would have a roast, either beef or lamb: chicken was still too expensive. This would be followed in the late afternoon by sandwiches of ham or tinned salmon and a dessert: usually tinned fruit with evaporated milk. Without fail, Monday was a cold version of the Sunday joint. Other regulars were mince, chops and liver. I yearned for some of the convenience foods that began to be advertised on the new commercial television station, ITV, but met parental resistance. Mom always cooked and the food was plain and wholesome. The main meal was taken at lunchtime and referred to as 'dinner'. The evening meal, referred to as 'tea', was usually based around sandwiches. Every week or so Mom had a rest from the cooking and we had fish and chips from another of the Rooker Avenue shops. While Mom and I loved our fish, Dad preferred battered roe, an acquired taste which I never acquired. As a youngster, the fish and chip shop came a close second in popularity to the sweet shop, run by an elderly lady, Mary Jones, and her brother. Inside were shelves with jars of all the old favourites: Everton Mints, Humbugs, Sugar Almonds, Pineapple Chunks, Black Jacks etc, etc. Aniseed balls costing a farthing (¼d) were particular favourites, as were packets of Spangles (preferably Old English). You made your choice and bought 'a quarter', or maybe opted for a sherbet dip, or kali, in a paper cone, gaining a brightly stained finger and tongue as a souvenir.

As time has progressed, I have picked up the bill at dentists across the country for my childhood addiction to sweets and my dislike of toothpaste.

The shops not only sold food. The young hairdresser provided a 'short back and sides' and finished off with a singe, a peculiar practice among hairdressers which involved scorching the ends of the hair with a lighted taper. It was supposed to have all sorts of beneficial effects such as helping the hair to grow or even fending off colds – I never understood how it was supposed to work and it certainly did nothing for the longevity of my hair. A visit to the hairdresser, every 3 or 4 weeks, also provided a chance to 'read' his copies of Parade, a 'men's' magazine with photos of ladies exposing plenty of cleavage but little else – innocuous by today's standards but a treat for a young boy entering puberty.

The two remaining shops were the cobblers where extra life was put into our shoes and the hardware. My father did not enjoy DIY and, apart from doing the painting and the wallpapering which was always a traumatic experience for all concerned, we used tradesmen, so very few visits were made to the shop and I have no recollection of it.

Alongside the shops was a red telephone box, just about the nearest to our house, and a means of instant communication with the outside world. Very few of our relatives had a telephone, but it proved invaluable for ordering goods and services and contacting the doctor.

Robbie Bennett who lived further up Cheviot Road recalls his visit in the 60s to the shops on Rooker Avenue.

As a lad I liked (to) run and found an errand a challenge. If it was a chip shop tea we were having, my mom would give *me the order and off I went. About 200 yards down our road was the garages and an alley that led to a piece of wasteland alongside the Rough Hills Tavern, now sadly adrift and derelict and most probably will soon be gone. That wasteland we called the patch is now houses. In Rooker Avenue, which stretched from Dixon Street to Parkfield Road, was a line of shops with the chippy at the far end. The obvious challenge in the chip shop was how quickly could I get back home with the family tea.*

This childhood memory inspired his poem, **Home in Hundred Seconds** © *Robbie Kennedy Bennett.*

Council house building continued well into the 1930s, although it never reached the scale of the 1920s. Leading up to the outbreak of WW2 in 1939, housing policy had become increasingly difficult for local authorities to administer. The housing subsidies provided by Government were inconsistent. The control of Council housing was divided between the Housing Committee, the Health Committee and the Medical Officer of Health. Finance was shrouded in an assortment of overlapping Housing Acts. A document from March 1934 listing rent arrears had to be broken down for each estate into those which came under the three Housing Acts of 1919, 1923 and 1924. A complaint by the Parkfield Road Tenants Association in November 1934 referred to the 1919 Housing Act, thus:

'As no practical effort has been made to reduce the overwhelming high rents of this Act houses, which have been patiently borne for so many years, it is proposed to organise a protest, by each 1919 Act tenant withholding half a crown weekly of their rent, ... You will agree that the amenities and the high rents of the 1919 Act houses are really bad when compared with other type houses of good conditions and low rents.'

Plans were also set out in March 1934 for a Dixon Street Estate on a plot of land bordered by Dixon Street, the canal and Mount Road. The estate would have consisted of 56 houses but it did not get beyond an inquiry stage.

Houses were still being built in and around the Parkfield Estate. In December 1935 plans were published for building 44 houses at Pond Lane, predominantly in what is now Pond Grove. The contract was awarded in March 1936 to Mr A. M. Griffiths. The council was in danger of running out of letters to designate the different designs and the plans show a mix of Type D, E, F and G houses, presumably of ever decreasing size. These were ready for tenancy by mid-

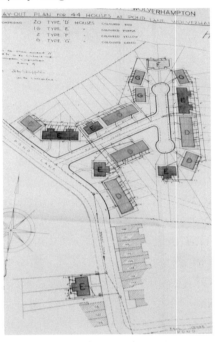

Figure 41: A map of the first stage of the Pond Lane housing development. (Photograph reproduced with the permission of Wolverhampton Archives and Local Studies).

September. This was the first of three developments in Pond Lane.

The second, much larger, development consisted of 92 houses centred on what is now Pond Crescent, extending into Kent Road in one direction and towards Silver Birch Road in the other. Once again the contract was awarded to Mr A. M. Griffiths. The last phase which started in January 1939 consisted of 32 houses with the contract awarded to Mr. A. Poole.

In January 1938, plans had been published for 48 houses on Dixon Street. These were mainly on the north side of the road near to the junction with Kent Road but 10 of the houses were to be built around its junction with Rooker Avenue. The photo

shows a small selection of those houses on Dixon Street, looking towards Kent Road.

In the rest of the town, there was limited development on the fringes of the major estates to accommodate the residents of slum clearance areas. More two bedroom properties were now

Figure 42: The final Dixon Street housing development.

built and the three bedroom properties continued to get smaller. The Housing Act of 1935 led to a continuation of this policy with estates built between 1935 and 1937 in the north of the town at Elston Hall, Marsh Lane and The Scotlands. The house building programme was brought to a halt in 1940 by the Second World War.

From 1918 to 1931 the local authority had overwhelmingly been the most important provider of housing. 966 new houses in 1926 and 1,280 in 1927 represent the two peaks of rented accommodation in the Borough. From 1933, however, Council house building was overtaken by the private sector, apart from an exceptional year in 1938.

21

LIFE DURING WW2

When war broke out in 1939, no-one knew for certain what might happen. Olwen Medlicott recalls that fear of the unknown.

> *I was nine when it started and I asked my Mum what it would be like and she told me the Germans would drop bombs on the houses and buildings and they would be demolished. I remember waking up next morning, pulling back the curtains and looking through the window, expecting to see the 18 houses in the Crescent demolished, but it didn't occur to me that ours would be too.*

In the first two years of the conflict, the threat of invasion was never far from people's minds and eyes. Large concrete blocks, to be used as tank traps, were placed on the side of the road at the junction of the Parkfield Road and Birmingham New Road. Barrage balloons were placed above factories such as Stewarts and Lloyds. Although no-one I spoke to can remember any incidents, the RAF archives for 30 August 1940 include the following report:

'Messrs Stewart and Lloyd's factory at Bilston was bombed causing some casualties, numbers not known. Water mains and electric cables were affected and there was some damage to a locomotive shed.'

John Thompson was also hit but fortunately the bombs did not detonate. The company expected to be attacked as a German manufacturer had installed machinery at the Motor Pressings works just before the war started and would have been aware of the factory layout. Like most factories in the country, their manufacturing energies were directed towards the war effort. One of their main products was the 25 pounder gun trailer. In addition, they made chassis frames for military vehicles, anti-tank shields and pontoons as well as a wide variety of components for planes including the Spitfires, Hurricanes and the Wellington bombers. The company were also responsible for manufacturing the casing for the 'Dambuster' bouncing bombs. Men worked overtime to reach production targets but many were also engaged in fire watching or as members of the Home Guard section.

Joan Underhill who lived in Myatt Avenue and Olwen Medlicott who lived in Rooker Crescent both remember the night of the Coventry bombing when they heard wave after wave of German bombers making their way to their target.

Wolverhampton did not suffer the same fate as Coventry and Birmingham but isolated attacks took place and enemy aircraft faced shelling from anti-aircraft gun batteries stationed in the town.

Sheila Cartwright was by the Rough Hills Tavern one evening when two searchlights picked out a German plane and bystanders started clapping and cheering. On his daily walk to All Saints School Barry Marchant recalls picking up pieces of shrapnel, the remnants of shells fired by the anti-aircraft guns, and comparing his collection with everyone else's when he arrived in class.

Public air raid shelters were set up around the town. In the Rough Hills area communal shelters were found in Rooker Avenue near the Tavern as well as in Dixon Street and Mount Road, the original part of D'Urberville Road. Constructed of thick brick walls with a concrete roof, they were built to accommodate up to 50 people. Individual households were provided with shelters. The Morrison indoor table was a reinforced cage-like construction with a steel top, a dining table in the day and a shelter at night, designed to withstand the collapse of the upper floor of a house. The Anderson shelter, made up of corrugated steel sheets, was built and set up in the garden, providing protection against a bomb blast.

Barry Marchant recalls his father being the first in Whittaker Street to install one. They were 6ft 6 inches long and 4 ft 6 inches wide and designed to accommodate six people. This did not stop twelve people crowding into their shelter when the first air raid siren went off. Barry recalls that his father maintained his daily routine despite the air raid sirens. It was not unusual for his father to walk home from the ECC factory while the siren sounded and sit down to his evening meal before he retired to the shelter in the back garden.

Barry can remember only one bomb landing in the area. Around 1941, a bomb was dropped in Caledonia Road and although it caused serious damage to a house, it did not explode. Wolverhampton Archives web site shows a photograph of the bomb damaged house taken on 1 August 1941.

He also remembers the plane which crashed a few days earlier in Parkfield Road on 21 July 1941 near to its junction with the Birmingham New Road. On crash landing the plane's engine hit a nearby house. Later in the day, Barry's curiosity got the better of him and when he visited the crash site, he made off with the plane's radio. Reprimanded severely by his father, the radio was taken to the police.

The plane crash is also remembered by Derek Shorthouse who was born at The Beeches in Parkfield Road and a pupil at Dudley Road School at the time of the tragedy:

'One day we heard at school that a plane had crashed at Parkfield Road and I ran, very apprehensively, with another boy Dennis Lawton to the end of Thompson Avenue when we realised that the aircraft had come down on his house. Fortunately, none of his family were in the house at the time but the pilot was dead.'

The Oxford V 3973 plane was on a training flight from the Service Flying Training School at Brize Norton and flown by two Czechs. Their names were Miroslav Drnek aged 24 and Joseph

Figure 43; Looking towards the site (to the right of the red car) of the
1941 plane crash in Parkfield Road.

Melena aged 23. The Air Ministry and RAF Command records show they were on a map reading and instrument flying practice flight. The crash was attributed to 'a lack of discipline'. The official Air Ministry accident card reports, 'a collision with house tops when low flying. Deliberate breach of orders given as understood. Low flying in vicinity of 'girlfriend's house. Pilot to blame.' The rumour which had circulated after the incident that they were flying low to show off to their girlfriends who lived nearby was founded on truth.

The Express and Star described the grim details of the incident and the lucky escapes of two particular families. The house numbers have since changed.

'At No.179 – the first house to be struck - a Mr H.G. Chatfield was just preparing to lie down. He said later that his wife told him: "Don't go up yet. That aeroplane sounds very low. Let's go out and have a look at it." That saved their lives. Just as they got outside the plane demolished the bedroom where Mr Chatfield would have been.

Next door at No. 181, a Mrs Doris Willis was making a cup of tea for Private W. Lawton, who had returned on leave to find his mother and father at work. On hearing the plane, they left the house to have a look – leaving Mrs Willis' ten-month old baby Alan in the front room. When she saw how low the aircraft was Mrs Willis rushed into the house and grabbed her child. A split second later the house was struck - with the plane's engine left resting partly on a chair in the bedroom. A flying helmet and leather jacket were also found in the room.'

Roy Holloway from Wanderers Avenue in Blakenhall recalls standing at the top of Buller Street with his Mother and Aunty and seeing the damage that the plane had caused. He also tells of the bomb which fell in Veronica Close a few years later. It was suggested at the time that it failed to explode because it fell on soft ground.

Incendiary bombs were used extensively in the war and residents in each street took it in turns to act as fire watchers in case any fell in the neighbourhood. Teams of three were trained up and responsible for the stirrup pump, buckets of water and sand and the water hose which it was hoped would put out fires. As well as the one which severely damaged the house in Caledonia Road, Barry can recall only one other being dropped nearby at the James Baker Boot and Shoe Factory located at the junction of Cleveland Road, Vicarage Road and Powlett Street.

School carried on as normal. Margaret Carroll was at All Saints School from 1939 to 1943.

During the war we all carried gas masks in cardboard containers and usually I.D. bracelets with our National Registration numbers on them. There were several public air-raid shelters in the district (e.g. Gower Street).

Olwen Medlicott started at her secondary school, the Municipal Grammar School, during the war. It did not go well.

I can remember my first day at that school very well. There was a war on and the brown tunic which I was supposed to wear was on order and had not arrived, so I wore the navy one I'd worn at my Junior School and my Mum gave me a letter to give to the Head Mistress, apologising and explaining. Before I had chance to find out where I could find the Head Mistress, we were all called out onto the playground for an Air Raid Drill, so there I was in line with the others in my class, my gasmask on my shoulder and Mum's letter in my hand, when this horrible woman hauled me out of the line and hollered "Don't you know our uniform is brown, girl?" Yes, you've guessed it, she was the Head Mistress, so I meekly gave her my Mum's letter. So that will give you some idea of the discipline, war or no war!

Roy Holloway's father worked at Sunbeam factory in Blakenhall during the war and was a centre lathe turner, a 'reserved occupation', which meant he was one of many excused military service.

A number of local men and women volunteered or were conscripted during the course of the war. Ben Owen, who was born in 1917 on Rough Hills around what is now Myrtle Street, was already an experienced professional soldier at the outbreak of the war. He had joined the Royal Artillery as a 15-year-old. Dissatisfied by 'orthodox' soldiering, he completed commando training and then volunteered and was accepted for a Special Forces unit, No. 1 Demolition Squad in 1942. Led by the charismatic Major (later Lieutenant-General) Vladimir Peniakoff, it became known as Popski's Private Army (PPA) and was involved in a number of clandestine and front line roles in North Africa and in Italy before they were disbanded in October 1945. In 1993, Ben wrote about his war memoirs in a highly regarded book called 'With Popski's Private Army'. The book was republished in 2006. In the preface to the book, Ben writes of how playing on the pit banks around Rough Hills prepared him for his life as a soldier:

'Today I live on an estate built on my boyhood playground, which then consisted of cinderbanks formed by the effluent from the heavy industrial factories of this part of the Black Country and the holes where I remember people digging for coal during the 1926 General Strike. I learned much of the field craft I would need in our war as we fought our Cowboy and Indian battles on this, then, rugged terrain.'

Many men, unable to join the Armed Forces because of age or occupation, joined the Home Guard. This was officially set up in May 1940 by Anthony Eden, Secretary of State for War, when he appealed for men aged 17 to 65 to join a new force, named the Local Defence Volunteers, the LDV. Within 24 hours, 250,000 volunteers had put their names forward. Irreverently known at first by phrases such as 'Look, Duck and Vanish' the force was renamed the Home Guard. Once enrolled, men went through a formal army training programme for several months after which they were issued with a rifle and uniform. The main function of the Home Guard was to defend factories and strategic points like railways, canals and road junctions and this included, for members of the 23rd Staffordshire (Wolverhampton) Battalion's 'B' company, guard duty at an eclectic mix of locations such as the Black Horse, Goldthorn Hill (at the top of the water tower) and Park Hall Hotel. Some of their training was carried out on the fields adjacent to the hotel.

Persuaded to do so by his friend, Ronnie Hill, George Paddock from Thompson Avenue was not quite 17 when he joined the Home Guard.

There was a recruitment centre nearby on the Birmingham New Road but I was concerned that the officials would know I was underage so I enrolled at a centre in Whitmore Reans. Following training which no-one seemed to treat too seriously, I was issued with a P14 service rifle and carried out security duty at places such as the electricity generating station on Bilston Road and at Molineux Stadium. I then transferred to an anti-aircraft battery unit stationed at Dunstall Park racecourse.

When it was stood down in November 1944, celebratory dinners were held by many units. The Black Horse in Thompson Avenue seems to have been a popular venue for these celebrations and the Wolverhampton Battalion's 'D' and 'B' companies enjoyed its hospitality in November and December. An Officers and Ladies evening was also spent there on the 2 December 1944.

Joan Underhill was called up when she was aged 17 for war employment. She had been working at Burtons, the tailors, in Victoria Street. She was given no choice as to where she was sent and found herself at Villiers in Blakenhall. Her job was chamfering the shells used by the Hawker Typhoon aircraft. She worked a 12-hour shift from 8am to 8pm with breaks for lunch and tea.

As the war progressed, resources that might aid the war effort were prized. Any metal was a valued commodity, required for conversion into munitions, and Roy Holloway remembers workers arriving in Wanderers Avenue with acetylene cutters to remove the iron railings. Everyone was encouraged to 'dig for victory' and growing your own food took on greater significance after rationing was introduced. This had a major impact on the daily lives of people across the country. The first foods to be rationed were bacon, butter and sugar in January 1940. Other items like meat, eggs and milk followed later. Families registered at chosen shops in their locality, and were provided with a ration book which contained coupons.

Margaret Jones lived in Legge Street and later Myatt Avenue during the war. Her parents registered with Lockley's at the corner of Myatt Avenue and Parkfield Road. The shopkeeper was provided with enough food for registered customers. Purchasers had to take ration books with them when shopping, so the relevant coupon or coupons could be cancelled. There were shopkeepers who were able to work around the system and Margaret mentions two from Parkfield Road, Mrs Hills and Granny Newton, who helped out families.

Bill Leighton's mother used her ration coupons for meat at Alf's butcher shop in Rooker Avenue.

To relax and attempt to forget the stresses of the war, Joan Underhill recalls that people went to the dances, to pubs and to the cinemas.

The Civic Hall in Wolverhampton was very popular for dancing. The big bands played there as well as good local bands. The cinemas opened on Sunday now and there were always queues to see the latest films The only snag; it meant walking home in the blackout as the last bus home was 9 pm. The pubs did well till they ran out of beer and had to close.

Figure 44: Mom (Violet) and Dad (Roland).

Life's traditions continued throughout the war and on 31 July 1943 my parents got married at Bushbury church. I was always too embarrassed to probe into their 'courting', but I believe my Mom and Dad met at the Hippodrome variety theatre in Queens Square, where he was a regular visitor with his brothers and my mother was an usherette. The war did not stop them enjoying a honeymoon at Budleigh Salterton on the South Devon coast. This resort always seemed a strange choice: like most coastal towns, it was still on an invasion alert with barbed wire plus anti-tank and anti-personnel mines to discourage any romantic walks on or near the beach. Nevertheless, they were able to enjoy nine months of married life before Dad received his conscription letter.

People also sought spiritual comfort at their local churches. From the beginning of the war, it was the custom of Rev. J. W. Barnsley, the vicar of St. Martins on Dixon Street, to read out at each Sunday service the names of those local men serving in the Forces. As the numbers increased, names were read out over the four services of each month. Relatives were invited to request special prayers if someone was reported wounded, missing or taken prisoner. Church business carried on as normal throughout the winters of WW2 and, despite the blackout, Evensong continued to be held at 6.30 pm.

VE Day marked the end of WW2 in Europe (but not the Far East) and the vicar's letter in the June 1945 edition gives an insight into the mood of people living around Rough Hills:

'On the day itself there was a steady flow of people in and out of the church from 3pm until midnight and it was noticeable how earnestly and devoutly everyone joined in the service and remained sometime after for silent prayer. The next morning there was a congregation at all three of the Masses of Thanksgiving, though not as many as I had hoped for, though perhaps ought not to have expected in view of the more secular rejoicings of the night before.'

This was not the end of the war for many servicemen. George Paddock had received his conscription papers on D-Day, 6 June 1944, and following training in Kent he joined the North Staffordshire Regiment in France. After the war ended in Europe, he returned to England where the regiment completed jungle training in the south of England in preparation for action in the Far East.

My father meanwhile was already stationed in Burma, a member of 'The Forgotten Army'. He had been conscripted on 18 May 1944 and following training with the North Staffordshire Regiment and Kings Shropshire Light Infantry, he embarked on a troop ship on 15 December 1944 at Liverpool, set for India. He recalls marching on a bitterly cold day, dressed in jungle uniform, from Lime Street station to the docks. The troop ship arrived in Kalyan, India on 12 January 1945. Following jungle training in India, he was posted to Burma.

My uncle has spoken to me about letters that were sent home to his wife and relatives. He was at pains to play down any dangers he faced. 'The Gurkhas are looking after us', 'It's safer than a Saturday night in Wolverhampton' were typical reassurances.

Both for George Paddock and my father, the dropping of the atomic bombs on Hiroshima and Nagasaki brought a welcome end to their active service. George was sent to Italy to help deal with the aftermath of the war in that country. My father who had served in the Burma campaign with the 2nd battalion Worcestershire Regiment was posted to India before finally leaving the country on 5 January 1946. Like the majority of Burma veterans, he spoke very little about his war experiences. By all accounts it had a deep effect on him and in 1946 he came back a different man to the cheerful, chatty lad who left Wolverhampton in 1944.

22

WOLVERHAMPTON AND ROUGH HILLS FROM 1945 TO 1971

The Beginning of the End

As WW2 moved towards its anticipated conclusion, domestic issues took on greater prominence. Once again a world war concentrated the minds of politicians on the importance of housing for the working classes. As early as June 1943, the Labour Party at its annual conference was declaring 'Plan Now' for post war houses. In 1944, William Beveridge, a member of the wartime Coalition Government, declared: "The greatest opportunity open in this country for raising the general standard of living lies in housing." The post war Labour government eventually adopted the Beveridge proposals and the Minister for Health and Housing, Aneurin (Nye) Bevan, directed his energy towards building good quality council homes and council flats.

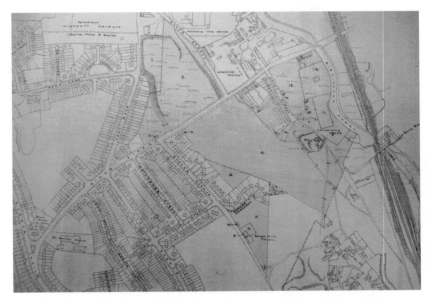

Figure 45: The Area in pink, showing the Rough Hills Compulsory Order.
(Photograph reproduced with the permission of Wolverhampton Archives
and Local Studies).

Wolverhampton's response was to identify sites at Bushbury, Warstones and Willenhall Road for council housing. More significantly, it also earmarked the remaining area around the derelict collieries of Rough Hills and in 1946 the Corporation made a Compulsory Purchase Order on the land adjacent to the 1920s Parkfield (Rough Hills) estate.

The shaded areas on the map covered 34½ acres comprising 21 plots which had not been bought by Wolverhampton Corporation in previous transactions in 1908 and the 1920s. The land belonging to the Corporation would now include:

■ Dixon Street, northwards, to the Moulders Arms pub and bordered to the east and west by Major Street and Kent Road respectively.

221

■ Dixon Street, southwards, to the Bilston Corporation boundary and bordered to the east and west by the Birmingham canal and Rooker Avenue, respectively.

Joan Underhill had been one of the first to move into Whittaker Street in 1930 with her Mom and sister. She describes Rough Hills then as 'a grey, desolate area of slag heaps and pit mounds.' The back of Thompson Avenue was used as a tip and had cart tracks leading to Steelhouse Lane and Silver Birch Road. There were 1920s houses on both sides of Thompson Avenue and a few 1920s houses in Dixon Street. By 1930 Whittaker Street together with Wheatley Street was developed. Beyond this was a large area of wasteland dipping down to the canal and the railway line. It was a great place to play as children, because although there were lots of pit mounds it was covered with grass and in summer, wild flowers. Children played across 'The Runners' all day in the summer, making camps, flying kites, picking wild flowers, but getting into trouble if you should go near the canal, which they did, especially the boys.

In winter, children played in the street. Tying a rope to a lamp post and holding the other end was a great way for ten or more to skip together. Then there was hop scotch, top and whip, hide and seek for the girls, football, marbles, jacks and swopping cigarette cards for the boys. No one had a car so it was safe. Everyone in the street knew each other and helped each other, especially in times of illness.

The pub stood out; it was the only building between Rooker Avenue and Parkfield Road'.

Olwen Medlicott lived in Rooker Avenue and could see right across to the railway line from her house. She would have a 'game' with her mother at guessing how many coaches the train would be pulling.

Locals like George Cartwright remember the landscape of Rough Hills in the 1940s.

The Rough Hills fields stretched from Dixon Street over to Hardy Square and from the railway right over to Myatt Avenue. Rooker Avenue finished just past the shops. You had the Rough Hills Tavern pub and a dirt track down to the Parkfield Road. ... They were up and down, mostly clay, rough terrain, little grass on there. Horses were tied on. ...

Barry Marchant described the ground as "solid. The only grass was by Rough Hills Tavern." The area near what is now Hardy Square was used for football matches by local teams. In the absence of proper goal posts, two 40 gallon drums were used instead.

The land was not without houses. Photographs taken in 1941 show small single storey dwellings, referred to as The Cotts, on land at Rough Hills and it is not known when these were demolished. George Cartwright who was born in Dixon Street in 1938 recalls making an unexpected visit to the Cotts.

The cottages were more or less at the end of Myrtle Street. Walking over there one day with my friends (we) walked over what we thought was a bank and found out we were on someone's roof and got chased off. They had a water standpipe in area to use. They looked very nice cottages, were well kept.

Barry Marchant who moved from Bushbury to Whittaker Street aged six months in 1929 remembers visiting the cottages in the 1930s and his impression of the houses was not so favourable.

They had no gas, electricity or water. The inside of the cottages had a dirt floor and were lit by oil lamps and candles. Outside, there was a communal standpipe for water.

These may well have been the same set of houses referred to in the Staffordshire Advertiser from 23 January 1915. The article on sanitary conditions highlighted a group of 40 houses at Rough Hills, still unconnected to a nearby sewer pipe, with some described as 'quite unfit for habitation'. Margaret Jones who lived in Myatt Avenue in the 1940s remembers about a dozen single storey stone built houses.

We knew the settlement as 'The Village'. We were never made to feel welcome and our parents warned us against visiting the area. I do remember seeing braziers burning outside the houses.

To the east of The Cotts settlement was a small estate of houses centred on Hardy Square. At the time these houses would have come under Bilston Corporation.

By November 1947, the layout of the 'new' Rough Hills Estate had been submitted to the Ministry of Health. In a reply, received in February 1948, the proposal was rejected: the

Ministry insisting that any revised plan must include a school site of approximately 2.5 acres. By September 1948, a revised layout approved by the Housing Committee and the Director of Education had been submitted to the Ministry of Health and approval by the Ministry was announced in a report from the Housing Committee to Wolverhampton Council dated 24 November 1948.

Following this belated approval, a levelling scheme covering four sites was put out to tender:

- ■ Rough Hills,
- ■ Major Street tip,
- ■ Pond Lane tip,
- ■ A small area near St Martin's church.

The high banks alongside Major Street could be the height of a two storey house and Barry recalls that they were used as an initiation ceremony for lads from All Saints.

> The challenge was to jump from the top of the bank to the bottom. Although the landing was covered with ash, it was not a challenge that the youngsters enjoyed and many had to be dragged to face their 'rite of passage'.

For Sylvia Enefer and her family in Pond Lane, the high banks which extended from Major Street to Kent Road created an insurmountable obstacle for a visit to the coal merchant on Dixon Street.

> When journeys were made with Mom to get 'emergency rations' from the coal yard by Millers Bridge, it was impossible

to wheel the pram up the banks and take a shortcut to Dixon Street. Instead we took a detour along Kent Road, past the Monkey House pub and down the entire length of Major Street. Having collected the coal in their pram, we had the return journey to look forward to.

By February 1949, K.E. Millard and Co. Ltd had commenced levelling and the scheme was completed in mid-summer.

In 1949 Wolves won the FA Cup for the third time, beating Leicester City at Wembley.

Council house building was already taking place in other parts of the town and by the end of 1949, 2,600 new houses had been built on sites at Bushbury, Warstones and Willenhall Road. During

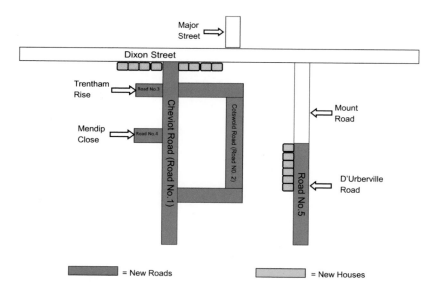

Figure 46: The First Phase of the New Rough Hills Estate.

the next five years, the Rough Hills estate took shape and, over three phases, 308 houses and flats were built. It began in earnest in December 1950 when the contract for the construction of roads and sewers was given to Asphalt & Public Works Ltd from Worcester. On 1 August 1951 the contract for the erection of 40 houses on the Rough Hills Estate was awarded to Austin & Co of Rushall, Walsall at a cost of £48,648-1s-6d.

The estate plan shows that this development comprising 32 houses and two blocks of 4 flats was to be built on a new section of Dixon Street, extending west of its junction with Major Street and an extension of Mount Street to be named D'Urberville Road. Building started in 1952 and in a report by the Housing Committee to the Council in July 1952, rents were fixed, in preparation for their imminent occupation, at £1 0s 0d for the three bedroomed semi-detached houses and 12s 0d for the flats. By September 1952, 4 properties had been completed.

In March of that year, the Council issued a Development Plan report. It included two proposals relevant to the new Rough Hills Estate. The first was to build a new primary school at Rough Hills on land belonging to Bilston Corporation. The second was to rebuild All Saints Primary School on existing playing fields on Pond Lane and to provide new playing fields on land between Thompson Avenue, Dixon Street and Pond Lane.

The development plan showed the now familiar layout with roads to be named as Cheviot Road (formerly Road Number 1 on the 1951 plan), Cotswold Road, Mendip Close, Trentham Rise, Rough Hills Road, Rough Hills Close and Lawn Road.

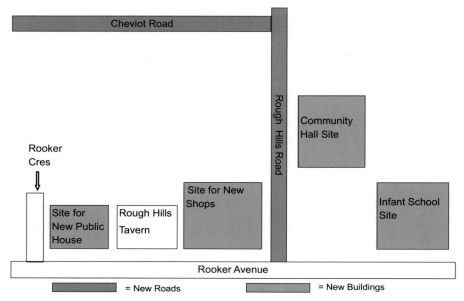

Figure 47: The New Facilities on the Rough Hills Estate.

The plan also showed that in addition to the houses, the following facilities would be provided:

- new pub to replace the Rough Hills Tavern
- new shops on Rooker Avenue to the east of the Rough Hills Tavern
- a pedestrian walkway from the garages behind Cheviot Road to the new shops on Rooker Avenue
- an Infants school on open land east of Rough Hills Road
- a Community Centre on open land immediately to the east of Rough Hills Road.

On 19 December 1952 the second phase began with a contract for the erection of a further 204 houses, awarded once again to

Austin & Co. at a cost of £238,631-17s-2d. This was the main section of the building project, leading to the creation of the three main roads that made up the estate: Cheviot Road, Cotswold Road and Rough Hills Road. Work started at the Dixon Street end of the estate and proceeded down towards the boundary with Bilston.

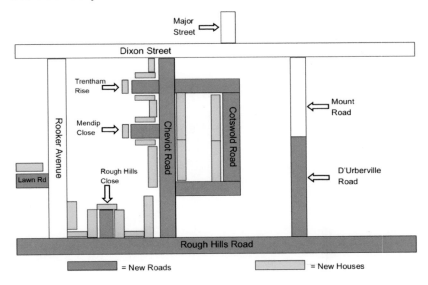

Figure 48: The Second Phase of the new Rough Hills Estate.

Building the houses on the estate posed civil engineering challenges. A Report by the Housing Committee to the Council dated 19 January 1953 described how 'the houses now being erected on the Rough Hills estate have to be constructed on special reinforced concrete rafts and wall foundations in order to overcome the difficult ground conditions.' A similar technique had been used in 1939 to build St Martin's Church at the top of Dixon Street.

The problems that had to be overcome were not necessarily

evident at the time. Sixty years later, as they prepared to build a social housing development behind Cheviot Road, Bromford Housing Group discovered the existence of a 100-foot mineshaft in the back garden of a house in Rough Hills Close.

On 19 January 1953 the contract for the last phase of 64 houses was signed, but this time it was awarded to Bishop Burns & Co, from Goldthorn Park at a cost of £83,453-15s-4d. Most were built on the east side of Cotswold Road.

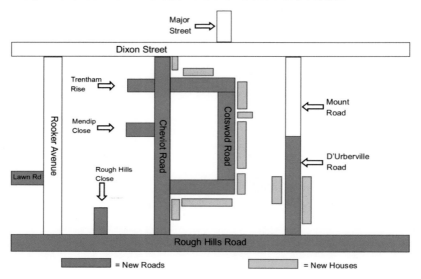

Figure 49: The Third Phase of the New Rough Hills Estate.

In July 1953 rents for newly completed houses at Tettenhall, Wednesfield and Rough Hills were fixed at a considerably higher level than for previous houses:

1 bed flats	13/6d to 14/-d,
2 bed flats and maisonette	19/-d,
2 bed houses	16/6d to 18/-d,
3 bed houses	19/6d to 20/6d,
4 bed houses	21/6d to 22/-d.

Everything (except for the bus service) was now in place. The Rough Hills council estate eagerly awaited the arrival of The Mills Family.

23

LIFE ON AND AROUND ROUGH HILLS

In the autumn of 1953, we moved to Rough Hills from 250 Bushbury Lane. Sixty years on, memories of Bushbury circulate in my mind: grandparents, on my mother's side, providing undivided love and attention; Uncles and Aunts coming and going; Mom disappearing to a distant hospital to be diagnosed with multiple sclerosis, a cruel debilitating disease which blighted the rest of her life; regular trips in a wheelbarrow to my grandad's

Figure 50: The ' Wild West' of Bushbury Lane.

allotment in Showell Circus; the back garden, my secure playground; glimpses of the Coronation on a neighbour's television. There are many more locked in the memory bank.

Grandad helped us to move and when he left in the afternoon, it felt very quiet. My life was to enter a new phase and I was not entirely happy.

The estate was far from finished. In October the Housing Committee highlighted the need to provide footpaths as soon as possible. Another report in November flagged up the provision of trees and the seeding of the open space at the junction of Rough Hills Road and Cheviot Road, adjacent to where the bus stop would be positioned.

On our arrival in 1953 we were greeted by the dirt, dust and noise of a construction site. I have few memories of that first year. The latest extension to the estate had started at the Dixon Street end of Cheviot Road. Number 48 was about two thirds down the road and as building work progressed, the layout of streets and houses took shape.

Figure 51: Grandad (Alf) and Nanna (Phoebe).

I was too young to take more than a passing interest in the new homes and certainly too young to take advantage of their adventure playground potential. My grandparents from Bushbury were regular visitors at weekends despite the lack of a direct bus service to the estate. Grandad revelled in the opportunity to work on the front and back garden. Landscaping the front garden of a council estate in the 1950s seemed to consist of planting a privet hedge (still there) to establish your territory, sowing grass seed for a lawn (most of it still there) and digging a narrow border (disappeared). The colliery may have closed over 70 years ago, but the gardening soon brought up nuggets of coal. The back garden provided more scope for his creativity and he planted a selection of flowers and vegetables plus a gooseberry bush that provided us with a regular supply of jam for years to come.

Figure 52: The Mills home at 48, Cheviot Road many years after we left.

The house was semi-detached with an attached outhouse. We used the door to our outhouse as our main entrance. The single story outhouse was built primarily as a storage area with one section bricked off for coal. It had a flat roof and a single layer of brick. Quite soon after our arrival it provided our first drama. I was woken in the late evening to be told that the ground floor was flooded. The neighbour's garden was way above the level of the damp proof layer (if it existed at all) in the outhouse and following heavy rain, the water seeped in.

From the outhouse, a door led into the first of two living areas. This one at the back of the house, shown on the plan as

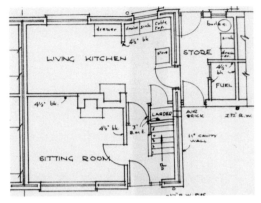

Figure 53: The Ground Floor plan of our house. (Photograph reproduced with the permission of Wolverhampton Archives and Local Studies).

'Living Kitchen', was adopted as the main living area. When I visited the homes of friends on the estate, this seemed to be the arrangement that most families chose. A wall partition partially separated the room into a lounge and a kitchen area. Fitments were minimal. There was a set of wall cupboards in the 'Living Kitchen' area and a sink, pantry and gas supply to confirm that the other part of the room was earmarked as a kitchen. The open fireplace was opposite the fitted cupboards and two windows looked out onto the back garden. Beyond the garden was a wasteland which eventually became an area for garages, building dens and playing football or cricket. A door from this main living area led to the hallway. On the right was a door leading to the front room, a room left for 'best', with a window looking out onto the small front garden and main road. At the end of the hallway was the main door, used only on special occasions. The stairway led from the end of the hallway to a small landing with doors to the two bedrooms and the combined toilet and bathroom. Another door gave access to a store room. My parents took the larger bedroom facing the road while mine faced out to the back garden. The house had fireplaces in both downstairs rooms but fires were only ever lit in the living room. Behind the fire was a boiler. To get running hot water, a coal fire was required. In the summer, you boiled

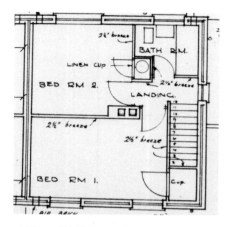

Figure 54: The First Floor Plan of our house. (Photograph reproduced with the permission of Wolverhampton Archives and Local Studies).

up kettles of water to wash up plates and pans or have a wash in the sink. If you wanted a bath, you boiled up pans of water and carried them upstairs. Without a cavity wall or roof insulation, the house was cold. Even when sitting in front of a coal fire, the back of your body refused to warm up. Regular coal deliveries were critical. On occasions, it would be necessary for Mom or Dad to walk down to the coal merchant, W.T. Webberley & Company on Bilston Road, by the canal bridge, to check on their next delivery. Many years later, the coal fire was replaced by a gas fire. As the provider of hot water had now disappeared, we had an electric immersion heater installed in the store room upstairs. We could now enjoy the promise of instant heat on a cold winter's morning and hot running water for washing up and bathing. My parents were proud of these innovations and neighbours were invited around to admire the new additions to the house.

On reflection there was never any pressure to 'keep up with the Jones' on Rough Hills estate. We were part of a one-class community. No-one was overtly well off or poor. Dads worked at one of the local factories and moms worked at home, looking after the children and house. If there were any examples of social deprivation on the estate, they were well hidden. Most of my clothes were bought on credit from mail order catalogues: Mom was an agent for Freemans and Grattan and a few of the neighbours would drop around to buy items. I remember most of my clothing with a tinge of embarrassment; the ladies' lingerie pages in the catalogues with teenage affection. A few families had a car but most travelled round by bus. Not everyone had a bike and those that did were happy to share. I learned to ride on a bike belonging to the Bodleys, who lived a few doors down. Only a small number of families enjoyed a week's seaside holiday every year staying in distant resorts like Bournemouth and Torquay where I assumed that the sun shone every day. I recall a couple of holidays in static caravans near Rhyl, but normally the long summer break was interrupted by a day's train excursion to somewhere like Blackpool or Weston-super-Mare. As it provided an opportunity for trainspotting, I was more than happy with the arrangement. I regarded my life as normal, unaware of alternatives; my first few weeks at the Grammar School were to change all that.

The community spirit on the estate is described by Sheila Morris who grew up in Cotswold Road in the 60s.

'I lived at the bottom end of Cotswold Rd. Many of the neighbours, along with my parents had lived there since the houses had been built. I was told that my mum became a bit of an unofficial midwife at one point, after helping to deliver the next door neighbour's baby. In the early days hardly anyone had a car or phone, so when the neighbour went into labour, mum popped round while her husband went on his bike to a phone box to call for the midwife. The baby came quicker than expected of course. After that, when some women went into labour, they fetched my mum for backup. I seem to remember she was also called to be there when neighbours were near to death (although this wasn't spoken

about in front of the children). When I was at primary school, I can remember my mum organising a day out for the children of Cotswold Rd (and one or two from other nearby streets). We went to Southport and it was really exciting. Some of the children never went on holiday, so they really loved it. I helped mum make up little goodie bags of sweets for all the children to take on the coach. Towards the end of the day, we all met up on the beach and played games and had races. Some of the mums took part in a sack race.'

Figure 55: Sheila's mom, Freda Burt, is the 4th lady from the left. The other moms are Rose (?), Margaret Hill, (?) Whicherley, Betty Morris, Connie Shrabonz (no idea of spelling), Edna Cowell and Ivy Jackson.

If you did not want to travel to the shops, there were regular visitors to satisfy your food and drink requirements.

My parents may not have been regulars at the Rough Hills Tavern but they were regulars with the ice cream vendors that visited the estate during the summer months. It did not matter if the van was Mr Softee or Mister Whippy, the chimes from the ice cream van were enough to get them off their armchairs and out onto the pavement. Usually, it was a plain cone but as a treat, we might have a '99' with the stick of chocolate while a special treat was a sundae with a mix of ice cream, syrup and a sprinkling of nutty flakes.

Another regular visitor to the estate was the 'Corona' man who delivered a selection of fizzy drinks in his van. We were big fans and regularly bought bottles of orangeade, lemonade and occasionally dandelion and burdock, a drink which combined a strange colour with an even stranger taste. Full of sugar, flavourings and other additives, they were not a healthy option but sitting in front of the television on a Monday night watching an episode of Wagon Train with a glass of orangeade and sharing a packet of Smiths crisps you were convinced that life could not get any better.

The milk float made his discreet daily deliveries. I have vague memories of the 'rag and bone' man with his horse and cart and instructions from my grandad to collect any horse droppings with a bucket and spade.

In December 1953, the Housing Committee reported an exchange of land covering Rough Hills housing estate between Wolverhampton and Bilston Corporations. Bilston Corporation would receive 1,593 square yards whilst Wolverhampton Corporation would receive 2,325 square yards without payment from either side.

By April 1954, the Housing Committee reported that 294 of the 308 properties had been completed. Kerbing, channelling and flagging of footpaths was now well advanced and the road would be ready for surfacing in the next few weeks. Tarslag Ltd of Wolverhampton had been invited to submit a quotation for the work.

Wolves claimed the league championship for the first time in 1954.

Driven by the slum clearance of areas close to the town centre, the council housing programme of the 1950s attempted to keep pace with a rising housing list and population size. The housing list had climbed to its maximum in 1952 at 6,682 coinciding with the town reaching its highest population of 162,300.

While it was not designated for imminent clearance, land around Steelhouse Lane was bought up in 1959 by Wolverhampton Council in a Compulsory Purchase Order. Most of this area dated back to the 1870s, with the housing dominated by terraced dwellings privately owned by landlords. Jenner Street, Dartmouth Avenue, Granville Street, Eagle Street and Steelhouse Lane, in particular, were identified in the Order. This was to represent a watershed for the immediate area. In the first half of the 1900s, it had developed into a thriving neighbourhood with the Royal Hospital and All Saints Church roughly forming its north and south boundaries. Enclosed within was a community of factories and houses, served by shops, pubs and schools, attracting workers, pupils and families from a wide area.

Margaret Carroll who lived in All Saints Road from 1937 to 1954 recalls life in and around Steelhouse Lane.

Pubs in Steelhouse Lane included The Summer House, which was large and roomy, but could not compare in popularity to The Hen & Chickens in Eagle Street, a very small (originally home-brewed) pub where people would pack in every time they opened. Some of the local women used to fetch their vegetables from Phoebe Buxton's shop in Steelhouse Lane and be banging on the pub doors at midday, where they would shell the peas for lunch! The Why Not at the Bilston Rd end of Steelhouse Lane was also a popular pub and opposite that was Rogers' Fish & Chip Shop, and further along a shop where a lady whose name I have forgotten made large meat pies which you could buy by the portion.

Other shopkeepers in the area were Mr Cooper, Mrs Milroy, All Saints' Road, Emms Newspapers (junction of All Saints Road and Vicarage Road), Mr. Pittaway who was the greengrocer in Vicarage Road. My grandfather, Thomas Bosworth had been moved from his shop in Warwick Street to 4 Mills Close, a private council house, but still continued to sell vegetables from his house and also, after visiting the Wholesale Market at 6.00 am he would continue hawking his vegetables on a cart in the area. He was well-known and I'm sure he must have been breaking every byelaw in the book!

In the area, of course, were the Royal Hospital and a home for single mothers in Sutherland Place. All Saints Vicarage in Vicarage Road eventually became the HQ of Patients Aid Association, nearby was James Baker & Sons (shoemakers) while Nicholls on the Birmingham Road dealt in timber and rope.

Our house, 242 All Saints Rd, was one of three houses built around the turn of the century for the church. 242 All Saints Rd was where I grew up from the age of 4½ until I married at 22. I understand that the houses numbered 241, 242 and 243 were built by the church and I believe that originally they were for curates and clerics of the church, although someone did tell me that Miss Lucy Smith, headmistress of All Saints' School had once resided at 242. We used to attend Sunday School up to the age of 11, in All

Saints' Junior School premises but as we grew older we attended the services in the church.

It was a cross section of families, mainly working-class but proud, some in business or trade and then a few poorer families. I remember our teacher asking boys' mothers if they could fit out one boy who belonged to a large family with clean and tidy clothes for the Maypole and the moms promptly did. They told the boy he could keep them and his mother pawned the whole lot the next day, for drink. The 1950s saw the arrival of Jamaicans, mainly men, who came to work on the menial jobs which our people did not want to pursue. Once a man was established he could then send for his family from Jamaica and the family would then settle into life here. Within a few years, the Asian population began to arrive and many white families moved out. There was a lot of resentment at the beginning because of culture differences. My own mother was horrified to see an Indian neighbour giving birth in the garden! The larger houses became lodging houses where a room was let on a half-day basis. A man working at, say, Goodyear, would do his shift, come home and then get into the bed which had just been vacated by the man on the alternate shift. There was a great deal of exploitation of these people and they had a lot to put up with. By this time, I had left the area (1954) and eventually coloured people became more established in business etc. and many of our old neighbours had moved into more modern houses (though not all).

Colin Jackson lived in Steelhouse Lane (No.187) from 1940 to 1962.

Our house was at the top of Cable St. end opposite Marandola's ice cream works where free broken wafers and biscuits (sometimes) were on offer. Further down Steelhouse Lane there was a small shop in Eagle St that sold vinegar from a barrel. You took your own bottle and they filled it for you.

There were local characters such as Mr Tye, the owner of the off licence at the bottom of Caledonia Rd, who had been head groundsman at the Wolves football ground. Just a short way up Caledonia Rd was a large house and yard which had horses, pigs and chickens owned by Wally Hales and he used to ride on a pony and trap around the streets near us. There was also a well-known lady named 'Nellie Cox who would come from The Summer House pub singing at the top of her voice, to the amusement of us kids.'

Opposite the off-licence was Adeys, a shop remembered affectionately by all workers and schoolchildren on their way to and from Bayliss, Jones and Bayliss' and All Saints School. On one occasion we stole some chocolate from the shop and ate it on the Rec on Pond Lane, the chocolate was called Ex Lax, we found out later that it was a laxative.

The decline of the Steelhouse Lane/ All Saints area was to continue into the mid-60s and beyond. In 1971, to halt further deterioration of the housing properties, the Council designated the zone bounded by Gordon Street, Steelhouse Lane, All Saints Road and Vicarage Road as a General Improvement Area (G.I.A.). This led to the Council investing nearly £350K on the environment and its council-owned housing. However, only 43 out of the 245 properties in the private sector were improved and by 1975, a proposal was put forward to designate it as a Housing Action Area. The report highlighted its scale of deprivation, describing the area as having 'a significant number of social problems which interact with the poor quality of the housing and that these problems are likely to increase.'

While the area around All Saints began its wretched downwards slide, the new estate at Rough Hills quietly bedded in. It is conceivable that the construction of a new estate with over 300 houses and the arrival of approximately 1000 people might have caused tensions amongst the residents of Parkfields and beyond. This was not the case. For residents on the Parkfields estate, the new housing development replaced the eyesore of a derelict landscape and the new network of roads provided a safer, more convenient environment for travelling around the area. In a very short period of time, the residents on the two estates integrated. This was due in part to the Council's failure to build the promised school and shops for the residents. Their shared dependency on All Saints School for education, Rooker Avenue for shopping, and the pubs such as the Rough Hills Tavern for entertainment helped families to mix socially. Many residents gained employment in the nearby factories and found themselves working alongside their new neighbours from Myatt Avenue or Pond Lane. Visually the estates were different but the new estate gelled with the surrounding area. Rough Hills estate was mainly populated by young working-class families, many of whom were moving into their first home as a result of slum clearance or overcrowded accommodation. The lack of new facilities may have caused some initial disappointment but many, like my parents, had been on the council waiting list for several years and were grateful to be in their first new home. These were the families who by 1957 'had never had it so good' according to Harold Macmillan, their Tory Prime Minister; families with two or three young children, the 'baby boomers', who would enjoy greater social mobility and material wealth than their parents could ever have dreamed of.

But what exactly did Rough Hills Estate offer those parents and children who arrived in the early 50s?

24

WORK, REST AND PLAY

Work ...

Three large factories representing the heavy industry that dominated the area were found within walking distance of the Rough Hills estate. They were in alphabetical order: Bayliss, Jones and Bayliss, Stewarts and Lloyds and John Thompson.

Bayliss, Jones and Bayliss

One of the major employers for people living on Rough Hills estate was Bayliss, Jones and Bayliss or BJB, as it was known. Established in 1826, it became a subsidiary of G.K.N. in 1922 but retained its name. By the time I started school in 1954, the firm employed about 1,500 people and occupied a vast expanse of land extending from All Saints to Monmore Green

Figure 56: The BJB magazine.

in one direction and towards Rough Hills in the other. Walking to and from school, it was never out of one's sight. As if to reinforce its presence, the start and finish of each shift was signalled by a siren which echoed around the neighbouring streets.

The post-war period was probably the heyday of the workers' social organisation, with many of the larger employers offering a whole range of activities for their staff. People were likely to spend as much time with their colleagues outside work as they would in work-time and many companies promoted a 'family' identity that would bind staff together. Bayliss, Jones and Bayliss was no exception and it was not unusual to find employees who had worked 30, 40, 50 or even 60 years at BJB.

For people like Val Peel who lived in Pond Lane, Bayliss, Jones and Bayliss was the centre of their social and working life. All her family including grandfather, father, mother and brother had worked there at some point and when she left school, a place was 'reserved' for her. Despite an unhappy and fruitless education at St Mary's and St. John's, Val was encouraged by BJB to enlist at classes at Wulfrun College and gain qualifications which proved invaluable as her career progressed elsewhere.

The company provided for every need. When Val broke her leg as a child in the grounds of the social club, medical care was immediately on hand. She was taken to the company's surgery, given preliminary treatment by the resident matron before being transferred by a BJB van to hospital.

The BJB News magazine, known as 'Under the Clock Tower', came out every month. As well as keeping staff up to date with company news, it contained details of births, weddings and obituaries, plus reports on its clubs and social activities. There were clubs to suit all sporting and leisure interests. Her dad, Noah, was the secretary of the angling club. Known as 'The Vicar', he was a regular contributor to the magazine.

It also catered for their families. There was a Sports and Social Club building in Cable Street which organised regular entertainments at weekends as well as productions by a highly successful drama society. The pantomimes and parties at Christmas for the children were remembered with affection.

Stewarts and Lloyds

The Steel Works at Spring Vale, Bilston went back even further.

With the opening of the Birmingham to Wolverhampton Canal in 1770 industrial activity in the area increased, and by 1780 the first blast furnaces for making iron were in use.

In 1866 the Hickman family acquired the works, then known as the Springvale Furnaces Ltd. It consisted of three square brick furnaces, known locally as 'The Hot Holes'. Between 1866 and 1883 six new blast furnaces were built. The furnaces were hand-fed and the molten iron was run off into pig beds. Despite the crude nature of production, the furnaces were recognised for producing large quantities of iron of a good quality. By the early 1880s five blast furnaces on the site produced 24,944 tons of iron a year. In 1897 the Springvale Furnaces and the Staffordshire Steel & Ingot Iron Co. were amalgamated to become Alfred Hickman Ltd. The site continued to expand and in 1907 the first mills powered by electricity were installed. This was followed in 1911 by the building of an open-hearth furnace. In 1920, the works were sold to Stewarts & Lloyds Ltd.

The Bilston works was a major industrial site and during the Second World War the company was an important shell-making centre. In the early 1950s a £16 million development scheme was put into place. A new blast furnace 'Elisabeth', named after the daughter of the chairman of Stewarts & Lloyds Ltd, was lit in 1954 replacing three smaller blast furnaces. 'Elisabeth' or 'Big Lizzy', as it was known by the workmen, produced 275,000 tons of steel a year and more than 5.5 million tons of pig iron her lifetime. 212 feet in height, it dominated the skyline to the south; the release of smoke and flames into the night sky providing an awesome sight from the safety of Rough Hills estate.

In 1967 the British steel industry was nationalised. The Iron and Steel Act brought into public ownership about 90% of

British steelmaking to form the British Steel Corporation (BSC) and Stewarts and Lloyds became part of BSC in July 1968. With the completion of major redevelopments, the Bilston works became one of the most modern integrated works of its kind in the country.

Some classmates from All Saints left secondary school at 15 years of age to work at Stewarts and Lloyds on the shop floor alongside the furnaces. I knew these were tough, dangerous jobs. You saw the grime on their faces at the end of a shift and imagined the intensity of the heat and white glow from the molten metal. Despite the attraction of beer vouchers to replenish the fluids they lost through sweat, I had no desire to swap my text books for a day at S and L. This is what you passed your 11 plus to avoid.

John Thompson

Another major employer for the residents of Rough Hills Estate was John Thompson. As with Stewarts and Lloyds, it was based outside the original town boundary at Millfields, Bilston. The founder of the company was William Thompson born in 1811 in Wolverhampton. Sometime between 1834 and 1840 William established himself as a boilermaker and maker of canal boats at a works situated on the Birmingham Canal at Highfields near Bilston. When the company got into business difficulties, it was initially taken over by his brother Stephen and then, in 1860, William's son John bought the company from Stephen. At first the company manufactured a variety of items including sheet iron, casks and air pipes for collieries but around 1870 a decision was made to concentrate on the production of steam boilers. A new site was acquired a few miles along the canal at Ettingshall and equipment was moved to the new works by canal boat and hand cart. Rapid expansion followed and Head Offices were built on Millfields Road.

The company was very much a family concern and when John Thompson died in 1909, his sons, William, Stephen John, James and Albert were already taking a leading role. They and their sons in turn, ran, and mostly owned, the company, for much of the twentieth century.

At the start of the twentieth century, the company diversified and began to manufacture chassis frames and pressings for the expanding motor industry. Their products became an outstanding success, supplying frames to just about every car manufacturer, including the local firms: Star Engineering, A. J. Stevens and Turner Manufacturing. In November

Figure 57: Long service medals awarded to members of the Shorthouse family.

1921, it made its first appearance at the London Motor Show. When the Golden Arrow, driven by Henry Seagrave, broke the World Land Speed record in 1929 on Daytona Beach, the vehicle's main frame and sub-frame as well as other components were made by John Thompson Motor Pressings Ltd. Even when car manufacturing in Wolverhampton went into decline, John Thompson maintained strong ties with clients such as Rolls Royce, Rover and Vauxhall. Back in 1908, Thompson's Motor Frame department had supplied the chassis frame of Rolls Royce's first car. Fast forward to 1965 and Motor Pressings works produced the sub-frame and cross-members for the new Rolls Royce Silver Shadow. The company was also involved with other motoring icons like the Land Rover, the London taxi and when the Austin Mini was introduced, Motor Pressings made the suspension struts.

By 1930, the Thompson site covered over 35 acres and employed 3000 workers. It was building a reputation for long service and family traditions: John Thomas Shorthouse, the grandfather of Stella Shorthouse, joined the company in 1893 and went on to work there for over 50 years, earning the company's long service medals after 30, 40 and 50 years. Stella's father, three uncles and brother were to join the company in later years.

During WW11 it was heavily involved in the war effort manufacturing over 35,000 components for aircraft such as the Wellington and Blenheim bombers and the Gloster Gladiator. The John Thompson factory at Dudley produced a great part of the mechanical equipment used at ICI's Trafford Park works in Manchester for the mass production of penicillin, the antibiotic that was to have such a dramatic impact on combating serious diseases.

After the war, the company moved into the construction industry and flourished. By 1947, there were over 6,000 employees and it expanded to the other side of the railway at Ettingshall. By 1953, the John Thompson Ltd site covered 80 acres and the handbook published in that year was subtitled, "We Cover the World" with an overseas presence in Australia, India, South Africa and Brazil. When the first nuclear power stations were built in the 1950s and early 60s at Berkeley, Bradwell and Dungeness, John Thompson Ltd was actively involved as a member of the Nuclear Power Group. The future looked rosy.

My father spent most of his working life at John Thompson and its proximity to Rough Hills was probably a major factor for moving to the estate in 1953. My father's brother, Jim, also spent most of his working life there. Jim had a management role in the Motor Pressings division while Charlie, his other brother, also worked there for many years. Companies like Bayliss, Jones and Bayliss and John Thompson provided not only employment but also sporting and social opportunities for its workers and their families. As well as an athletics ground, there were tennis courts and two bowling greens. My father worked in the Beacon Windows division of John Thompson and played for many years in their football team. I have dim memories of attending their matches at Aldersley. The Sports and Social club also organised coach trips and I particularly remember a visit to Stratford-on–Avon, not for its cultural delights but for the lunchtime stop at Evesham where I reluctantly sampled ox tongue for the first time.

What particularly stick in my memory, however, are the children's annual Christmas parties. The staff canteen was decked out in bunting and we enjoyed an afternoon of food, drink and raucous chatter. Entertainment took the form of cartoons or a film starring the likes of Old Mother Riley. The highlight, however, was the collection of our Christmas present. These were always top notch, heavily subsidised I imagine by the company. Two particular presents stick out in my memory: roller skates which I loved but never mastered and a set of carpentry tools in a sturdy wooden box that I kept and used well into my married life, much to the amusement of my wife and two sons.

There was a long tradition of Christmas parties for the children of John Thompson's employees dating back to 1915.

Stella Shorthouse remembers attending them between 1939 and 1948.

> *I can remember waiting with lots of other children for the doors to be opened so that we could rush in. There were very long tables (canteen tables I suppose) and we were given a paper bag which contained our food. It was very noisy. We sometimes had a magician, Punch & Judy and the John Thompson band. They were very good and played Christmas carols beautifully. Towards the end we formed a line to get our presents. It was very exciting!*

Steelway

In the 1950s, Wolverhampton enjoyed economic prosperity and there were many small and medium sized businesses near the estate providing employment for its residents. One such company was Steelway which occupied a prominent position on Bilston Road at the bottom of Dixon Street. This was a leading engineering and fabrication company and had a significant claim to fame. When the UK's first pedestrian safety barriers were installed at the busy junction of Princes Square in the town, Steelway was responsible for their manufacture.

Midland Tar Distillers

The company which had started on the site almost 100 years earlier as Major and Company finally closed in 1955.

MEB

In the late 1950s the Midlands Electricity Board (MEB) started building their offices, stores and workshops along the Major Street boundary on the site originally occupied by the Midland Tar Distillers. Many problems beset its construction and it finally opened in January 1961.

This was a big bonus as my Mom could walk along to pay the bills – much better than a bus journey to town and a steep walk up and down Darlington Street.

Unknown to the people who turned up to pay their bills, the building was floating on a bed of tar. Staff recall tar seeping through the gaps in the floor. When it closed there was talk of it being converted into a community centre but the unstable foundations made this inadvisable and the building was demolished in the 80s.

Rest

Pubs

Pubs were an important part of the social life on Rough Hills. Four of these 'locals' were the Rough Hills Tavern, Monkey House (Moulders Arms), Black Horse and Silver Birch at the top of Pond Lane. Residents had their personal favourites but by all accounts, they would freely move from one pub to the next. A typical Friday night for Barry Marchant would start his pub crawl with a drink or two at each, finishing off with a bag of fish and chips from the chippy by the Silver Birch pub.

Rough Hills Tavern

The Rough Hills Tavern in Rooker Avenue dates back to at least 1851 and its early history has been described in an earlier section.

The Tavern was again demolished in the 1920s. In August 1926, plans were approved for a new building and it gained its full licence from the Royal Oak, Stafford Street in 1929. By 1939, there were plans to build new premises but these did not materialise and later on, in 1950, another application by Wolverhampton and Dudley Breweries to rebuild the pub was refused by the Town Council and the pub carried on trading.

Margaret Jones who lived in Myatt Avenue from 1942 to 1953 remembers the pub in those days.

The landlord was Mr (Joseph Leonard) Washbrook. The pub had two rooms, a bar and a smoke room with a small garden area outside. The bar was a man's domain and women were not expected to be there. Sawdust was put down on the floor each day and swept out into Rooker Avenue the following morning. Youngsters would search among the sawdust for coins. Couples used the smoke room. In the passage was an 'outdoor' with a serving hatch window for anyone who wanted to buy a drink and take it home.

On a Sunday afternoon, when the pub had closed, some of the men would start an impromptu game of football on the field outside.

Olwen Medlicott lived close to the Rough Hills Tavern in the 1940s but did not frequent the place.

> *.....my friend who lived in Rooker Avenue had a drink in The Rough Hills Tavern with me. We only went the once and we sat in the passage, although I think we were in our 20's at the time, but it wasn't the "Done Thing" for young ladies to drink in Public Houses on their own in those days.*

Carole Bridgen was born in Rooker Avenue in 1945 and remembers that the Tavern held a large party for the local children on the day of the Coronation in 1953.

> *I remember going to the Tavern for the Queen's Coronation. We had a party in the yard and all the children were given mugs full of boiled sweets.*
>
> *I remember that the tavern yard was full of trestle tables and a lot of the children had to bring their own dining room chairs to sit on (because the Tavern hadn't got enough stools). I think maybe at least seventy kids were there.*

Carole has close connections with the pub. Her father looked after the cellars and pipework at the Rough Hills Tavern and on one occasion took a horse into the tavern bar; a talking point with the regulars for quite a while. Her mother worked at the old Tavern and then the new one until she was 72 years old.

My parents were not regular drinkers and did not frequent any of the local pubs. On occasions I would be sent to the 'outdoor' at the Rough Hills Tavern to get a bottle of beer, usually Double Diamond, a bottle of pop, usually lemonade, and a packet or two of crisps, always Smiths with a blue sachet of salt tucked away inside. Life was simple in those days and finding a packet of Smiths crisps with extra packets of salt was deemed a worthy topic of conversation. Empty bottles were

Figure 58: The old and new RH Tavern side by side.

stored as some carried a 3d (1p) refund when you returned them to the pub.

In 1963 it was once again demolished. On a neighbouring site the third Rough Hills Tavern was built in 1964 and a photograph from Peter Phillips shows the old and new pubs side by side. Under the ownership of Wolverhampton and Dudley Breweries, the new building, in the foreground, was designed as a large multi room pub to cater for what had become the large housing estate of Rough Hills.

The pub had a flourishing darts team. George Cartwright was the team's secretary in the 60s and a look at the fixture list from 1966/67 shows a healthy list of competitors such as the Waggon and Horses on the Cannock Road, Ash Tree Inn by Fighting Cocks and the Gate Hangs Well near Sedgley, most of which have gone the same way as the Rough Hills Tavern.

The Moulders Arms (Monkey House)

The Moulders Arms dates back to at least 1860. In 1871 the owner was John Richards and it was run by Richard Knot. In 1892, it was sold to W. Sherwood with the new owner installing G. Till as the new landlord. Following his death in 1896, his widow took over, and then his son from 1909 until 1924. The ownership of the pub had changed in 1900 to Wolverhampton and Dudley Breweries who remained its owners until it was demolished in 1937. It was in the 1930s that the pub earned its nickname as the Monkey House. Two monkeys were kept by the landlord in small cages in the pub garden and children would peep in if the door was open. Its replacement, a much larger pub, was built in 1938 to a design by architect Bertram Butler on the same site, which by then had become part of Kent Road. Like many built in the inter war years, it was an example of the 'reformed' or 'improved' public house which attempted to change the image of drinking and attract 'respectable' customers.

Figure 59: The back of the Monkey House, complete with Adventure playground.

The Monkey House pub was where many of us were introduced to the joys of Banks' beer. An evening session of football on the Dixon Street fields was often followed by an invitation by the older members of the group to try out the Mild and Bitter beers. We each had our favourite for refuelling after a tiring game. Despite the warning that the 'mild' was made from the leftovers, I would happily share a half pint of Banks' finest before setting off home.

Black Horse

The Black Horse was the 'baby' of the three. It occupied a prominent position on Thompson Avenue near to the junction with Dixon Street. It was a large interwar pub built to a plan by architect W. Norman Twist for John Davenport & Co of

Birmingham in 1931 and opened in 1932. However when the pub opened it was as a Mitchells & Butlers house, not Davenport's, as it was difficult to obtain new licences for firms which had no other pubs in the licensing area. It became a very popular pub drawing customers from a wide area. Over the course of the years several alterations, mostly internal, were carried out to cater for more diners and functions on the first floor. Downstairs there was a large but basic bar and a smart lounge which drew big crowds in the evening.

We frequented the Black Horse on a regular basis during the late 1960s. The bar was handy for a drink and a game of cards or dominos. One evening Eddie Clamp, the ex Wolves and England player from the 50s, made an unexpected appearance, playing dominos in the same dour, uncompromising style that had graced football grounds at home and abroad.

The lounge bar was more suitable for impressing a girlfriend. Pub food in the form of scampi (or sausage or chicken) in the basket was yet to make an appearance and your choice was usually limited to crisps, cobs and the delights of pickled eggs. If you were lucky the man from Grimsby Fisheries would appear at some point in the evening, selling packets of cockles, mussels and shrimps, liberally covered with vinegar.

Sport

Monmore Green

Monmore Green Stadium opened on 30 May 1928 as a speedway track with a meeting organised by the Wolverhampton Dirt Track Motor Cycle Club. The sport had originated in Australia and meetings in the UK soon attracted big attendances. The first meeting at Monmore Green drew around 5,000 spectators. Speedway events initially consisted of individual tournaments, scratch and handicap races. The programme for 20 August 1929 announces "the illumination of the track for the first time in Wolverhampton". This floodlit meeting included a team competition between Wolverhampton and Leicester. Each team had four riders; the winner of each race was awarded 4 points while the rider coming

second gained 2 points. Wolverhampton's association with speedway was short-lived and in 1930 the last meeting before the war took place.

Figure 60: Looking across to Monmore Green Stadium from the railway bridge. Taken around 2012.

Speedway did not return to Wolverhampton until 1950 on the back of a post war boom in the sport. A new track was laid down and competitive speedway returned in 1951 with a meeting between Wolverhampton Wasps and Sheffield. The management had wanted to identify the team as Wolverhampton 'Wolves' in line with the football club but the name was already being used by Walthamstow speedway club.

Roy Holloway and his friends were big fans of speedway at the time. He remembers Jimmy Grant and Eric Irons as two of the top riders for the Wolverhampton Wasps. Roy was not content with watching speedway at Monmore Green.

> *We used to catch the train on a Saturday night to watch the (Birmingham) Brummies at Perry Barr. Their top riders included Graham Warren and Alan Hunt who was killed taking part in a meeting in Australia.*

Once again the popularity was short lived and the Monmore Green track closed in 1954. It was not until 1961 that speedway returned to Wolverhampton and apart from a spell in 1982/3 the sport has prospered in the town.

I was introduced to speedway in 1962 by a friend from Cotswold Road, Derek Lawrance. Derek was convinced that I needed to get out more and off we went one Friday evening to the Stadium. At the time, Wolverhampton was in the second tier of professional speedway, the Provincial League. I was told to look out for their star riders: Graham Warren, the 'blond bombshell' in his day, an old campaigner from Australia who just missed out on the world championship in 1950 and Tommy Sweetman, the fans' favourite and a master of the Monmore Green circuit. But my first speedway meeting is remembered not for Graham or Tommy but for the smell of the engine fuel, methanol. This was my first experience of solvent abuse and I was determined to go again.

Before too long, I had been indoctrinated into the rituals of watching speedway: acquire a clipboard for attaching your race programme, take a pencil for filling in the results of each race. No need to arrive too early for the 7.30 start. As you walked over the railway bridge on Sutherland Street at 7.15 you were quite likely to catch one or two riders arriving by car with their bike on a trailer. Many speedway riders were sporting mercenaries, based somewhere in the country, moving from club to club each season and clocking up thousands of road miles as they travelled slowly from venue to venue without the benefit of the network of motorways we now take for granted. Go through the turnstile and buy the programme, and once a month the Speedway Star. Meet up with the regulars, a mix of friends and acquaintances, at your favoured spectator spot. Mine was the enclosure on the far side of the stadium, directly opposite the start/finish line. When it rained, everyone retreated ten yards to take advantage of a sheltered area with a corrugated iron roof. When I now watch the TV coverage on Sky, I notice with disappointment that this section of the stadium has been demolished. By now the ground staff would be raking the track and at 7.30pm the March of the RAF boomed over the tannoy system as the two teams walked out and lined up by the starting tape. The teams were presented to the crowd and the match was ready to commence. Each race provided one minute of gung-ho action: the charge to the first corner where races were won or lost, skirmishes at each corner as riders wrestled with their machines and the cinder track, the sprint down the straights with the roar of the engines almost blocking out the noise of the crowd - plus that all pervading smell of methanol. As each result was announced you wrote the details into your race programme. Between each race there was enough time for a pop single to be played. This was 1962, pre Radio 1, and Friday night at the speedway provided a rare fix of pop music. It was slightly cheaper than an afternoon at Molineux and attended by far more schoolgirls who walked about in small groups, unaware of the races but not unaware of teenage boys. Home teams at a speedway meeting had a clear advantage so victories were taken for granted, unless the opponents were the local rivals, Cradley Heath, the Heathens. Inspired by their captain, Ivor Brown, a close contest was to be expected and *savoured. Brown was instantaneously recognisable with a white jumper worn under his leathers. Idolised by the Heathen fans and reviled by the Wolverhampton faithful, he carried out a one-man campaign to claim victory for his team. Cradley apart, we could expect a match to end with loud celebrations as the team completed their lap of honour in the groundsman's lorry.*

A break in the proceedings ensued and when the gate into the more expensive enclosure by the start line was opened, we wandered across for the second half. It might have a head to head race like the Silver Helmet trophy for the best individual riders but the real highlight would be the reserves' races. These gave newcomers to the sport a chance to show off their skills. A regular at these races had been Howard Cole who rode under the pseudonym of Kid Brodie. Howard was a sixth former at Wolverhampton Grammar School and used the pseudonym to avoid detection by the school staff. As a pupil at the school, I was aware like everyone else of Howard's extra-curricular activities on Friday evenings and I expect the school staff were as well. Kid Brodie went on to enjoy a successful career in the sport, riding in the 1969 World Final held at Wembley Stadium. For us, the real 'star' of these races in the early 60's was a young rider called Fred Priest. We waited in anticipation for Fred. You knew what to expect from Fred and what you got was his inability to complete the four laps of the track. At some point in the race we knew that Fred and his bike would part company. The fall was predictable but it always generated great amusement and thankfully for Fred's self-esteem his helmet and the din from the other bikes blocked out the laughter and jeers. Fred would get up, check for broken bones, dust himself down and take the ride of shame back to the pits. Fred would be back next week and we would be there to share his misery.

The Stadium is also associated with greyhound racing with the first meeting taking place in 1932. Compared to speedway racing the history of greyhound racing at the stadium is less well documented. Dave Simpson who spent much of his childhood living near the Stadium on Bilston Road recalls his father, Jack, who started working as a trainer in the 1940s.

My dad was one of five trainers based at the stadium, the others included Major Baker, Prentice and Brown. Major Baker was ex-military, a distinctive figure around the stadium with his pipe, trilby and knee length leather gaiters. A trainer would have up to 60 dogs under his control, owned by individuals or syndicates. Despite the betting revenue that the sport attracted, trainers did not make a lot of money; probably less than a skilled working man.

Most of the dogs were bred in Ireland and sold to individuals or syndicates in the UK. The dogs would be given trials at a stadium to assess their potential. Some of the trials took place at Willenhall greyhound track on a Monday. The training consisted of trial races for dogs on their own to see if they would chase the electric hare. I saw one young trial dog run out of the trap box. When it got to the first bend, instead of following the hare around the bend, it ran over the rail and straight into the fence. The dog died of its injuries.

Success at the trials was not a guarantee that the dog would do well. Some of the owners operated a ruthless 'payment by results' policy and if their dogs did not race up to their expectations, they were transferred at short notice to another trainer. Prize money went to the owner or syndicate.

The dogs were kept in kennels alongside the stadium and would be walked each day along Bilston Road, Stowheath

Lane and Willenhall Road and back to the kennels. The stadium also employed kennel boys and girls to work alongside the trainers. While the trainer took responsibility for the exercise walk around the streets near Monmore Green, the kennel boys and girls cleaned out the kennels, fed the dogs and walked them inside the stadium. My Dad had three big paddocks which all of the dogs in the kennels were permitted to use for around twenty minutes at a time, allowing them to stretch their legs.

The return of speedway racing to the Stadium in the 50s and then the 60s was greeted with dismay by the trainers. Many dogs were disturbed by the noise of the bikes and consequently they did not get the sleep and rest they required for the next day's racing.

Dog racing night was Thursday and a popular sport in the late 50s, early 60s. The meeting would start at 7 pm and by the time it finished around 9 pm, six or seven buses would have lined up along Bilston road near to my grandmother's house to take people back into town. On Friday nights, racing took place at the Willenhall stadium. That meant the dogs had to be transported to Willenhall for the race meeting and then returned back to Monmore Green Stadium afterwards. The racing life of a greyhound was about five years.

My father continued to work as a trainer up to around 1980 when the stadium owners decided to withdraw all greyhound training from Monmore Green.

... and Play

The area around Parkfields and Rough Hills had found fame not only as a sporting venue but also for producing a number of famous sportsmen.

Jack Holden an international runner who competed for Tipton Harriers trained around the area and both Barry Marchant and Stan Whitmore recall seeing Jack on his training runs along Thompson Avenue.

The Rowley brothers, Jack and Arthur, lived at 83, Myatt Avenue in the 1930s before becoming professional footballers. Jack Rowley scored 211 goals in 424 post war appearances for Manchester United and represented his country 6 times. Their legendary manager, Sir Matt Busby once said, "Jack Rowley would rank as one of the greatest players it has been my good fortune to handle." Arthur Rowley still holds the record as the most prolific goalscorer in English football. In a career spanning 19 years and a total of 619 appearances for West Bromwich Albion, Fulham, Leicester City and Shrewsbury Town, his total of 434 goals surpassed the previous record of 380 by the legendary Dixie Dean. Arthur died aged 76 in 2002.

George Paddock from Thompson Avenue recalls the time he played alongside Arthur Rowley for Dudley Road School in the 1930s.

In 1937, we were winners of a Junior League competition. As the school's right back, I had the pleasure and privilege of playing in the same team. Arthur was captain and could play either in defence or attack, but scoring goals was his forte. I particularly remember one occasion where he took the ball up to the goalkeeper, dummied him and calmly shot into the goal.

Don Howe, who died recently, lived at 82, Thompson Avenue near to the Black Horse pub. Howe spent most of his playing career at West Bromwich Albion, joining the club as a youth player in December 1950. Although he turned professional in November 1952, Howe did not make his first-team debut until 1955. A full back, he played nearly 350 games for the Baggies in twelve years, as well as becoming a regular in the England team, representing his country 23 times including appearances in the 1958 World Cup. On our shopping expeditions to Rooker Avenue in the 50s, we occasionally met Don and made puerile comments about the Baggies in a futile attempt to taunt him. Howe retired from playing and became Arsenal's reserve team coach under Bertie Mee before stepping up to become first team coach after the departure of Dave Sexton in 1968. Arsenal won the elusive 'Double' of league and cup trophies in 1971 with Howe playing a crucial role.

Hugh Porter lived in Rooker Avenue. He was probably the most successful track cyclist of his generation but first represented Great Britain in 1963 on the road. He switched to track cycling and gained selection for the 1964 Olympic Games in Tokyo but was hampered by injury and illness. After winning a gold medal in the track pursuit event in the 1966 Commonwealth Games, he turned professional a year later. Between 1967 and his retirement in 1973 Hugh went on to win four world championship pursuit medals. In recent years he has worked extensively as a TV commentator, covering not only cycling but also speed skating and swimming. His voice became synonymous with the success of the GB track cycling teams in the Olympic Games in Athens, Beijing and London.

In 1965, while still living in Rooker Avenue, Hugh married Anita Lonsborough, a gold medallist in the 200m breaststroke at the Rome Olympics. After their marriage, Anita was employed for a time as a swimming teacher at Regis School and she was a regular companion on the No.30 morning bus from Rough Hills into town.

Dixon Street Playing Fields

Aware of these and other sporting role models, we did our best to emulate them. The Empire and Commonwealth Games of 1958 encouraged us to improve our running skills. I struggled on the sprints by the bus stop in Cheviot Road but was more comfortable with the 'long distance' races around a lap of Cotswold Road and Cheviot Road.

However, come winter or summer, there was only one sport for a Wolverhampton lad to play and that was football. When your local team were league champions, allegedly the best club team in the world, captained by the legendary Billy Wright (captain of his country and the first professional footballer to win 100 caps), the choice was easy. Nobody played rugby and a decent game of cricket was scuppered by the lack of grass and a flat surface. Despite the fact that the pitches on Lawn Road were better, we favoured Dixon Street. As part of the preparation for the construction of the Rough Hills Estate in the 1950s, a considerable amount of levelling had taken place on a triangle of wasteland bordered by Dixon Street, Major Street and Kent Road to set up the Dixon Street playing fields.

Our kit was cheap and cheerful. A leather football, a 'casey', was too heavy and far too expensive so we opted for a red plastic football which was cheaper, easier to kick and more forgiving when you headed it. The commercialisation of football was still decades away so youngsters (and adults) did not wear the latest home or away strip to walk around the streets or play on the park. We dressed for a session of football by putting on a pair of football socks and old shoes. Football boots would have given us better grip on the grass but in those days they were constructed in the style of an alpine walking boot. No danger of broken metatarsals but no chance to show off your latest ball control tricks. Unless there was rain, we made a daily trip up Cheviot Road to the Dixon Street playing field. After a warm up of 'keepy–uppy', we started our favoured game, 'cup ties' with one in goal and three or four outfield players who could only score by heading. The goalposts used by the local Works teams were too big, the goalmouth too hard and bumpy so it was jumpers for goalposts and on-going arguments about dubious goals. 'Cup-ties' relied on spectacular diving headers and acrobatic saves, so we always played over by Major Street near the corrugated iron changing rooms where the only lush stretch of grass was to be found. On a warm day, thirst was quenched by visits to one of the local shops on Steelhouse Lane, Dixon Street or even Rooker Avenue. If possible we bought a frozen Jubbly – 3 pennies worth of orange heaven. The juice was sucked from the ice and before too long your tongue and lips were numb. A particular highlight was to wait for juice to melt and collect in the triangular carton. Then, with huge pleasure, it was poured down the throat – pure magic.

We only played in Cheviot Road on occasions. The goals were the width of the road so matches tended to be high scoring with regular interruptions by the number 30 bus and

Figure 61: Dixon Street playing field in 2012,
much improved since the 1950s.

other traffic. As a result, such games were discouraged by our parents. The other recreation area was the garages behind Cheviot Road. There were spaces for about twenty cars but not many residents owned cars and games of football, cricket and cycle speedway were not usually interrupted by traffic. The downside was the surface of rough cinder which shortened the life expectancy of the plastic football and did no favours for your knees if you fell over.

As we grew older, we moved on to setting up matches on Dixon Street or joining in an established one. We chose sections of the playing field with a reasonable amount of grass; not always easy. The proper goalposts were rarely used. In the best traditions of childhood football, jumpers were used for the goal posts and a sense of fair play was used to judge disputed goals. To join in a game, the unwritten rule was to turn up in pairs. We all knew each other's ability and that same sense of fair play which was used for goal decisions was used to maintain two fairly equal sides. More often than not the game would start with a small number which increased as the match and day progressed. Newcomers were rarely turned away. The rules were simple: no offside (but 'goal hangers' were frowned upon and likely to become social outcasts); first to five, ten or some random number depending on the length of the game. Once we started, we played till we 'ran out of steam' but more often

271

than not it was meal time, fading light or 'curfew time' that dictated when we drifted away. As the days shortened, evening games were played alongside Major Street with the street lights providing our floodlights as dusk approached.

Games could materialise at any day or time in the week but in the early 1960s Sunday afternoons often became a focal point for the big game. After finishing their roast dinner, folk from far and wide would congregate on Dixon Street and a game would unfold. High on the list of memories would have to be the occasional influence of the Alan Freeman 'Pick of the Pops' radio show. This was pre Radio 1 days and it was arguably the only genuine pop programme on BBC radio. A 'trannie' (transistor radio) was positioned behind one of the goals and at 4 o'clock, the programme's signature tune started up. Alan Freeman or 'Fluff' as he was to be known in later years, began by playing the new songs which were ready to 'burst into the top 10'. At 4.30, he started the countdown of the nation's top 10. The momentum of the match slowed down as music and football competed for our attention. Some would ignore the ebb and flow of the match completely and take up a convenient position near to the radio. Fluff cranked up the tension and we had the countdown leading up to the top three. Would Elvis stay at No.1 for the fifth week with 'Return to Sender' or would one of the new British groups spoil the party? There was time for one final countdown from Fluff before the all-important No.1 was played to a background of jeers or cheers with a few singing along. Fluff bade his farewells, the signature tune died away, the radio was switched off and normal service was resumed on Dixon Street.

In 1963, Wolverhampton Wolves won speedway's Provincial League. Inspired by our heroes at Monmore Green, the main summer sporting activity around 1963 to 1965 became cycle speedway rather than cricket. As the football pitch alongside Kent Road lacked any significant amounts of grass, its conversion to a cycle speedway track rather than a cricket pitch was relatively easy. The design of the cycle speedway bike was unique with 'cow horn' handlebars, no brakes and 2 to 1 gearing There were some very expensive cycle speedway bikes for sale but I can recall only one lad, Tony Marandola, with one. Most of us acquired an old discarded bike and customised it. Dugmore's on Bilston Road could provide the parts and fit the gearing. Cycle speedway was not only tough on your knees and elbows, it was very tough on the bike and your pocket money. If wheels and pedals came together, it was a major repair job for the spokes. Some people used Dugmore's for repairs but we started to frequent someone off Steelhouse Lane who did the repair for a fraction of the cost.

We were not the first youngsters to be inspired by the Wolverhampton club. Roy Holloway and his friends took up cycle speedway in the 50s in the wake of the return of speedway to Monmore Green.

We had already got bikes to get around on but we had to have another bike to use as a track bike so we went around scrounging old bike frames and other parts, some we had to buy to make a bike up, then we made a rough track with half enders for the inner and outer perimeter. We used to get plenty of spectators as they were walking up and down Parkfield Road. We had two teams of eight, A and B teams, and called ourselves Parkfield Panthers. On most occasions we rode against each other. The sport was catching on and although there was no league we rode against other teams in the area such as one from Windsor Avenue near Coalway

Road and another from Goldthorn Hill. We also had another track behind The Ash Tree. On the back wheel you had a twenty-two tooth cog and a 44 tooth chainwheel on the front to make it a lower gear so it would be easier to pedal to get around the track.

One day a bloke out of Buller Street approached us and told us he had connections with Monmore Green and would we like to appear on Monmore Green track on one of the Friday nights during the interval. Of course we jumped at the chance and I was one of the lucky eight who was chosen to go round the track in a cycle speedway one lap race. I forget where I came, I wasn't first but the bike being in a low gear made it all the harder to get around because it was a big track.

The popularity of cycle speedway took off in the late 50s. The British Cycle Speedway Federation (BCSF) had formed in London in 1958 and the sport flourished across the country. Wolverhampton was no exception and teams such as Dixon Street Demons, Monmore Green Demons and Wolverhampton Wolves were formed in the early 60s. The most successful was probably Wolverhampton Wolves who raced in the Birmingham League, winning the Beehive Shield in 1962. Their first track was at Inkerman Street near New Cross Hospital but as the surface deteriorated they moved on to other venues including Dixon Street. The local star was undoubtedly Arthur Price who lived in Dixon Street. Arthur went on to enjoy a successful speedway career, signing for Wolverhampton Wolves in 1968 before riding for Cradley Heath in the 1970s, and representing England in three internationals.

Rough Hills estate also has connections with one of the most successful cycle speedway teams in the country, Wednesfield Aces. It was founded in March 1962 by two schoolboys, one of whom was Paul Bodley who had lived on the Rough Hills Estate in Cheviot Road until 1960 and was one of our 'gang'. The club won the Wolverhampton league in 1968 and were British League Champions for the first of many times in 1972.

The Air Raid Shelter

This was your standard one storey, brick built construction which provided refuge during the air raids that Wolverhampton, for the most part, thankfully avoided. Despite the proximity of the estate to factories like Bayliss, Jones and Bayliss, there were no major incidents.

Carole Bridgen remembers 'playing hide and seek in the old shelter and having gang meetings in there'.

Our gang, a few years later, were not so confident. We were wary of what lay inside and generally avoided stepping beyond the entrance, the gateway to darkness. On occasions you were pushed inside by someone older or stronger but you immediately ran out: your worst nightmares were hiding inside.

Even the fear of the Cold War was insufficient to justify its existence for some residents who wanted it knocked down as soon as possible. Many complained to their local MP, Mr Enoch Powell, who put his concerns about racial harmony to one side and ensured that it was demolished once and for all in the 1960s.

Bayliss, Jones and Bayliss Sports Ground

If you wanted to play on a decent football or cricket field, the only place to go was the Sports ground belonging to Bayliss, Jones and Bayliss.

Positioned on the corner of Steelhouse Lane and Major Street, its impressive sports ground was built around 1950 on the site of allotments. It had a pavilion and pitches for football and cricket that a youngster brought up on the Dixon Street playing fields could die for. These were flat and grassy, our 'Lords' in the summer and 'Wembley' for the rest of the year. In reality, the ground was only open when the BJB teams were playing so the best you could do was to play on the outfield. Even the outfield was well maintained and it was probably the best and safest place to play cricket. Safe in the sense that the cricket ball would not rear up erratically as it did on Dixon Street and leave an imprint on your temple. For that reason, I recall that most of our cricket activity was played on the Lawn Road playing fields alongside the Rough Hills Tavern where the patches of grass exceeded the patches of bare earth. By the time I was about 10 my cricketing hero was Peter May and I happily became a glory hunter, following the fortunes of Surrey CCC via the Express and Star. Prompted by my mounting interest in the game, my parents bought me a 'Richie Benaud' bat from Beatties in town, a big extravagance in retrospect, and later on some proper stumps. I do not recall any organised competitive matches like we had for football. A small group might assemble and you took your turn to bowl two or three overs or to bat until you were dismissed or everyone got fed up with your defensive prods. Otherwise you stood around as a fielder. We still kept to a tennis ball unless older lads brought

276

along a cork cricket ball and tried to flatten us. 'Bodyline' bowling was alive and well around Rough Hills and my interest in cricket never matched my passion for football.

East Park

Wolverhampton's first large park, West Park, had opened in 1881 and there was pressure from the public and local politicians for a similar park to serve Wolverhampton's 'east end'. In 1892 Sir Alfred Hickman and the Duke of Sutherland each donated 25 acres of land between Willenhall Road and Monmore Green to the Corporation. The park would provide 'good open spaces' which were 'of great advantage .... to the working classes'.

As with West Park, the council held a competition for the design, but all the entries far exceeded the budget allowed for the project. One design by Thomas Mawson did, however, catch the eye of the judges. Mawson had recently completed two public parks in the Potteries, and was to become recognised as one of the outstanding landscape designers of his time. The council decided to use his basic concept and retained his services to assist the Borough Surveyor in the development of the final scheme. Mawson remained closely involved with the project by attending site inspections, and was a guest at the opening ceremony.

The final design showed 11 acres of sports grounds, a children's play area, an open air swimming pool, a lodge, toilets and areas of shrubberies and flower gardens. The crowning glory was a 10-acre boating lake. A bandstand was also erected in the park, paid for from the proceeds of the annual floral fete. It was a difficult scheme to implement with the site consisting largely of collapsed and exhausted mine workings of the former Chillington Colliery. Considerable reclamation was required and the old mines were filled in with 14,787 loads of soil brought by rail from the nearby excavations at the Great Western Railways works at Oxley. Eventually on 21 September, 1896, crowds gathered on a rainy afternoon to witness the grand opening by Alderman Dickinson.

The East Park, as it became known, was beset with problems from the outset. To reach the main entrance from the Willenhall Road required a walk of over 200 yards across rough ground, ankle deep in dust in the dry weather and deeper still in mud in the wet. The lake, however, created the biggest setback. Even during construction there were issues with leakage into old mine workings and, despite efforts to retain levels, the lake gradually disappeared. The loss of the lake was a major blow to its popularity and East Park never gained the same success as its western counterpart.

The area surrounding the park was not developed with housing until the middle years of the 20th century, and there was a revival in its fortunes in the post war period when a paddling pool and new sports facilities were introduced to serve the new housing estates which had grown up around the park.

In the mid-1960s, Jack Nicklaus was our golfing hero and East Park was where we went to recreate his magic. Its pitch and putt course became our par 72 championship course. With no hole longer than 75 metres, many considerably shorter and some little better than crazy golf in construction, its similarity to a proper golf course was non-existent. This did not spoil our enjoyment and armed with a couple of clubs, a few tees plus a scorecard and pencil, we made our way around the course. For one hour or so we played with full commitment; good shots were acknowledged but no holes were conceded and scorecards were checked. The 'outstanding' golfer was Sid McDonald and the rest of us challenged for second place. We talked of travelling to Bantock Park which had a more challenging pitch and putt course but we never quite made it. We weren't that serious about golf.

Phoenix Park and the 'Range'

Phoenix Park did not exist as such in the 1950s or 60s. The area it now occupies was a wasteland of brooks, weeds and one prominent water filled quarry. Linked to an industrial heritage covering 150 years, the Park has been a site for coal mining, clay extraction, brick manufacture and land fill. The earliest plans dating back to 1842 show the site consisting of fields with a few pools next to the hamlet of Blakenhall, formed at the crossroads of the Dudley and Parkfield Roads. By 1884 the area was within the bounds of the Cockshutts colliery. The 1887 Ordnance Survey shows a heavily worked area of pits, shafts and old workings interspersed with small enclosures. By the turn of the century there were two brick works extracting the marl and clay deposits present on the site. These developed into the Phoenix Brick and Tile works and the Premier Tile works. Some records claim that mining continued until 1922 with approximately 31 shafts across the site of Phoenix Park.

There were things you did not tell your parents about. One was playing around any railway line or canal. This was described earlier. Another was playing on the 'canyons' behind Thompson Avenue, on the site of what is now Phoenix Park. The 'canyons' were a set of deep pits, some of which were filled with water.

Bearing in mind that none of us could swim, the place stank and rats scurried about, it is hard to work out its attraction. Nevertheless, we were drawn to similar spots near Monmore Green and behind Parkfield Road and they became one of our adventure playgrounds.

The 'canyons' had been an adventure playground for youngsters for many decades. George Paddock from Thompson Avenue remembers his 'gang' making good use of them in the 1930s.

Our gang, boys only, was led by Ronnie Richard Hill. We spent a lot of time there: fishing in one of the pools for sticklebacks with a line, matchstick and worm or just chucking stones at each other. We camped overnight on one occasion to the amusement of passers-by and a game of cricket was in full swing by 6.30 in the morning.

Roy Holloway also remembers using the area as an adventure playground in the late 40s, early 50s when he was a lad.

There was a path from Dudley Road, almost opposite Wanderers Avenue where I lived, across to the Black Horse pub. As you made your way across, there were vivid reminders of its industrial history. Near the end of Phoenix Street was one of the 'canyons'. This particular one was not flooded with water and had a wooden frame which I presumed was the remains of a horse gin, a legacy from its mining past. Near to this canyon, the ground was covered in roof tiles with Premier embossed on them. The Premier Tile Works was one of two tile making factories which occupied the area. The other one, the Phoenix Brick and Tile works which is clearly seen on photographs taken in 1927, had been demolished and I have no recollection of the building. Back towards the Ash Tree pub was a water-filled 'canyon'. Alongside Parkfield Road, near to the cycle speedway track we constructed, was located the most prominent 'canyon' known as Washbourne's pool, a good place for catching tadpoles.

By the mid 1960s the 'canyons' were landfilled after which the site was capped and covered in a thin layer of soil. This allowed for the establishment of Phoenix Park which took its name from the brick works, originally situated on Phoenix Street at the north end of the Park.

Adjacent to Phoenix Park near the start of Cockshutts Lane are the remnants of the Jewish Cemetery and Chapel which lie hidden behind a high brick wall and locked gates. The tithe map of 1842 shows the site before the development of the cemetery. A long thin strip of land, numbered 1014, is shown running east-west. It is described as 'Slang at Blakemore', a slang being a long, narrow strip of land. It was

Figure 62: Phoenix Park - the Dudley Road entrance

presented to the Jewish community in 1851 and while the owner of the land was the Duke of Sutherland and the occupier John Underhill, there is some suggestion that it was donated by the Duke of Cleveland. The building first appears on the

1887/88 OS maps and is first labelled as 'Jews B(urial) G(round)' on the 1902 OS map. An inscription attests to the fact that 'new walls and buildings (were) erected in the year 1884 and the 'Ohel cum Bet taharah' (chapel cum mortuary) was erected by Jonas Hart May in 1906'. The Jews 'had each to subscribe a large amount in order to encompass it with a high wall'. The original 'slang' was around 280m length and 12m width but only the easternmost 90m was given for the cemetery. The earliest grave stone to survive is dated 1851, and the last burial took place in 1993.

On occasions we ventured even further to the 'Range': open fields beyond Parkfield Road and Fighting Cocks near to the Park Hall Hotel. It gained its name from being a First World War rifle range, also used by the Home Guard during WW2. We never found any old .303 shells but we did find many fossils in an old limestone quarry. The 'Range' almost marked the edge of our known world and we walked there with some trepidation. It was worth the journey. This was a proper adventure playground with trees, hedgerows and fields galore providing endless possibilities for hiding, chasing and playing at war games. It was a long trek to get there and by the time we arrived, it was almost time to go back before any parent noticed our disappearance. We were too young to take proper advantage of the 'Range'.

Years later the 'Range' took on another, less attractive, identity as it was used by the Grammar School as its venue for the Inter-House cross–country races, with a punishing uphill finish by the Park Hall Hotel to complete the annual challenge.

Scouts and Guides

Personally unaware of its existence, many youngsters from the area were attending Scout, Cubs, Guides or Brownie groups based at St. Martin's church. The Scouts' section was set up by two local men, George Paddock and Bill Leighton. It was a very successful troop with Bill acting as George's assistant. When the cub master left, George was asked to take over leaving Bill in charge of the scouts. Bill Leighton from Blakenhall recalls the start of the troop.

Having left Graiseley School in 1950, I started a 5-year apprenticeship at John Thompson. Not long afterwards a chest X-ray revealed that I had contracted pulmonary tuberculosis (TB). This took me completely by surprise as I considered myself fit, being very keen on cycling. During my convalescence I was visited by Father Parker from the church. I had never shown any special interest in religion but his visits made a big impression and when I recovered from the illness, I began to attend the church on a regular basis. I was in my early teens when I was politely 'press-ganged' by the Father into helping to set up a Scout Troop in 1956.

There was sufficient interest in the neighbourhood for scouts, cubs, guides and brownies' sections to form and it soon took over my life, outside of work.

The scout section met on Mondays. Regular weekend visits were made to Patshull Park or to the county site at Beaudesert. During the school holidays, we ventured further afield with camps lasting one or two weeks in National Parks such as the Lake District. Most 'recruits' came along voluntarily but I remember one lad who turned up around 1959 with his probation officer. The officer said the boy needed some 'direction' in his life. We got off to a bad start with the lad showing me his knowledge of the 'f' word and me demonstrating the power of the slipper. However, scouting provided a positive outlet for the lad and a few years later I proudly accompanied him to London to receive his Queen Scout award.

The photograph below was taken in 1960 and shows Bill, second from the left, with a group of scouts showing off their certificates. Bill maintained a long involvement in scouting at St. Martin's. Having started as an assistant to the Scout Leader, he became a Scout Leader himself and later a Group Scout Leader. The Scout Troop was eventually disbanded in 1992.

Figure 63: Bill Leighton, second from left with a group of scouts.

25

WOLVERHAMPTON AND ROUGH HILLS FROM 1971 TO 2015

THE END

Factories

The iconic factories which dominated the skyline around the estate no longer exist. Bayliss, Jones and Bayliss, Stewarts and Lloyds and John Thompson provided a protective arm around the estates of Rough Hills, Parkfields and Pond Lane and while they may have created the noise and air pollution that blighted the area, they were also the sources of income and stability for so many of the families on the estates.

Bayliss, Jones and Bayliss

In 1968, the company was rebranded as GKN Machinery Ltd and despite losing its name, there was justifiable optimism amongst the workforce. Significant investment had updated the buildings and plant equipment and the company became engaged in the design, development and manufacture of a wide range of new engineering products.

By the 1980s it became another casualty of the government's economic policies. GKN decided to close the steel side of the business and the works were sold. To look at the remains of BJB is to look at the industrial decline of Wolverhampton. The majority of the buildings have been demolished particularly on the site of the Monmore Works where an open vista across to All Saints church is broken only by the drifts of wild flowers. In their place are industrial and commercial units scattered piecemeal across the landscape.

Stewarts and Lloyds

By the late 1970s steel production in the UK had become uncompetitive and factories like the one at Bilston were increasingly expensive to run. On 12 April 1979 the last steel billet was cast at Bilston, ending more than 200 years of iron and steel production on the site. Eighteen months later, on 5 October 1980 the last blast furnace affectionately known as 'Big Lizzie', was demolished. It would no longer light up the winter sky; a boost to cleaner air around Rough Hills but a major blow to employment and the economy of the area.

John Thompson

Increased competition from abroad, the government cutback on nuclear power stations, over-manning and increasingly outdated manufacturing practices were some of the factors cited for the decline of the company in the 1960s. In 1970 the Thompson family relinquished control of the Thompson organisation. They had always been well regarded by the workforce and viewed as courteous, formally friendly and approachable. Members of the Thompson family were affectionately known by employees as Mr Pat, Mr Jack and Mr Chris. Bill Leighton remembers how the company kept his job open for 18 months as he slowly recovered from TB.

The first merger resulted in Clarke Chapman – John Thompson Pressings Division Ltd, the family name relegated to second place. Redundancies, up to then a comparative rarity in the organisation, followed. Over the next three decades the company became caught up in a complex series of amalgamations, conglomerates and financial manoeuvrings. Other players in this economic merry-go-round included Rockwell Standard of America and the Parkfield Group, an engineering and entertainment company based not locally but in Surrey. The failure of its entertainment division in 1990 led to the company going into receivership. A management buyout and the creation of United Pressings and Fabrications Ltd (UPF) followed. A recovery ensued but despite ongoing contracts for Land Rover's Discovery and Vauxhall's Frontera, problems mounted in the late 90s. GKN stepped in during 2002 but it was another false dawn. The Ettingshall works closed in 2004 bringing to an end the Thompson enterprise as well as GKN's equally long association with the Black Country.

On 20 January 2008, a church service was held at St. Leonard's church, Bilston to celebrate the substantial contribution that the company had made to Britain's industry and the local area. A former company chairman, Christopher Thompson (Mr Chris), joined over 100 former employees to attend the service: a mark of their respect for the Thompson family, the company and its achievements.

Churches

Parkfield Road Methodist Church

In its centenary year in 1975 the church was said to be thriving but by 1990 it had ceased to be used as a place of worship. It has recently reopened for worship as the All Saints Bethel United Church of Jesus Christ Apostolic.

All Saints

The church has undergone major changes since 1990. Its main body, the nave, has been redesigned to provide a number of facilities for holding meetings and houses the All Saints Community Centre. The eastern part is still used exclusively for worship.

Figure 64: The west end of All Saints church and community centre.

St Martin's

Unlike the other two churches, it has a relatively short history dating back to 1939. It is an Anglo-Catholic church and advocates the Forward in Faith movement which is opposed to the ordination of women as priests or bishops.

Bill Leighton has been the churchwarden periodically since the 1950s. Now in his 80s, Bill has seen a steady decline in the congregation with around 25 now attending the services. It acts as a base for clubs such as the 'over 50s' which provide some income for the church. Nevertheless, it is in urgent need of investment with the removal of asbestos an immediate priority.

Schools

All Saints School

It was still functioning as a school in 2002. The photograph taken in that year shows a group of pupils standing outside what would have been the Infant section when I started school in 1954. I

Figure 65: All Saints School, taken in 2002.

suspect this building was the original Boys school opened in 1895. Out of sight, to the left of the old Infant building is the larger, taller Junior School building, presumably the 'new premises' of 1894, housing Girls and Infants in separate departments. Car parking for staff and visitors now occupied the space used in my day as playgrounds.

The failure of Wolverhampton Corporation to build a new Infant School next to the estate and to rebuild All Saints School on a new site near Pond Lane meant that children from Rough Hills estate continued to make the long trek across Dixon Street playing fields and down Steelhouse Lane for the next 40 odd years. The legacy of the Reverend Henry Hampton lived on until July 2002 when the school closed and its pupils transferred to Grove Primary School in Caledonia Road. This brought to an end nearly 140 years of education on or near the site of the converted barn in Steelhouse Lane.

Thankfully, the Junior and Infant School buildings, along with ancillary buildings, survive. Following major refurbishment, it reopened as The Workspace in 2009. This community enterprise owned by All Saints Action Network provides office and conference facilities for local and national businesses.

Shops

On a visit in 2012, the shops in Rooker Avenue were being renovated, with scaffolding and skips in evidence. When I

Figure 66: Rita and Winnie's
Fruit and Veg shop

returned the following year, the scaffolding that had shrouded many of the businesses had been removed. There was nothing to ring the nostalgia bells except for the signage of V.E. Cotton, the greengrocer shop run by Rita and Winnie during my childhood. Its shop window was caught in a 50s' time warp while on either side you looked for signs of familiarity. However, Alf's butcher shop was now a Chinese, Cantonese, Thai food Takeaway. Before the advent of Vesta foods in the 1960s, very few of us would have considered eating foreign foods. I remember the cooks at the Grammar School offering a curry dish in the early 60s; the food went back to the kitchens barely touched. The shop where Mary sold sweets was now selling keys, while pizzas were now available where the cobbler would once have repaired our worn shoes.

Pubs

One might have expected there would be sufficient demand for at least one of the pubs to survive but they have gone the way of so many other city centre and neighbourhood pubs across the country. While the shells of these derelict buildings still exist, a visual reminder is left of when they were an integral part of the estate.

Rough Hills Tavern

Figure 67: The Rough Hills Tavern shortly before demolition.

It would trade for another 42 years before it closed its doors in October 2006 and was boarded up, its future uncertain. An application was granted in 2007 to demolish and erect 7

291

houses, a three storey building containing 6 apartments and a bungalow. A further application in 2008 to build a care home was granted. Neither of these plans proceeded and in 2014 Bromford began a housing development that now extends from Rooker Avenue across the 'patch' to the site of the garages behind Cheviot Road. More about the outcome of that development later.

Monkey House

In 2007 it officially changed its name to the Monkey House only to close a year later in August 2008 when it was boarded up and put up for sale for £650,000. The following year, it suffered internal damage caused by a fire started by vandals. It was sold and an application to demolish and build four homes for adults with learning or physical disabilities on the site was granted in November 2009. Work unfortunately did not commence.

In the last five years, the derelict site has continued to be targeted by arsonists but fast forward to August 2015 and another planning application has been submitted to Wolverhampton council to convert the pub into two care homes at a cost of £3M.

Black Horse

From 2000 onwards a change of ownership and management resulted in a decline in trade. After the closure of the nearby Silver Birch pub it appears that anti-social customers moved to the Black Horse, causing problems for the local residents and a further decline in its fortunes. Matters became so bad that an application was made by the police to revoke its licence. This

Figure 68: The site of the Black Horse, following demolition.

was granted and the pub closed in June 2006. The building was submitted for listing in 2008 but the application was turned down by English Heritage. Sitting on a large site the pub was sold for £550K. The new owners submitted a planning application to demolish and build houses and flats which was refused. The pub suffered fire damage in 2009 and, amid concerns for safety of the building, permission was given to demolish it shortly afterwards. A new plan to build a small development of private housing on the site was granted in May 2010 and this has recently been completed.

EPILOGUE

Figure 69; A familiar view: looking down Cheviot Road from Dixon Street.

It would be easy to finish on a downbeat note, but as I drove down Cheviot Road with my son on our annual pilgrimage to Molineux in 2016, it was clear that the estate was in good shape. Sixty years on since they were built, the houses were all occupied, clearly in sound condition; a testament to the builders in the 1950s and their occupants and, dare I say it, the 1980 Right to Buy legislation. Many front gardens were now paved to accommodate the family car but those that existed were well maintained. A number of the houses had garage extensions where space permitted.

At the bottom of Cheviot Road, I turned into Rough Hills Road. A Council office now occupies a position at the top of the road. Moving onto Rooker Avenue, there was a sad inevitability about the new building development which came into view. Rough Hills Tavern, a sorry site to behold since I started researching the book, had finally been demolished. In its place a small housing

Figure 70: The Bromford housing development on the site of the Rough Hills Tavern.

development by Bromford Housing Group Ltd filled the land between Rooker Crescent and Rough Hills Close. A new road, Tavern Close, had been constructed which will remind later

Figure 71: The site of garages, football matches and 'dens' behind Cheviot Road in 2013.

generations of the original beer house from 1860 and the community pubs that succeeded it.

My other disappointment in 2013 had been to see the garages behind 48 Cheviot Road cleared away and the ground a wasteland of weeds. One year later and closer examination revealed that the new houses actually extended back to the site of the old garages behind Cheviot Road and the eyesore I had viewed in 2013 had been replaced by a small development of 'affordable homes' for rent. Moreover, a stunning set of mosaics, created by a local artist

Claire Cotterill, were installed around the development, celebrating its industrial and sporting past. Indeed, among the figures in the mosaics were two runners and a cyclist on a penny farthing: a fitting reminder

Figure 72: The mosaics by Claire Cotterill

of the Victoria Grounds that occupied the site of the new homes.

Opposite Tavern Close, Lawn Road playing fields looked slightly neglected but the same could not be said of the Dixon Street playing fields at the end of Rooker Avenue. The area has been landscaped with trees which are close to reaching

Figure 73: Dixon Street playing fields – fencing long overdue.

maturity. A measured walkway wound around the edge of the fields closed off by a smart perimeter fence. If only it had been in place in the late 1960s when a young lad from Rough Hills Close chased a football onto Dixon Street and was fatally injured by a passing police car. The land had far more grass than I remember from the 50s and 60s and was crying out for groups of youngsters to set up games of football or cricket. Near the Monkey House the corner of the playing field was occupied by an adventure playground. I hoped the local youngsters respected these facilities and used them with the same enthusiasm that we would have done. Wearing my rose tinted glasses, I am convinced the estate had more vitality then: a young estate with young families who worked hard in the factories and played hard in the pubs and sports fields that surrounded the estate.

And where does the estate and its surroundings fit into the city nowadays? When I passed on my home details at the start of each academic year at the Grammar School, the form teacher would inevitably ask where the estate was. An address in Finchfield would not have created that annual bout of embarrassment. If one assumed that its profile, low in the 50s and 60s, could only rise, one would be incorrect. Rough Hills continues to sit below the radar of most Wulfrunian's awareness. Lying between the route of the Metro and the start of the Birmingham New Road there are no obvious reasons for non-residents to divert there. The original Wolverhampton Marathon route would once have taken thousands on an annual trip along Thompson Avenue and down Dixon Street. Unfortunately, major industry, the MEB offices, the pubs and the sports pitches which in the past may have drawn visitors, even temporarily, to the area are gone.

A large sign at the junction of Dixon Street and Major Street informs visitors that the estate was now on the edge of the ABCD regeneration zone, the All Saints and Blakenhall Community Development Partnership, set up in 2001 to provide improved services and a better environment within which to live and work. However, its big hope for regeneration recently received a major blow when the landmark redevelopment of the Royal Hospital site in Cleveland Road as a supermarket was abandoned by Tesco. Given their financial predicaments, Tesco's scheme, proposed way back in 2000 to include additional shops as well as offices and community facilities, is unlikely to restart in the near future. Described recently in The Guardian as 'Wolverhampton's red-light district' the All Saints neighbourhood in 2014 desperately needs economic and social support. One's mind goes back to the 1860s when the Rev. Hampton established a Mission church for the area, saying it was 'not really decent for a woman with any sense of propriety to walk down Steelhouse Lane' and inevitably one reflects on whether the wheel of history has turned full circle.

I read through the Black Country Core Strategy, adopted in February 2011, with its detailed proposals for Regeneration Corridors and Strategic Centres and my fears about Rough Hills' identity are confirmed. Rough Hills and Parkfields apparently form part of Regeneration Corridor 4 in this scheme but at no point in this section of the document does it mention the estates or even the areas by name. Nevertheless, there are grand plans for this specific corridor with the creation of 2,180 family homes in 'Aspirational Canalside Suburbs'. It proceeds to say: 'By 2026, one third of the large swathe of industrial land stretching along the canal between Wolverhampton City Centre and Bilston Town Centre will have been transformed into new residential communities, continuing the metamorphosis that began when the collieries and foundries dominating this area

were redeveloped at the beginning of the 20th century.' An incentive, indeed, to be around in another ten years and evaluate the success of this laudable vision.

Figure 74: ABCD and other acronyms.

In the meantime, I am

reminded that Wolverhampton City Council has built its first new set of council housing for 30 years. It chose a site behind Thompson Avenue, between Dixon Street and Silver Birch Road. Forty new council homes form part of a development which also incorporates 80 private houses. By coincidence, the completion of these council houses in 2015 almost marks the centenary since council house building started in Parkfield Road, a stone's throw away. More importantly, it means the last of those parcels of land that made up the pits, furnaces, spoil heaps, houses and gardens of Rough Hills and Cockshutt has been developed. The final piece in the 1842 Tithe jigsaw has been put into place.

BIBLIOGRAPHY

Maps

1750   Plan of Wolverhampton surveyed in MDCCL
by Isaac Taylor

1775   Yates. W, A Map of the County of Staffordshire.

1788   Godson, Plan of the Township of Wolverhampton

1827   Wallis, Map of Wolverhampton

1831   Lt Robert K Dawson, Reform Act Survey
Plan of Wolverhampton

1842   Wolverhampton Tithe Map and Award.

1850   Bridgen, Plan of the Township of Wolverhampton

1855   Henery, J D, Plan of the Township of Wolverhampton

1852   Map produced in connection with Health of Towns Act

1864 Peel & Cobbett map

1871 Steen & Blacket, Map of Wolverhampton

1884 John Steen's Map of Wolverhampton

1884 Ordnance Survey 1st edition, 25" (Staffs) LXII.10 & LXII.11

1886 First edition 1:500 series, Staffordshire Sheet LXII (10.2, 11.6, 11.7, 11.11)

1888 Ordnance Survey (1887/88) Staffordshire 62.11

1901 Stephens and Mackintosh's Business Street Map

1901 Alan Godfrey Maps, Wolverhampton (SE)

1901 Alan Godfrey Maps, Ettingshall

1902 Ordnance Survey 2nd edition, 25" (Staffs) 62.10 & 62.11

1914 Ordnance Survey 25" edition (Staffs) 62.10 & 62.11

1937 Ordnance Survey 25" edition (Staffs) 62.10 & 62.11

Bibliographic references

ABCD Heritage Project: All Saints Trail.

Baker N, 1980, Wolverhampton, The Archaeology.

Ballard report (1874): Report to the Local Government Board on the Sanitary Condition of the Municipal Borough of Wolverhampton.

Barnett S A, 2004, A Century of Thompson in the Motor Industry.

Barnett S A, John Thompson Motor Pressings Ltd, A Historical Review 1904-1970.

Benson J, 1980, British Coalminers in the Nineteenth Century: A Social History.

Benson J (ed) 1993, The Miners of Staffordshire 1840-1914.

Brew Alec (compiler), 1998, Images of England, Penn and Blakenhall.

Brew Alec (compiler), 1999, Images of England, Ettingshall and Monmore Green.

Brook F, The Industrial Archaeology of the British Isles - The West Midlands.

Collins P, 1990, Notes on Buildings of Interest in Wolverhampton.

Crompton J, 1991, Guide to the Industrial Archaeology of the West Midlands Iron District.

DoE, 1992, List of Buildings of Special Architectural or Historic Interest.

Falconer K, 1972, Industrial Monuments Survey.

Greenslade M W & Jenkins J G, 1967, Victoria County History of Staffordshire, Vol. II.

Griffiths Guide to the Iron Trade of Great Britain, 1873.

Hadfield, 1969, Canals of the West Midlands.

Hanley Lynsey, Estates: An Intimate History.

Hooke & Slater, 1986, Anglo-Saxon Wolverhampton and its Monastery.

Hunt (1857), Memoirs of the Geological Survey of Great Britain.

Hunt (1858), Memoirs of the Geological Survey of Great Britain.

Malam JP & Thomas D M, 1981, Recording of a late 18th century-early 19th century ice house.

Mander G P & Tildesley, N W, 1960, A History of Wolverhampton to the early 19th century

Marshall John, 1833, A digest of all the accounts: relating to the population, productions, revenues, financial operations, manufactures, shipping, colonies, commerce, &c. &c., of the United Kingdom of Great Britain and Ireland.

Mason F, 1979, The Book of Wolverhampton. The Story of an Industrial Town.

Mason F, Wolverhampton, the Town Commissioners 1777-1848.

McMillan B, 1947, History of Water Supply of Wolverhampton.

Memoirs of the Geological Survey of Great Britain, 1855, 1857, 1859.

Mills M, 1993, Mapping the Past, Wolverhampton 1577-1986.

Mills & Williams, 1996, The Archive Photo Series: Wolverhampton.

Owen Ben (1993): With Popski's Private Army, published by Janus

Page W (ed), 1908, Victoria County History of Staffordshire, Vol. 1.

Pevsner N, 1973, Buildings of England – Staffordshire.

Rawlinson Report (1849): 'Report to the General Board of Health on a Preliminary Inquiry into Sewerage, Drainage, and the Supply of Water, and the Sanitary Conditions of the Inhabitants of the Borough of Wolverhampton, and the Townships of Bilston, Willenhall, and Wednesfield.'

Redford A, (1964) Labour Migration in England, 1800-1850.

Ritchie Andrew, The Origins of Bicycle Racing in England: Technology, Entertainment, Sponsorship and Advertising in the Early History of the Sport.

Roper J, 1976, Wolverhampton as it was, Vol. III.

Roper J S, 1966, Wolverhampton: the early town and its history.

Rowlands, 1967, Industry and Social Change in Staffordshire 1660-1760.

Seaby WA & Smith CA. Windmills of Staffordshire.

Shaw & Stebbing, 1801, The History and Antiquities of Staffordshire.

Shill Ray, South Staffordshire Ironmasters.

Short John, Housing in Britain: The Post-war Experience.

Jon Stobart, Neil Raven, 2005: Towns, Regions and Industries: Urban and Industrial Change in the Midlands, C.1700-1840, Ch. 8:

Staffordshire and Stoke-on-Trent Archive Service: Staffordshire County Record Office.

Upton C, 1998, History of Wolverhampton.

White Hilary, 1998, Wolverhampton Town Centre Action Area 10: The Archaeology.

White, Hilary, with Wade, Petra, 1997, Wolverhampton Town Centre Action Plan: Archaeology Phase 1

White Hilary, 1997, Archaeology of Wolverhampton: an update.

White William, 1834: History, Gazetteer, and Directory of Staffordshire.

Wolverhampton Archives and Local Studies Service

Wolverhampton Arts and Heritage Community Panel: The Blakenhall Trail.

Wolverhampton Chronicle

Wolverhampton City Council, Penn Road (Graiseley) Conservation Area Appraisal.

Wolverhampton City Council, Cleveland Road Conservation Area Designation Report: Fellows Street (Blakenhall) Conservation Area, Detailed Appraisal.

Wolverhampton Express and Star

Wolverhampton Industrial Development Association, 1936, Book of Wolverhampton.

Other Sources

A History of Housing in Wolverhampton 1750 to 1975, Barnsby G (1985):
http://www.gbpeopleslibrary.co.uk/index.php?option=com_content&view=article&id=9&Itemid=10&limitstart=1

Birmingham Archaeology: Fort and Towers Works, Wolverhampton:
http://archaeologydataservice.ac.uk/catalogue/adsdata/arch-502-1/dissemination/pdf/birmingh2-19113_1.pdf,

Birmingham Grid for Learning:
http://www.bgfl.org/bgfl/custom/resources_ftp/client_ftp/teacher/history/jm_jones/jmj_rotton/page39.htm

Black Country Core Strategy, Appendix 2: Detailed Proposals for Regeneration Corridors and Strategic Centres (2011):
http://www.wolverhampton.gov.uk/CHttpHandler.ashx?id=1493&p=0

Black Country History: http://blackcountryhistory.org

Black Country Muse:
http://www.blackcountrymuse.com/home.htm

The British Newspaper Archive:
http://www.britishnewspaperarchive.co.uk/

The Coalmining History Resource Centre:
http://www.cmhrc.co.uk/site/home/index.html

Collieries of the United Kingdom at Work 1869 –
www.anthony maitland.com/listapdx.htm

Donald Potter obituary:
http://www.theguardian.com/news/2004/jun/08/guardianobitu aries.artsobituaries

Doyle, Patrick Joseph: The Giffards of Chillington, a catholic landed family 1642-1861, Durham University:
http://etheses.dur.ac.uk/9887/1/9887_6681.PDF

Durham Mining Museum:
http://www.dmm.org.uk/books/ccci-154.htm

Education Act (1870): http://www.parliament.uk/about/living-heritage/transformingsociety/livinglearning/school/overview/1 870educationact/

The Free Library: http://www.thefreelibrary.com

The Governance of Wolverhampton, 1848 – 1888: A PhD Thesis by John Butland Smith:
https://core.ac.uk/download/pdf/42016432.pdf

Grace's Guide: http://www.gracesguide.co.uk

The Inland Waterways Association:
https://www.waterways.org.uk/waterways/canals_rivers/birmi ngham_canal/historical_information

The London Gazette: http://www.london-gazette.co.uk/issues/25171/pages/5466/page.pdf

Memoirs of the Geological Survey of Great Britain ... South Staffordshire coal-field (1859):
http://babel.hathitrust.org/cgi/pt?id=hvd.32044102950672;vie w=1up;seq=7;size=125

Memories and Information – Staffordshire 23rd
(Wolverhampton) Battalion:
http://www.staffshomeguard.co.uk/DotherReminiscences13st
affshg.htm

RAF Commands: http://www.rafcommands.com

RAF:
http://raf.mod.uk/history/campaign_diaries.cfm?diarymonth=
8&diaryyear=1940&diaryday=30

Report into State of Public Health in Wolverhampton, 1840:
http://www.newmanlocalhistory.org.uk/wp-
content/uploads/history14-vol11.pdf

Staffordshire General and Commercial Directory 1818:
http://specialcollections.le.ac.uk/cdm/ref/collection/p16445co
ll4/id/339965

St. Martin's Church: http://www.smcommunity.org.uk/st-
martins-church

Wolverhampton History and Heritage Society website:
http://www.historywebsite.co.uk/

Wolverhampton, Bilston and District Trade Union Council:
http://wolvestuc.org.uk

Wolverhampton City Council, Planning Committee, 1
December 2009: http://Wolverhampton.moderngov.co.uk

The Workhouse:
http://www.workhouses.org.uk/Wolverhampton/

ACKNOWLEDGEMENTS

Four years ago, I placed an enquiry in the Express and Star newspaper asking if anyone had memories of the Rough Hills estate and its surrounding area. A number of individuals promptly responded and over the next two years this network of local expertise expanded. The book includes many of the personal recollections and photographs which they kindly passed onto me. I believe they each makes a significant contribution to our knowledge of the communities in and around the estates of Rough Hills, Parkfields and All Saints during the period from 1930 to 1970.

I sincerely thank the following for their involvement in this project and I apologise profusely to anyone who has been overlooked.

- Robbie Bennett
- Carole Bridgen
- George Cartwright
- Sheila Cartwright
- Margaret Carroll nee Williams

- Claire Cotterill
- Sylvia Enefer
- Brian Hall
- Roy Holloway
- Colin Jackson
- Joan Johnston nee Underhill
- Margaret Jones
- Bill Leighton
- Barry Marchant
- Olwen Medlicott
- Mary Mills
- Shirley Morris nee Burt
- George Paddock
- Val Peel nee Darby
- Peter Phillips
- Rosemary Phillips nee Stevens
- Stella Shorthouse
- Dave Simpson
- Stan Whitmore

I should also like to thank the staff at Wolverhampton City Archives who, over a period of four years, have provided invaluable assistance during my research on the historical aspects of this book. Finally, many thanks to Ray Lipscombe and Antonia Tingle at Mereo Books who have invited me into the world of publishing. Without their considerable support and expertise, this project would not have been completed.